UNITED STATES CRYPTOLOGIC HISTORY

Series IV
World War II
Volume 8

A History of U.S. Communications Intelligence during World War II: Policy and Administration

Robert Louis Benson

CENTER FOR CRYPTOLOGIC HISTORY

NATIONAL SECURITY AGENCY

1997

Table of Contents

List of Illustrations v
Foreword vii
Introduction and Acknowledgments ix

Chapter 1: U.S. COMINT, 1939–1945 1

    The U.S. Intelligence Organizations Prior to Pearl Harbor 1
    The Other COMINT Organizations: Coast Guard, FBI, and FCC 7
    Prewar COMINT Agreements with the British 14
    Toward Pearl Harbor 22

Chapter 2: The First Year of War 31

    The Impact of War 31
    The Expansion and Reorganization of Army COMINT during 1942 32
    Navy COMINT Reorganization and Expansion in Washington during 1942 43
    The Army-Navy-FBI COMINT Agreements March–July 1942 47
    U.S.-British COMINT Agreements in Washington – 1942 56
    Navy COMINT in the Pacific 62

Chapter 3: Army-Navy Policy and Organizational
            Development during 1943 77

    The Combat Intelligence Division and OP-20-G 77
    The Army COMINT Breakthrough in 1943 80
    Central Bureau Brisbane 85
    Proposals for Closer Army-Navy Cooperation 90

Chapter 4: The Army-British COMINT Agreements of 1943:
            The ENIGMA Crisis 97

    The Crisis in British-U.S. Relations 97
    An Agreement Is Reached 108
    The Implementation of the Agreements 110

Chapter 5: British-U.S. Navy COMINT Agreements of 1943–1944 119

Chapter 6: Continued Jurisdictional Problems regarding
            Clandestine Communications 123

    The Radio Intelligence Division 123
    The Navy-FBI Controversy and the Attendant
        Disputes regarding the British 125

**Chapter 7: The Army and Navy Move toward
   Full Cooperation, 1944–1945** 133

   The Army and Navy Formalize Cooperation 133
   The Workings of ANCICC and the Creation of ANCIB 135

**Chapter 8: Internal Army and Navy Organizational Developments,
   1944–1945** 141

   SSOs in the Pacific 141
   Developments at the War Department 143
   Attempted Army Consolidation in the Theaters and the
      Creation of ASA 148
   Developments in Navy COMINT Organization in Washington
      and the Pacific 155

Glossary of Abbreviations 163

Sources 167

List of Illustrations

Page	Illustration
2	Colonel Raymond Eliot Lee, Army attaché in London, 1935–1939, 1940–1941
5	RED machine analog. This cipher device was used for high-level diplomatic traffic until it was superseded by the PURPLE machine in February 1941.
5	The Japanese PURPLE machine
7	Elizebeth Friedman
11	General J. O. Mauborgne, chief signal officer
15	Bletchley Park, Headquarters, Government Code and Cipher School
19	Abraham Sinkov
23	Lieutenant Commander A. D. Kramer headed the OP-20-G translation section.
33	Major General Dawson Olmstead, chief signal officer
35	Carter W. Clarke, wartime chief of special branch (1954 photograph)
38	Aerial view of Arlington Hall Station, 1945
41	George Bicher, director, Signal Intelligence Division, Signal Section, HQ ETOUSA
42	Cryptographic and security personnel, 849th SIS
44	Rear Admiral Joseph Redman, director, naval communications
58	Solomon Kullback, chief B-2, SIS
64	Lieutenant Commander Luther L. L. Dilley, USN Cryptanalysis Section, FRUPAC
66	Admiral Chester W. Nimitz, CINCPAC

80	W. Preston Corderman, chief SSS, (1955 photograph as major general)
84	Arlington Hall Station employee at a decipherment machine
98	Dr. Alan Turing, cryptanalyst and mathematician
102	Casablanca Conference, January 1943
104	German ENIGMA cipher machine exhibited at the National Cryptologic Museum, Fort Meade, Maryland
110	Lieutenant Colonel Frank B. Rowlett
144	Major General Clayton Bissell, assistant chief of staff, G-2
150	SID ETOUSA, Headquarters SI Division, 59 Weymouth Street
155	Captain Joseph N. Wenger, assistant director naval communications, OP-20-G
157	Captain Jack Holtwick, Jr., USN, officer in charge, RAGFOR

Foreword

The revelations about World War II cryptology – begun with the publication in 1974 of F. W. Winterbotham's *The Ultra Secret* and continued with extensive declassification of original documents – sparked a great reevaluation of wartime events. Most wartime decisions, operations, and events, even those long considered settled, have had to be reconsidered. The ULTRA revelations have also sparked a cottage industry of books, monographs, and articles based on the wealth of original documents declassified over the past two decades. A great many of these books have concentrated on the information content of communications intelligence reports, relating newly released COMINT to a particular commander, operation, or theater.

One lacuna in the study of world war COMINT, therefore, is an examination of the organizations that produced communications intelligence and how they changed under pressure. Both the U.S. Army and Navy had relatively small COMINT organizations in the prewar period, and both expanded rapidly with the advent of hostilities. Expansion was only one aspect of the institutional challenges they faced: the processes which attended peacetime were inadequate for support of military operations on a global scale. With national survival and individual lives at stake, the services demanded more information – both tactical and strategic – and more timely distribution than ever before.

The U.S. military COMINT organizations for the first time engaged in close cooperation with a foreign ally, the United Kingdom. By the end of the war, the United States and the United Kingdom were linked in communications intelligence activities at levels perhaps unprecedented in international affairs, at least on a voluntary basis. To achieve this advantageous situation, the U.S. Army and Navy had to make considerable adjustments in organization and policy.

Rapid expansion, urgent requirements for information, international agreements – these factors forced the American COMINT organizations into profound changes. While the services never completely solved the problems posed by these challenges, by war's end they created structures and implemented policies which, however cumbersome, achieved high levels of combat support. Understanding how the services changed from the organizations of 1940 to those of 1945 is an essential undergirding for understanding the production and use of COMINT product in World War II as well as the postwar movement toward centralization.

Mr. Robert L. Benson has produced an important monograph about these changes. His careful research and writing about the what and why of institutional changes and their far-reaching effects constitutes fundamental study of these complex issues. Mr. Benson's book is strongly recommended for all who wish to understand the origins of modern COMINT, how it has grown, and how COMINT policy has developed.

David A. Hatch
Director,
Center for Cryptologic History

A History of U.S. Communications Intelligence during World War II: Policy and Administration

INTRODUCTION AND ACKNOWLEDGMENTS

The objective of this study is to provide an authentic and reliable guide to U.S. communications intelligence (COMINT) during World War II. A complete history of this subject would be an overwhelming task; therefore, I have limited this effort to matters of high-level policy, administration, and organization. I have tried to show how communications intelligence was controlled and directed by each service and how these services related to each other and to their British counterparts. This is not a history of cryptanalysis or COMINT operations, nor is there much here about the specific uses made of COMINT.

Nevertheless, within these limits, I have tried to be complete. That is, I have made an effort to show not only how Army and Navy COMINT activities were run but also how COMINT was structured in the Coast Guard, FBI, and Federal Communications Commission (FCC). There is also a great deal here on the non-COMINT producing agencies – the Military Intelligence Service (MIS) and the Office of Naval Intelligence (ONI). In fact, my account as it relates to the Army has more to do with the MIS than with Arlington Hall. I hope the reasons for this will be made clear in the text.

Much of this study seems to be concerned with service politics and interservice disagreements. I can only say that I recognize that COMINT was often produced *in spite of* certain high-level maneuverings. On that same theme, I also recognize that the people who produced the real COMINT product are, in this study, quite secondary figures. There is little here about Frank Rowlett, Solomon Kullback, or Frank Raven.

A word about the British. This study could almost be subtitled "The Development of a COMINT Alliance." The emphasis on British intelligence is an absolute must for a policy and administrative history, because there is no understanding of the development of U.S. COMINT without continually reporting and examining the role of the British.

The sources used in this study are adequately identified in the footnotes and the sources section. I have used the footnotes to report a great deal of supplementary information, and I hope that the reader will turn to them.

The research for this study and the preparation of a draft manuscript were done from August 1975 until August 1976 under the auspices of a Cryptologic

Education Fellowship at the National Cryptologic School, NSA/CSS. It would have been impossible to have completed a study of this scope but for the fact that so many documentary sources had been gathered together in previous years by Vincent J. Wilson, Jr., and Henry F. Schorreck of the History Department at NSA and their predecessors, especially Dr. George Howe and Ed Fishel. Throughout my fellowship, which allowed for complete independence in my work, Messrs. Wilson and Schorreck were most helpful in suggesting research leads, critiquing the project, and providing general encouragement. Mr. Wilson edited the study.

I want to thank the following persons who provided or suggested sources of valuable information: Thomas F. Troy, CIA; Captain Wayman F. Packard, USN (Ret); Dr. Jack Mason, U.S. Naval Institute; James McKinney, FCC; Pat Paddock, FBI; D. Finke, Center for Military History; and Jerry Hess, National Archives. In addition, Mr. Bob Hilbish, Naval Field Office for Intelligence Operations, and Mr. Owen Crowder, NSA, kindly allowed me to have material couriered through their offices.

My only regret is that I was not able to obtain certain material stored at Crane, Indiana, by the Naval Security Group.

I wrote this study between 1975 and 1976, and some of it appeared in various Agency journals during the 1970s. However, this is the first complete edition to be published. If I were writing this today, I would use some additional sources, especially U.S. Navy materials, that were not available to me at the time. Also, the Center for Cryptologic History (CCH) has conducted many excellent interviews since that time. However, it seems to me that the study can still be interesting and useful as is. Therefore, I made very few changes. Finally, I especially thank Barry Carleen, Jean Persinger, Laura Clark, Vicki Adair, Tom Johnson, and Dave Hatch of the Center for Cryptologic History for getting this to press.

ROBERT LOUIS BENSON

Chapter 1
U.S. COMINT, 1939–1941

THE U.S. INTELLIGENCE ORGANIZATIONS PRIOR TO PEARL HARBOR[1]

By the time the United States entered the Second World War, significant measures had been taken toward establishing an intelligence structure. On 26 June 1939, President Roosevelt issued to the Army, Navy, and Federal Bureau of Investigation (FBI) an order restricting investigation of espionage and sabotage. These agencies clarified their relationship in the Delimitations Agreement of 5 June 1940, whereby the Military Intelligence Division (MID) and the Office of Naval Intelligence (ONI) were to have cognizance over the services' military and civilian personnel in espionage/counterespionage and sabotage matters, while the FBI would have that responsibility for civilians. The Army would have authority overseas in the Philippines and Panama, the Navy in Guam and Samoa, and the FBI in the other territories (Hawaii and Puerto Rico). The consultative or exchange body that acted on the Delimitations Agreement became known as the Interdepartmental Intelligence Conference (IIC), composed of the director, FBI, or a senior assistant; the assistant chief of staff (ACS), G-2, who headed MID; and the director of naval intelligence (DNI). The overall coordinator of the IIC, if only informally, was Adolph A. Berle Jr., assistant secretary of state.[2]

On or about 24 June 1940, President Roosevelt made broad foreign intelligence assignments. The FBI was to collect intelligence and conduct counterintelligence operations in the Western Hemisphere, while all other foreign intelligence was to be the responsibility of the Army and Navy. To fulfill its role, the FBI formed the Special Intelligence Service (SIS), which operated in Latin America throughout the war.

In a final prewar directive, the president authorized the formation of the office of the Coordinator of Information (COI) in June–July 1941. The COI, renamed the Office of Strategic Services (OSS) in 1942, was headed throughout its existence by William J. Donovan, a prominent New York attorney and well-known hero of the First World War. The role of COI (and OSS) was often ambiguous, but it became the primary U.S. intelligence agency, for other than communications intelligence (COMINT), during the Second World War. Donovan and the COI were not popular with the IIC members, who in fact made a last-minute effort in May 1941 to stop Donovan from forming the organization. The IIC members held that as their own relationship was satisfactory (though it really was not), a superagency and a formal coordinator were unnecessary.[3]

The COI, though a Donovan creation, was inspired by British intelligence personnel, especially through the medium of British Security Coordination (BSC). The BSC, established in 1940, was the Western Hemisphere arm of the British Secret Service (also known as the Secret Intelligence Service and MI-6) and was headquartered in New York City. It acted as a more or less independent body under the direction of William Stephenson, a Canadian millionaire who, like Donovan, was a hero of the last war. Stephenson and Donovan became close friends and established a U.S.-British partnership in intelligence that would help OSS establish itself almost worldwide. Stephenson also courted J. Edgar Hoover and the FBI. None of this pleased the Army and Navy. These early relationships strongly influenced U.S. COMINT policy, particularly because the latter remained in the hands of the Army and Navy.

Whatever the agreements and divisions of responsibility, the actual intelligence assets of the U.S. before Pearl Harbor were rather thin – except for communications intelligence. ONI was by no means inexperienced in covert operations and counterintelligence techniques, but these were largely limited to the U.S. and its possessions. Overseas the Navy depended on attachés and observers whose success in intelligence collection was quite modest. The Army also depended on its attachés and was quite ill-served. Attachés were selected largely on the basis of independent wealth and social acceptability. Army counterintelligence, especially in the overseas departments, was busy. Both MID and ONI had a tiny corps of experienced intelligence analysts, men who jeopardized their own advancement by their interest in this unpopular field. The FBI did quite well in counterintelligence and undoubtedly disrupted most German operations in the U.S. and later in Latin America. All the services received an ever-increasing amount of information from the British, though again largely in counterintelligence.

There was one more try to better coordinate the U.S. intelligence activities, this on a British model. The Army attaché in London, Colonel Raymond E. Lee, advanced the idea in 1941 of a Joint Intelligence Committee (JIC),[4] which was to act as a "clearinghouse" for intelligence coming to the U.S. from British agencies. The JIC, which initially included only MID and ONI representation, did not become active until after Pearl Harbor, and it was only briefly involved in U.S. COMINT activities.[5]

Colonel Raymond Eliot Lee
Army attaché in London, 1935–1939, 1940–1941

Thus on the eve of war, the U.S. had a fledgling foreign "secret intelligence service" (the five-month-old COI) and a modest counterintelligence effort. There were as yet no significant secret sources of intelligence – except for the communications intelligence organizations, which were then, as during the war, the most carefully guarded and vital source.[6]

Before the creation of the Second Signal Service Company on 1 January 1939, the SIS received its intercept from the First Radio Intelligence (RI) Company, which had been organized at Fort Monmouth, New Jersey, in 1938, and the radio intelligence detachments of the various signal companies – the Panama Signal Company in the Canal Zone; the Seventh Company at Fort Sam Houston, Texas; the Ninth Company at Fort Shafter, Territory of Hawaii; the Eighth Company at Presidio of San Francisco; and the Tenth Company at Fort Mills, Philippines.[7] Except for the First RI Company, which was under the office of chief signal officer (OCSigO), the radio intelligence detachments of the signal companies were under the command of the signal officers of the appropriate corps or department. Personnel of these detachments were transferred to the Second Signal Service, which was also augmented from other sources.

By the end of 1939 the following monitoring stations (MS) were available to the SIS:

MS-1:   Fort Monmouth/Fort Hancock, New Jersey[8]
MS-2:   The Presidio of San Francisco, California
MS-3:   Fort Sam Houston, Texas
MS-4:   Corozal, the Canal Zone
MS-5:   Fort Shafter, Territory of Hawaii
MS-6:   Fort McKinley, Philippine Islands
MS-7:   Fort Hunt, Virginia (near Mount Vernon)

These seven monitoring stations remained the basic source of SIS intercept traffic until after Pearl Harbor.

At SIS in Washington, the raw traffic from the stations was worked by four cryptanalytic sections under the general supervision of Mr. William F. Friedman, the chief assistant to Colonel Spencer Akin.[9]

	Section	Supervisor
J	Japanese diplomatic	Mr. Frank B. Rowlett
G	German diplomatic	Mr. Solomon Kullback
I	Italian diplomatic	Mr. Abraham Sinkov
M	Mexican (and other Latin American) diplomatic	Mr. H. F. Bearce

The assignments seem not to have been rigid, and the various sections assisted each other. As can be seen, the main SIS effort was against foreign diplomatic traffic. Other intercept and cryptanalytic coverage was added before Pearl Harbor: the diplomatic traffic of Vichy France, Spain, and Portugal, and espionage systems of Germany and Japan. The SIS lacked the means – personnel, equipment, and monitoring stations – to cover German or Italian military communications. Japanese army traffic, however, was intercepted by MS-6 (and its predecessor detachment) from the Philippines. In September 1940, Mr. Friedman learned that Station 6 was doing good work on Japanese army traffic.[10] The traffic was sufficient to enable SIS to tentatively reconstruct certain Japanese army radio nets in China and Japan.[11] According to a report prepared after the war began, the following numbers of Japanese army messages had been available to SIS before the war.[12]

Year	Number of Messages	
1935	500	
1937	1,200	
1938	6,000	
1939	77,000	
1940	106,000	
1941	61,000	(34,000 from British sources)

But there were no solutions or translations.[13] The Japanese army codes were extremely difficult, and, in spite of the seemingly high volume of messages available, coverage was perhaps erratic and unsystematic. Most important, the SIS's solution of the Japanese PURPLE system during 1940 required that army resources be turned to its exploitation. PURPLE was the highest-level Japanese diplomatic system, and its breaking was undoubtedly the greatest achievement in prewar COMINT.

The SIS successes with diplomatic systems were truly impressive. All Japanese diplomatic systems were solved (PURPLE, RED, LA, and many more) as were the systems of other countries (though not Germany). Japanese espionage messages, sent in *diplomatic systems*, and German espionage traffic were also read.

All this material, decrypted and translated by SIS, was forwarded to MID for analysis and dissemination to an ever-shrinking circle of authorized readers.

RED machine analog
This cipher device was used for high-level diplomatic traffic
until it was superseded by the PURPLE machine in February 1941.

The Japanese PURPLE analog machine

The Navy's COMINT organization during the prewar period was rather more complex than the Army's. There were three COMINT processing centers (as opposed to one for SIS) and a greater number of intercept stations. The Navy's COMINT targets were also more extensive: Japanese naval, German naval (primarily U-boat), Axis merchant marine, and diplomatic (mainly Japanese). In addition, work was done on Vichy, Portuguese, and Spanish naval systems. The intercept sites serving OP-20-G during this period were as follows:[14]

Station A	Shanghai, China (disestablished in October 1940)
Station B	Guam
Station C	Corregidor (previously at Cavite), Philippine Islands
Station G	Amagansett, New York
Station H	Heeia, Territory of Hawaii
Station J	Jupiter, Florida
Station M	Cheltenham, Maryland
Station O	San Juan, Puerto Rico
Station S	Bainbridge, Washington
Station W	Winter Harbor, Maine
Station U	Toro Point (previously Balboa), Canal Zone

In addition, there were direction finding (DF) facilities located at many of the above stations and elsewhere. Sites involved solely in DF included Poyners Hill, North Carolina; Guantanamo, Cuba; American Samoa; and Point St. George, California.

Most of these intercept and DF sites were in operation by the end of 1939. Some had a particularly long history. Station B, Guam, dated to 1929, and there had been intercept operations in the Philippines even before that.[15]

The processing centers where cryptanalysis (CA), traffic analysis (TA), and translation were performed were at Corregidor (known as the Cast unit), Pearl Harbor, and Washington. The Cast unit supported the Asiatic Fleet, commanded by Admiral Thomas Hart. Cast was under the military command of the Sixteenth Naval District.[16] The Pearl Harbor unit supported the Pacific Fleet, commanded by Admiral James O. Richardson and later by Admiral Husband Kimmel. It was under the military command of the Fourteenth Naval District. Both Cast and Pearl Harbor were guided and supported by OP-20-G, which was itself a processing center. Traffic and solutions and translations were forwarded to 20-G by Cast and Pearl Harbor.[17] Cast was also in contact with the Army's MS-6 at Fort Mills, and there was an exchange of traffic. It should also be noted that Cast supported General MacArthur in the Philippines, as it had far greater capability than MS-6. Cast, unlike the SIS station, had a "copy" of the PURPLE machine, and before Pearl Harbor, it had been assigned to cover and decrypt Japanese diplomatic traffic.[18]

By the end of 1941, OP-20-G had some 300 people (this figure may or may not include the Continental United States (CONUS) intercept and DF personnel).[19] The Pearl Harbor unit had about thirty officers and enlisted men with an additional fifty to sixty at the intercept and DF facility.[20] The Cast unit's strength was seventy-six, of whom twenty-six were involved in processing.[21]

A necessarily broad summary of naval COMINT processing during the immediate prewar period is represented in the following chart.

Center	Officer in Charge	Material Being Worked
Washington (OP-20-G)	Commander Laurance Safford	Japanese naval systems, especially JN-25, the general fleet system; naval systems of other countries; diplomatic systems (mainly Japanese)
Pearl Harbor	Lieutenant Commander Joseph Rochefort	Japanese navy fleet officers' code; TA; other Japanese naval systems
Cast	Lieutenant Rudolph Fabian	JN-25; PURPLE; other Japanese naval systems; TA

Analysis and dissemination of the COMINT product were performed for the Navy Department by ONI, and for the fleets by the appropriate staff intelligence officers (Commander Edwin T. Layton for Admiral Kimmel; Commander Redfield Mason for Admiral Hart).

THE OTHER COMINT ORGANIZATIONS: COAST GUARD, FBI, AND FCC

The United States Coast Guard (USCG) became involved in COMINT through its law enforcement responsibilities. In 1924 the Coast Guard's communications personnel began intercepting the radio traffic of rumrunners. Various groups of smugglers used elaborate ship-to-shore communications and code and cipher systems. A cryptanalytic unit was established in the 1920s, and this unit was placed in the intelligence division of the Coast Guard in 1931.[22] The chief cryptanalyst of the unit was Elizabeth Friedman, wife of William F. Friedman.

Elizabeth Friedman

She hired and trained several college graduates to assist her, and they solved most of the rumrunner systems and testified in many successful prosecutions.[23]

Following the repeal of Prohibition in 1933, the Coast Guard continued to use radio intercept to detect other types of smuggling activities. The cryptanalytic unit continued to function, on a reduced basis, and included code and cipher development in its work.[24] During the Munich Crisis of 1938, the secretary of the treasury directed the Coast Guard to monitor radio traffic "... for any clues pointing to sudden changes in the international situation."[25] Similar directives were made by the secretary before the outbreak of war in September 1939.

In 1939 the Coast Guard cryptanalytic unit was transferred from the intelligence division to the communications division. During that year Coast Guard radio monitors began to cover "nonneutral" communications of merchant ships as part of the Coast Guard's responsibility to enforce American neutrality laws. This type of work led to the detection of clandestine stations operating in the Western Hemisphere. By late 1940 the Coast Guard was regularly intercepting and cryptanalyzing messages to and from these stations, which were operated by German and Italian intelligence agents.[26] This type of COMINT became a Coast Guard specialty and would remain so throughout the war. Stations were detected in the U.S., Brazil, Chile, Argentina, and other Latin American countries.

In keeping with the Delimitations Agreement and President Roosevelt's counterintelligence directive of 1939, the FBI was initially the chief consumer of Coast Guard COMINT. But when it became apparent that the FBI was not properly sharing this COMINT with other interested agencies, the assistant secretary of the treasury directed on 17 June 1941 that Coast Guard intelligence disseminate this material to the State Department, Army, and Navy.[27] Soon afterwards, Captain James Roosevelt, COI liaison officer, was also placed on distribution for Coast Guard COMINT.

USCG-FBI relations were particularly strained during 1941 by the "VVV TEST-AOR" case. The Coast Guard had been monitoring clandestine stations using the callsigns VVV TEST and AOR. In July 1941, when the FBI arrested members of a German espionage ring in the U.S., the Coast Guard learned that TEST was an FBI-controlled radio station communicating with Hamburg, Germany (AOR). Much of the FBI-transmitted material being relayed from German intelligence station GLENN in Mexico City seemed to the Coast Guard to be good intelligence of demonstrable value to German U-boat operations.[28] The resultant espionage trials exposed information concerning U.S. cryptanalysis and German cryptographic technique. Many of the suspicions concerning FBI security practices would crop up again and again in the relationship between the armed forces and the bureau and may be traced to that trial and circus of publicity.

The FBI itself had a COMINT effort in the prewar period. In October 1939, Mr. Paul Napier was hired by the FBI as its first full-time "cryptographer" (i.e., cryptanalyst). For a time cryptanalysis of criminal and foreign communications was conducted by the cryptographic element of the FBI technical laboratory, which also prepared the FBI's secure systems. In December 1940, a separate cryptanalytic section was formed, under the direction of W. G. B. Blackburn, who reported to Mr. E. P. Coffey, laboratory director, and ultimately to FBI associate director Edward A. Tamm (who later became a federal judge). By the time of Pearl Harbor, the cryptanalytic section had twenty people.[29] The main interest of the section was German espionage traffic, but attempts were also made to solve German and Japanese diplomatic systems.[30] In June 1941 the FBI solved "certain codes used by the Vichy government of France."[31] During this period the FBI cryptanalysts received training from the SIS and from Mrs. Friedman.[32]

The FBI's sources of raw traffic in the prewar period are not definitively known. However, on 11 October 1940 J. Edgar Hoover wrote Federal Communications Commission (FCC) chairman James L. Fly to suggest that Japanese, French, Italian, German, and Russian cables should be obtained (by the FCC). Mr. Hoover offered FBI assistance in cryptanalysis should the FCC be unable to "break the codes." Mr. Fly suggested a personal conference on the matter. Instead there followed correspondence between Hoover and Fly into January 1941, with inconclusive results. It was Mr. Fly's contention that the FBI proposition involved legal, administrative, and budgetary problems.[33] What is certain is that before Pearl Harbor the FCC was providing the FBI with intercept, including that from established international circuits.[34] But there is no evidence that the FCC was obtaining cables from the cable companies, as Mr. Hoover seemed to be suggesting in his initial letter to Mr. Fly. If the FBI had access to the cable companies, it was through their own, or perhaps British, efforts.

After Pearl Harbor the FBI experimented with both intercept (from sites in Maryland and Oregon) and field processing (in Oregon).[35] The FBI also had benefit of the traffic developed in the TEST-AOR case and later controlled radio station cases. Nor should we overlook the FBI's ability to use surreptitious means of obtaining foreign cryptographic materials in both the U.S. and Latin America. This was done for the FBI's own intelligence objectives and, whether requested or not, for the Army-Navy COMINT organizations.[36]

As we have seen, another organization involved in COMINT was the FCC. According to FBI records, as early as 16 October 1939, Chairman Fly was planning a COMINT organization to be based in New York City.[37] In a meeting that day with FBI representatives, Fly claimed that a presidential order gave the FCC the sole responsibility for "intelligence received through international communications." The FBI could not agree to that portion of his plan, which called for FBI agents to be assigned to his organization working under FCC control. Whatever the origin of Mr. Fly's plan (there is nothing on this matter in FCC COMINT files reviewed by the author), it came to nothing. The alleged presidential order cited by Mr. Fly has not been identified.

In June 1940, immediately after the fall of France, FCC supervisor George Sterling conceived the plan to use FCC monitoring capabilities to detect possible Axis spies, saboteurs, and infiltrators.[38] Sterling, an Army reserve officer who served in the Army COMINT organization in France during World War I, promptly wrote a $6 million budget proposal for this new operation and cleared it through E. K. Jett, FCC chief engineer, and Mr. Fly. He received more funds than requested, and he set about procuring equipment, personnel, and new sites. His base was the existing FCC network heretofore involved in enforcement of U.S. radio laws. The Sterling organization was originally called the National Defense Organization (NDO) and was renamed the Radio Intelligence Division (RID) in early 1942. Ultimately RID had twelve primary and eighty secondary radio-monitoring stations throughout the U.S., Alaska, Hawaii, and Puerto Rico. Sterling obtained the best receivers, recorders, and DF equipment then available and set the organization to work on its mission: detection, location, and interception of foreign intelligence radio stations in the U.S. and in other areas where the national defense was affected. As an enforcement agency, the RID could act on its own product. Most often its efforts were on behalf of the intelligence organizations of the Army, Navy, Coast Guard, and FBI.

The RID, like the other secondary COMINT organizations (USCG, FBI) became involved in the TEST-AOR case. Again the lack of coordination was revealed. Through DF, RID located the apparent German station on Long Island. The FBI was apprised of the situation and was told that the FCC would raid the station if the former took no action. At the last moment, FBI associate director Ed Tamm revealed that the station was being operated by the FBI.[39] From late 1940 through 1941, the RID intercepted German intelligence traffic between Germany and Portuguese, West Africa, Central America, and Brazil. Their work against German agents in Honduras and the Canal Zone during 1940 assisted in the neutralization of a group supporting U-boat operations.[40]

Although there is no record of a presidential policy directive (in writing, at least) governing COMINT before July 1942, the Army and Navy made efforts in the prewar period to reach agreement concerning their respective responsibilities.

In a document dated 8 December 1939 entitled "Agreement Regarding Special Material," signed by Colonel E. R. W. McCabe, ACS, G-2, and Rear Admiral Walter S. Anderson, the DNI, the services agreed to take special care in disseminating COMINT.[41] MID and ONI were to have sole responsibility for handling the COMINT that they received from their own service agencies. But if the material to be disseminated was jointly produced (i.e., by OP-20-G and SIS) or was to be disseminated outside the Army or Navy, then there was to be coordination, and each service was to be informed of the action taken. This of course was an agreement on security rather than on COMINT production.

During July 1940, Commander Safford of OP-20-G and Colonel Akin of SIS began serious discussions on division of intercept, cryptanalysis, and other aspects of processing, and they appointed a small study committee. But, as Safford reported on 25 July to

Admiral Noyes, the director of naval communications (DNC), no agreement could be reached.[42] Safford noted that it was mutually agreed that the Army would attack foreign military systems while the Navy would attack foreign naval systems. The matter of contention was diplomatic traffic. The lack of agreement was especially important, wrote Safford, because foreign military traffic was virtually uninterceptable at long distances, because of the low-powered transmitters commonly used. Thus the Army, unlike the Navy, had only diplomatic traffic to work. Safford suggested to Noyes that the best division of diplomatic effort was along national lines; the Army should deal with German, Italian, Mexican, and Latin American traffic, and the Navy with Japanese and Russian traffic. But Akin had told Safford that General Mauborgne, the chief signal officer, would not agree to this. Safford then outlined for the DNC the other possible methods of division. Included were division by cryptographic system or on the basis of radio transmitting stations.

General J. O. Mauborgne, chief signal officer

On 27 July 1940, Safford again addressed Admiral Noyes on this matter.[43] He suggested three alternative plans in order of preference:

1. The Army was to intercept Japanese, German, Italian, Mexican, South American, and Russian army traffic, as well as the international circuits carrying diplomatic traffic.

The Army was to "decrypt" foreign military traffic and the diplomatic systems of Germany, Italy, Mexico, and other Latin American countries. The Navy was to intercept Japanese, German, Italian, and Russian naval traffic, as well as the international circuits carrying diplomatic traffic. The Navy would "decrypt" the foregoing naval systems and the diplomatic traffic of Japan and Russia.

2. If General Mauborgne would not accept the foregoing, the Army would be offered responsibility for all Japanese diplomatic systems.

3. Failing in the above, Japanese diplomatic systems were to be divided. The machine systems (RED and PURPLE) were to be worked by the Army and the other Japanese systems by the Navy.

On 31 July the services again appointed a joint panel to study the problem. The committee was composed of Lieutenants Earle F. Cook and Robert E. Schukraft, SIS, and Lieutenant Commander E. R. Gardner and Lieutenant Junior Grade J. A. Greenwald, OP-20-G.[44] The committee was charged with examining all possible methods of division, but especially the Mauborgne plan, which was to divide intercept on the basis of transmitting station, and a plan to pool all traffic and arrange for an equitable basis for "translation." There was no mention of cryptanalysis. The study committee was also to report about the current status of each service's operations in other than military/naval intercept.

The committee submitted a report on 24 August and a revision on 27 September. The final report was approved by Akin, Safford, Noyes, and Mauborgne on 3 October 1940.[45] Basically the report was an acceptance of the Mauborgne plan. Particular international commercial circuits being jointly covered were to be assigned exclusively to the Army or the Navy (however, some joint coverage was to remain), virtually eliminating duplication. The report, which became an agreement with the signatures of Noyes and Mauborgne, addressed the matter of processing of intercept to a very limited degree. This was to assign the Russian problem to the Navy and the Mexican problem to the Army. It was further agreed to continue delivery of traffic from the intercept sites to Washington by the existing means, which were radio, airmail, regular mail, and courier, rather than turn to teletype, because the latter was too expensive.

The report revealed in great detail the intercept assets of the Army and Navy, at least in diplomatic coverage, as of the summer of 1940. The following personnel and receivers were being used:

	Number of Operators	Number of Receivers
Army	105	63
Navy	56	62

While the FBI (or FCC or USCG) does not seem to have entered into any formal COMINT agreements with the services, the matter was under discussion at the time of these

Safford-Akin conversations. On 5 July 1940, a conference had been called by General Sherman Miles, ACS, G-2 (he was chosen by General George Marshall, chief of staff, in April to replace McCabe) and attended by Admiral Noyes, Admiral Anderson, General Mauborgne, and FBI associate director Ed Tamm.[46] Miles explained that the president, through his military aide, General Edwin Watson, had expressed concern about the lack of intelligence coordination and exchange between the Army, Navy, and FBI. Miles and Anderson then revealed to Mr. Tamm the existence of "radio telegraph monitoring stations," which were intercepting "international radio messages," and that the Army and Navy were coordinating these efforts to avoid duplication. Admiral Anderson also told Mr. Tamm that special arrangements had been made with the commercial cable companies to obtain copies of messages. Admiral Anderson provided no details.[47] Tamm stated that the FBI was not receiving any results of these operations. While the FBI had no interest in foreign military or naval matters, Tamm continued, he expected that matters of interest to the FBI must be appearing in traffic. Admiral Anderson assured him that ONI had furnished the FBI general intelligence concerning the Western Hemisphere. Miles and Mauborgne agreed to search their records ". . . to make certain that the Bureau was receiving and had received everything that might be of interest to it."

At this conference some of President Roosevelt's views on COMINT activities were revealed. General Mauborgne stated that as Henry L. Stimson was about to be nominated as secretary of war, he (Mauborgne) had gone to General Watson to gain assurance that Stimson would not be allowed to dismantle Army COMINT as he had done once before (in 1929, when he was secretary of state). The president (either directly or through his military aide, General Watson) told Mauborgne that Army COMINT operations should be continued and that Stimson was not to be advised of these activities. Admiral Anderson also stated that he had briefed President Roosevelt about Navy COMINT and had been told that the program should be continued.

The FBI did not become a regular recipient of Army and Navy COMINT, although as has been described, the Bureau had access to COMINT from other sources in the prewar period. The precise nature of the COMINT that the FBI did receive from the Army and Navy deserves further study. It may be stated that the FBI did not have access to PURPLE or other Japanese diplomatic systems ("MAGIC"). But it seems likely that the Army and Navy did share with the FBI COMINT relating to clandestine activities in the Western Hemisphere (the SIS especially worked German clandestine traffic, sometimes in concert with the Coast Guard).

During 1940, Admiral Noyes and General Mauborgne reached an unwritten agreement for "decoding and translating Japanese intercepts" on this basis: the Army would process Japanese diplomatic and consular traffic on even days of the month and the Navy on odd days. This agreement may have been reached in August, though contemporary documentation is lacking, and that date seems at odds with the aforementioned 3 October agreement, which makes no reference to an odd-even day understanding.[48] Whatever the date of the agreement (and it was certainly made by the end of 1940), its simplicity created problems. For what was to be used as the determining date – transmission date or receipt date by the COMINT center? The agreement was refined so that the date became the Japanese cryptographic date based on the numbering system of the Japanese originator.[49]

There was considerable additional Army-Navy cooperation attendant on the solution of the Japanese PURPLE machine (September 1940). The Navy helped build copies of the PURPLE machines, and the Army then released copies of the machine to the Navy. The Navy had PURPLE machines at OP-20-G in Washington and at the Cast operation in the Philippines.

On 25 January 1941, the dissemination agreement of 8 December 1939 was superseded by a new agreement signed by General Miles and Captain Jules James, the acting DNI. This agreement was in chart format accounting for dissemination, retention, and destruction of each copy of a translated intercept. While the agreement did not so state, it applied mainly to Japanese diplomatic-consular traffic. On external distribution for these intercepts (that is, outside of OP-20-G/ONI and SIS/MID) were the secretary of war, chief of staff, and military aide to the president.[50]

PREWAR COMINT AGREEMENTS WITH THE BRITISH

U.S.-British COMINT agreements, like other intelligence arrangements between the two countries, were fragmented and uncentralized. The Army, Navy, FBI, and Coast Guard had independent contacts with the British. Nonetheless, the key event of this period was a joint undertaking. This was the Army-Navy mission to Bletchley Park (BP), the home of the British COMINT organization, the Government Code and Cipher School (GC&CS).

The reader should bear in mind that what follows is an account of COMINT activities, almost to the total exclusion of the larger matter of the growing alliance between the United States and Britain and the extraordinary confidential relationship between President Roosevelt and Prime Minister Winston Churchill. Two events are offered as guideposts: Mr. Churchill became prime minister on 20 May 1940; by the end of June 1940, President Roosevelt had determined to release fifty overage U.S. destroyers to the Royal Navy.

While the U.S. Army's, and to a lesser extent the Navy's, "mainstream" COMINT relationship with the British from 1940 to 1941 can be described in some detail, there are separate, and confusing, relationships resulting from the presence in the U.S. of a large, covert British intelligence organization. This was BSC, referred to in Section 1, which was headed by William Stephenson. BSC became the main conduit for COMINT going between the U.S. agencies in Washington and GC&CS. Though the arrangement began before

Pearl Harbor, much of this is a later development. But it can be said of prewar BSC and COMINT that BSC obtained, surreptitiously, aids for British cryptanalysis by operations in Washington and New York (one target was the Italian embassy). BSC also passed information relative to certain "lower-echelon cipher systems" to the FBI via Captain H. Montgomery Hyde.[51] Other BSC involvement in COMINT, with or without FBI assistance, can only be surmised.[52]

Bletchley Park, Headquarters, Government Code and Cipher School

The formal British-U.S. COMINT relationship may have been initiated by the British in early 1940, when a proposal was made to the U.S. naval attaché (Captain Alan Kirk) calling for broad COMINT cooperation. Though the Navy saw this as an opportunity to learn about German naval systems, this approach was also rejected.[53]

The British now began their campaign, at a high level, to tap U.S. technical and industrial resources. On 8 July 1940, Lord Lothian, the British ambassador to the U.S., wrote President Roosevelt suggesting, among other things, that the British government would appreciate a broad exchange of secret technical information especially in the ". . . ultra short-wave radio field."[54]

The Lothian request was favorably received. As the chief of the Army's War Plans Division, General George V. Strong noted on 19 July the secretary of war and the president had adopted a stance that the U.S. should "give all information possible to the British to aid them in their present struggle and furnish them such material assistance as will not interfere seriously with our own defense preparations."[55] Strong suggested to General Marshall that the ACS, G-2, be designated as the Army's coordinator for technical exchange with the British. This was approved by the secretary of war on 22 July 1940, and the State Department was advised of this arrangement the same day.[56]

Two weeks later General Strong and General Delos C. Emmons, commanding general of General Headquarters (GHQ) Air Force, departed for London. At the same time, the Navy sent Rear Admiral Robert Ghormley, the assistant chief of naval operations (ACNO), to England as a special observer. These missions were of the highest level, and Ghormley, at least, received his instructions personally from President Roosevelt. These officers were to hold technical discussions, learn of British war plans, and generally observe the situation within Britain, then undergoing heavy bombing and facing possible invasion.[57] Whether Strong and Ghormley took with them specific instructions regarding possible U.S.-U.K. COMINT collaboration is uncertain, but it is improbable, considering subsequent events. Their main technical interests were probably general communications, radar, air defense techniques, and antisubmarine warfare.

On 23 August Strong cabled General Marshall to advise him that England was a "gold mine" of technical information that should be exploited.[58] Strong urged the assignment of a U.S. technical staff to London, as the attaché's staff was too small. He might also have added that the sudden demands of modern warfare were rather beyond the typical Army attaché. The attaché in London was Colonel Raymond E. Lee, soon to be promoted to brigadier general and subsequently (and very briefly) to become the ACS, G-2.[59]

On 29 August Assistant Secretary of War Robert P. Patterson notified the Army chiefs of arms and services and G-2 that General Strong's recommendations would be the topic for discussion at the War Department's weekly staff meeting, to be held the next day. Mr. Patterson reported that a secret British technical mission, headed by Sir Henry Tizard, was in the U.S. and that a reciprocal mission to England should be studied.[60]

In response to the growing sentiment for cooperation with the British, Colonel Akin and Mr. Friedman of SIS prepared an informal paper, divided into five parts, recommending an Army COMINT position. The paper was prepared on or about 1 September 1940 and was shown to General Mauborgne and Commander Safford of OP-20-G. The Akin-Friedman proposals were these:

1. *Cryptographic* – nothing secret to be disclosed to the British and specifically no mention to be made of the machines M-134-A, B, or C (the latter also known as the CSP-888);

2. *Training Material* – some exchange of texts;

3. *Cryptanalysis* – full exchange with the British on a reciprocal basis but only in conjunction with the U.S. Navy;

4. *General Cryptanalytic Technique* – reciprocal exchange of mechanical and machine information;

5. *Exchange of Intercept Traffic* – broadest possible exchange especially to obtain Japanese and German tactical traffic for U.S. study.

Safford disagreed with items three and four.

The matter was dramatically thrust before the War Department several days later when Strong cabled from London:[61]

London No. 401, September 5, 1940

Are you prepared to exchange full information on all German, Italian, and Japanese code and cryptographic information therewith? Are you prepared to agree to a continuous exchange of important intercept in connection with the above? Please expedite reply.

This message for the Chief of Staff from Strong

Lee

The Navy would later claim that Strong had acted abruptly and unilaterally. According to Captain Kirk, the naval attaché, General Strong, in addressing a British staff group, offered the British all U.S. information on Japanese diplomatic systems. The British were astounded, said Kirk, but readily accepted the offer.[62] That Strong acted without the Navy's agreement is likely, but he was following a policy quite acceptable to the Army.

General Marshall took no immediate action on Strong's message, seeking rather an opinion from the Signal Corps and MID. General Mauborgne was at the Signal Corps center at Fort Monmouth where he received a summary of events from Colonel Clyde Eastman. Eastman reported that General Miles would take no action until General Mauborgne had given his opinion. Colonel Eastman also advised Mauborgne that General

Strong's message had been shown to Admiral Anderson, the DNI. Anderson, and Admiral Noyes, too, tentatively rejected the proposal.[63]

General Mauborgne telegraphed his position two days later.[64]

23WVP – Fort Monmouth, N.J., September 7, 1940

Signals, Washington, D.C.

As a matter of utmost importance to National Defense strongly urge concurrence Chief Staff in proposal General Strong that this government exchange complete technical information re Japanese German and Italian codes and cipher systems but believe constant exchange of traffic unnecessary. Each government should rely upon own intercept services for collection material and translation. Unnecessary to discuss Paragraphs A, C, D and E of Akin's memorandum because not believed pertinent Strong's radio.

Mauborgne

On 9 September General Miles added his favorable endorsement to COMINT cooperation in a memorandum to General Marshall on various aspects of technical collaboration with the British.[65] General Marshall approved the exchange and the role of MID as coordinator for the War Department.

Probably because the Navy did not agree, nothing was done for some weeks to accomplish an exchange. The Navy's position was not unreasonable. The PURPLE machine solution was only weeks old when Strong proposed that it be given to the British – this before the British had made any specific offer to provide information of similar value. Strong returned to Washington before the end of September. He made a personal report to the president, and it seems likely (though there is no record) that the matter of COMINT cooperation was discussed.

The matter was renewed by General Miles on 4 October, when he wrote to Lieutenant Colonel W. M. Regnier, Secretary Stimson's aide, to urge, as absolutely essential, an immediate exchange with the British of ". . . information concerning military, military attaché and diplomatic codes, ciphers, cipher devices and apparatus, and code and cipher systems employed by Germany, Italy, and Japan together with all information concerning the methods employed to solve messages in codes or ciphers of the classes mentioned." The information to be furnished by the U.S. would include the PURPLE machine solution.[66] Miles noted the Navy's opposition and expressed the belief that it was based on a fear of aiding the British in solving U.S. systems.[67] Miles stated these reasons for his recommendations:

1. It would result in the Army being able to obtain (if the British cooperated) foreign army and air force traffic and solution data unavailable from U.S. resources.

2. With these expanded sources of intelligence, the U.S. could learn more of possible German and Italian plans regarding the Panama Canal and Latin America. German and Italian espionage in the U.S. might be exposed.

3. The British would be materially assisted by what the U.S. could provide.

A favorable decision was reached during December 1940. On 26 December orders were issued to Mr. Friedman (who was recalled to active duty as a lieutenant colonel) to travel to England. Because of Mr. Friedman's illness, however, these orders were cancelled on 17 January 1941, and orders were issued on the 17th and 24th, respectively, to Captain Abraham Sinkov and Lieutenant Leo Rosen, both of SIS, detailing them to MID for temporary duty with the U.S. military attaché in London. They were to take the PURPLE machine to the British.[68]

Abraham Sinkov

The timing of the Sinkov-Rosen mission was partly dictated by the availability of suitable transportation. On 15 January 1941, a British staff delegation, accompanied by General Raymond Lee and Admiral Ghormley, sailed from England aboard the new battleship, HMS *George V*. The British joint-service group included Rear Admirals Bellairs and Danckwerts, Air Vice Marshal Slessor, and Major General Morris. They formed the permanent British staff organization in Washington, later known as the British Joint Staff Mission. So began the formalization of the alliance.[69]

Rosen and Sinkov, joined by naval officers Robert Weeks and Prescott Currier of OP-20-G, departed for England on the *George V* in early February with a PURPLE machine and other COMINT material in their possession.[70] Upon landing in England, the party visited the office of the military attaché, delivering a letter from General Strong that indicated they were on a special mission. They were then driven to Bletchley Park where their presence was explained, except to a small group of initiates, as being a Canadian delegation.[71] As Sinkov would later recall, the circumstances of the mission were so secret that he never knew if the British expected to receive the PURPLE machine or even knew that the U.S. had solved the system.

The mission remained at GC&CS for ten weeks. They received information about German, Italian, Russian, Latin American, and Japanese systems, military and civil, and learned about the status of various British COMINT operations. Weeks and Currier spent much of their time studying intercept and DF operations and obtained equipment used for the latter. The group was briefed concerning the greatest British secret: that the German ENIGMA, used by all the German armed forces, had been solved and was being exploited. They were not permitted to take notes about the ENIGMA, nor was the technical briefing they received adequate to allow the U.S. to duplicate the British success. The officers gave a special pledge of secrecy regarding ENIGMA, and the Army members agreed to reveal the secret only to General Miles, Colonel Akin, and Mr. Friedman. General discussions were held concerning future cooperation, and the British requested COMINT assistance in the Far East, where they were hindered by a lack of Japanese linguists. The mission returned to the U.S. in April 1941, this time on a British destroyer.[72]

This mission, carried out by junior officers, was one of the most important events of the prewar period. It would be hard to imagine an action more likely to cement an alliance than one in which two countries exchange their most vital secrets. The mission was revealed, in general terms, to the public during the Pearl Harbor hearings after the war. Its significance was not lost on historians seeking to find evidence for President Roosevelt's alleged perfidy in secretly leading the U.S. toward a war to rescue his British friends.[73]

At the time, the U.S. agencies seemed satisfied with the exchange. But two years later, when the Army was still not exploiting any foreign military traffic, there was considerable dissatisfaction at how little the British had shared concerning ENIGMA. This story is told in chapter 4.

In the Far East, the Cast unit in the Philippines and the British COMINT organization in Singapore entered into an informal agreement of mutual assistance early in 1941. This cooperation lasted until the two units were evacuated during the series of disasters that overcame Malaya and the Philippines in early 1942.

According to British sources, possible cooperation was first discussed within British intelligence circles in December 1940.[74] On 10 February 1941, the British DNI radioed the commander in chief of the China naval station authorizing immediate and full exchange with the U.S. of COMINT material and methods.[75] The timing is significant, for the Sinkov-Rosen group had just released, or was about to release, the PURPLE machine to GC&CS. A PURPLE machine went from Bletchley Park to Singapore soon after Cast received its PURPLE machine from 20-G.

At the end of February 1941, a U.S.-British COMINT conference was held in Singapore. Among the U.S. participants were Captain Archer Allen, the naval observer in Singapore, and Lieutenant Commander Jefferson Dennis, former head of the Cast unit, who had remained in the Philippines to help Cast with TA problems. The USN delegation released to the British a Japanese merchant ship code, a naval personnel code, and callsign information. The British, in turn, provided valuable information about JN-25, which was, for COMINT purposes, the most profitable Japanese naval system.[76] In April 1941, when the British commander in chief Far East flew to Manila for high-level staff conferences, he was accompanied by Lieutenant Commander Burnett of the Singapore COMINT unit. Lieutenant Commander Burnett visited Cast, where arrangements were made for a private one-time cipher system for radio exchange of COMINT data. This system supplemented the weekly bulk exchange of COMINT made by the Clipper airplane.[77]

With wide-ranging COMINT cooperation with the British now a fact of U.S. policy, additional arrangements were made in Washington. On 25 May 1941, the British DNI, Admiral John H. Godfrey, and his aide, Commander Ian Fleming, arrived in the U.S. Godfrey's mission was to encourage the U.S. to integrate its intelligence services.[78] The Godfrey-Fleming mission was undoubtedly aimed toward giving a boost to William J. Donovan's efforts to create a U.S. secret intelligence service. Fleming even wrote two memorandums to Donovan, suggesting how such a service might be organized and naming persons whom he (Fleming) thought should fill key positions.[79] The author has not found specific information to show that Godfrey and Fleming dealt with OP-20-G, but it is almost certain that in their meetings with ONI, which did take place, COMINT was discussed.

Very soon after, if not concurrently, Captain Edward G. Hastings, RN, came to Washington to head the working committee of the U.S.-based adjunct of the British Joint Intelligence Committee. Hastings, a representative of the chief of the secret service (CSS), was mainly concerned with British-U.S. COMINT relations until his recall in late 1943.[80] It is interesting to note that Ian Fleming recommended to Mr. Donovan that Captain Hastings be chief of communications for Donovan's planned organization (the COI). Hastings was a GC&CS veteran!

Admiral Godfrey's visit was returned by a special mission to the British Admiralty in August 1941, consisting of Captain Sherwood Picking, Commander Arthur McCollum, and Walter Chappell, all of ONI, and Archie Wrangham, an officer of the Royal Marines on duty at ONI. Picking and Wrangham were killed in an air crash in England, and it became McCollum's mission.[81] Unfortunately only Captain Picking had been given specific instructions in Washington concerning the objectives of the mission. Commander McCollum visited various parts of the Naval Intelligence Division and ultimately, through the personal intervention of Admiral Sir Dudley Pound, the First Sea Lord, gained access to British COMINT. McCollum then visited sites involved in COMINT production.[82]

Beginning in June 1941, OP-20-G and GC&CS began to exchange COMINT, first through the British embassy in Washington and later (perhaps in August) through British Security Coordination in New York City. The material went by air. Material for GC&CS from OP-20-G was called EWT, and that received by OP-20-G, PQR.[83]

In that busy August, Commander Alfred Denniston, head of GC&CS, visited the SIS in Washington. At a meeting on 16 August general discussions were held and a week-long itinerary laid out. Denniston was to visit all sections, observing the SIS efforts against German, Italian, French, Latin American, and Japanese communications. Denniston explained to his hosts the status of the cryptanalytic efforts at GC&CS, and a system for "... safe and direct forwarding and exchange of documents was agreed upon."[84] And in a concession undoubtedly welcomed by SIS, Denniston announced that GC&CS cooperation with its developing Canadian counterpart organization would depend on that organization discharging Herbert O. Yardley, the discredited American cryptanalyst, who had been seeking foreign employment for the past decade.

A listing of the U.S. personnel at the Denniston conference may serve to identify the SIS hierarchy just before the war:

Lieutenant Colonel Rex Minckler, chief of SIS

Captain Harold G. Hayes

Captain Earle F. Cook

Captain Abraham Sinkov

Lieutenant Leo Rosen

Mr. William F. Friedman

Mr. Frank B. Rowlett

Dr. Solomon Kullback

At the end of his visit, Commander Denniston arranged for Major Geoffrey Stevens's assignment to SIS as a liaison officer. Major Stevens, who probably was in Washington at the time, stayed with SIS until October 1944, when he was replaced by Major John R. Cheadle.[85]

Denniston also visited OP-20-G, which he discovered was where the ENIGMA was being worked on. Denniston had hoped that the U.S. would concentrate its COMINT efforts on the Japanese,[86] and he repeated this theme as late as mid-1943, to no avail.

TOWARD PEARL HARBOR

The intelligence aspects of the surprise attack on Pearl Harbor have been examined in such detail that one hesitates to say more.[87] Therefore, this section is only a broad outline of COMINT handling.

The COMINT product of the SIS – decrypted and translated messages – was given to MID for analysis and dissemination. There was very little analysis. In the months just before Pearl Harbor, COMINT derived from Japanese messages was personally delivered by SIS officers to Lieutenant Colonel Rufus Bratton, chief of the Far East section of the intelligence branch of MID. Bratton personally read each item and delivered the translations daily to a small circle of readers who included General Miles, General

Marshall, Mr. Stimson, and a very few officers in the War Plans Division of the General Staff.

Within MID itself almost no one except Bratton and Miles had regular access to MAGIC, the Japanese diplomatic material. The chief of the intelligence division, Colonel Hayes Kroner, claimed no regular access; the officer of the Japanese desk, Lieutenant Colonel Dusenberry, may have shared some of the reading, as he did the delivery, with Colonel Bratton, his chief; Lieutenant Colonel Thomas Betts, who headed the Situation Section of MID, did not see MAGIC. Each recipient had to read each intercept or perhaps a summary of intercepts. There were no written analyses, no special reports, no "finished" intelligence derived from MAGIC. Copies of intercepts were stored by Bratton; extra copies were destroyed.

The Navy's handling of MAGIC was similar to the Army's. Lieutenant Commander A. D. Kramer, an ONI officer on detail to OP-20-G as a translator, performed functions similar to that of Colonel Bratton. Within ONI proper, Commander McCollum, who had the Far East desks, was responsible for analysis of MAGIC and other COMINT derived from Japanese naval communications. The problem of COMINT handling was compounded in the Navy Department by the ongoing controversy between ONI and War Plans, headed by Admiral R. K. Turner, as to who was ultimately responsible for analysis. Turner won out, and he proved to be incapable as an intelligence analyst. To the professional intelligence officers who later gave testimony before Congress, Admiral Turner was the villain in the Navy's use, or non-use, of COMINT.[88]

Lieutenant Commander A. D. Kramer headed the OP-20-G translation section.

There was unquestionably greater dissemination and analysis of COMINT within the Navy. The Navy had far greater sources than the Army (the reader is reminded that the bulk of the naval COMINT effort was on naval COMINT, not on MAGIC) and had two overseas COMINT centers directly serving the fleets.

The Pearl Harbor material relative to that has been examined leads to several significant conclusions. No MAGIC or naval intercept available to the U.S. directly identified Hawaii as the intended target of a Japanese attack. Several espionage messages between Japanese intelligence in Hawaii and Tokyo, during the period late November to 6

December 1941, gave fairly strong indications that Hawaii might be in danger. However, the most important of these messages were not translated (in OP-20-G, as it happened) until *after* the attack.

In spite of the complexity of prewar intelligence organizations and arrangements that have been described above, they proved to be only an elementary framework for what would be needed. Many inadequacies were exposed immediately at the outbreak of war.

Notes

1. The major source for this outline of U.S. intelligence prior to Pearl Harbor (other than COMINT) is Thomas F. Troy, *The Coordinator of Information and British Intelligence*, published as vol. 18, No. 1–5, in the CIA journal *Studies in Intelligence*, Spring 1974. Troy's account is classified.

2. For Berle's view of his role, see extracts from his papers contained in Beatrice B. Berle and Travis B. Jacobs (ed.), *Navigating the Rapids, From the Papers of Adolf A. Berle* (New York, 1973). Berle was decidedly *not* the director of IIC, and no such position existed. Berle was an Army intelligence officer 1917–19 at the War Department and in Paris.

3. Troy, 99.

4. Ibid., 98–99. See also Vernon Davis, *The History of the Joint Chiefs of Staff in World War II*, vol. 1, JCS Historical Division, 1972, 50–53.

5. This was during 1942. See chapter 2. In theory the IIC was concerned with counterintelligence, and the JIC would be a higher body with broader interests, though of similar membership. The IIC actually dealt in both positive intelligence and counterintelligence, at least for the Western Hemisphere.

6. From 1939 until Feb. 1942, OP-20-G was known as the Communication Security Section or the Radio Intelligence Section. The commonly used term for the organization was OP-20-G, which will be used throughout this study.

7. George R. Thompson and Dixie R. Harris, *The Signal Corps: The Outcome (Mid-1943 through 1945)* (Washington, DC, Office of the Chief of Military History (OCMH), 1966), 333. See note 6.

8. *U.S. Cryptologic Activities 1941–46, Part 2: Intercept and Processing*, NSA historian, 1953. The lineage and development of the Army's intercept sites before World War II is by no means fully established. Intercept operations at Fort Hancock began in 1938, when a detachment from the First RI Company moved into an isolated building on the beach at Sandy Hook. Fort Hancock is only twenty miles north of Fort Monmouth, where intercept operations had previously been carried out. In documents of Oct. 1940, MS-1 is shown as Fort Monmouth again rather than Fort Hancock. I believe that MS-1 remained at Fort Hancock but that general administrative, and later teletype, support was at Monmouth. Thus the site was identified interchangeably as Fort Hancock/Fort Monmouth. (See especially the 1976 interview of Mr. Albert Jones, NSA employee. Jones was an intercept operator at Hancock 1938–1939.)

9. *History of the Signal Security Agency*, vol. 2, 2–3.

10. Memorandum from Sam Snyder to Mr. Friedman, 12 Sep. 1940, subject: Station 6 Traffic (classified), NSA Historical Collection (hereafter referred to as NSAHC).

11. Ibid., attached papers.

12. "Copy of report given to Lieutenant Rowlett, May 16, 1942," NSAHC.

13. The author does not suggest that there ought to or could have been solutions or translations. In an interview in 1975, Mr. Frank B. Rowlett opined that Japanese army traffic was too inadequate for solution to have been possible. There were probably never more than fifteen SIS intercept operators at MS-6, and covering both the low-powered (according to Rowlett) Japanese army traffic and the Japanese diplomatic traffic (which was exploitable) was impossible.

14. *NAVSECGRU Stations, 1922–1959.* Photocopy of an undated listing, presumably prepared by the Naval Security Group, NSAHC (classified).

15. Ibid.

16. Summary of interviews of Captain Rudolph J. Fabian, USN (Ret) conducted 1975–76 by Captain Wayman Packard, USN (Ret). Captain Packard, who has written a history of Naval Intelligence, provided much information to the author.

17. The prewar relationship of OP-20-G with the field sites was complex. It is addressed in great detail by Captain Laurance Safford in his testimony before the various Pearl Harbor inquiries. The focus of the author's study is on World War II policy/administration and not on intelligence preceding or related to the Pearl Harbor attack.

18. By far the best account of intelligence related to the Pearl Harbor attack is Roberta Wohlstetter, *Pearl Harbor: Warning and Decision* (Stanford, 1962). Mrs. Wohlstetter made an impressive study of the forty volumes of testimony – *Pearl Harbor Attack (PHA)* – resulting from congressional hearings in 1946.

19. Wohlstetter, 171. This figure probably includes the intercept sites (other than in the Pacific).

20. Rochefort testimony, *PHA*, Part 10, 4,673.

21. Fabian testimony, *PHA*, Part 36, 46ff; and memorandum from Joseph E. Wenger to Op-20-G, 26 Jan. 1942, subject: Reorganization, NSAHC (classified).

22. Memorandum from J. F. Farley, USCG to Commander John R. Redman, OP-20-G, 6 March 1942 (classified), NSAHC. Captain Farley was chief of USCG communications from 1937 to 1942 and later, as a rear admiral, was commandant of the Coast Guard. This memorandum gives a history of USCG COMINT.

23. Interview with Mrs. Friedman, Jan. 1976.

24. Ibid.

25. Farley memorandum. It is not stated just what type of communications were to be covered by the USCG.

26. Farley memorandum; also, memorandum from Commander L. T. Jones, OP-20-G, 7 Sep. 1944, subject: Clandestine Radio Intelligence, NSAHC (classified).

27. Farley memorandum.

28. Memorandum from J. F. Farley to Commander J. R. Redman, 28 Mar. 1942 (classified), NSAHC; also, *History of Coast Guard Unit 387*, NSA Cryptologic Collection, undated.

29. Interview of Paul Napier and I. Woodrow Newpher, retired FBI cryptanalysts, Oct. 1975.

30. Ibid.

31. Letter from Brigadier General Sherman Miles, ACS, G-2, to J. Edgar Hoover, 28 June 1941, National Archives, Record Group 165. The Miles letter acknowledges a 19 June 1941 letter from Hoover in which Hoover apprised MID of the solution and offered to help MID with unsolved traffic. Miles claimed the Army had "none on

hand for decoding." Miles was almost certainly being cagey in this reply as the SIS was working Vichy traffic. The Miles letter was drafted by W. Preston Corderman.

32. Napier–Newpher interview; Mrs. Friedman interview.

33. Correspondence between Mr. Hoover and Mr. Fly, Oct. 1940–Jan. 1941, in Box 9, Record Group 173 (RID Records), National Archives. Some of this correspondence has been declassified, but some remains under FBI seal (the author saw all the material).

34. Napier-Newpher interviews. Circuits included those carrying South America-Tokyo diplomatic traffic.

35. Ibid.

36. See vol. 2, the General Cryptanalytic Problems, in *History of the Signal Security Agency in World War II*, for material on FBI surreptitious assistance (classified).

37. Letter to the author from the FBI, 26 January 1976. The author has not seen the documents summarized in this letter. While a possible mistaken date, Oct. *1940* instead of Oct. *1939*, seems obvious, the FBI letter was in response to specific requests and discussions with FBI personnel involved in COMINT. Further, the correspondence cited in footnote 35 does not describe a meeting or proposal resembling that of 1939. RG173 contains no material earlier than summer 1940. Chairman Fly was a Naval Academy graduate and a former naval officer. My tentative conclusion is that Fly did make such a proposal and that it was unrelated to later FCC (from summer 1940 on) involvement in COMINT.

38. Interviews with Mr. Sterling by author, 1975.

39. Sterling interview.

40. George Sterling, "The U.S. Hunt for Axis Agent Radios," *Studies in Intelligence*, vol. 4, Spring 1960, CIA (FOUO).

41. "Agreement Regarding Special Material," filed in vol. 1 of *Catalog of Papers*, a collection prepared by AFSA in 1952, NSAHC (hereafter cited as *Catalog*) (classified).

42. Memorandum from Safford to OP-20, 25 July 1940, subject: Coordination of Intercept and Decrypting Activities of the Army and Navy With Detailed Appendix (same subject), vol. 1, *Catalog* (classified).

43. Memorandum from Safford to Noyes, 27 July 1940, vol. 1, *Catalog* (classified).

44. Memorandum from Commander Safford and Colonel Akin to Joint Army-Navy Committee, 31 July 1940, vol. 1, *Catalog* (classified).

45. The approval document, committee report, and appendices (all classified) are in vol. 1 of *Catalog*. This material is of exceptional historical interest. It shows virtually the complete picture of SIS intercept operations as of Oct. 1940: circuits covered, number of intercept operators at each station, amount and type of equipment, and number and type of messages intercepted. The information concerning OP-20-G is less complete, as there is no information on naval COMINT (i.e., anti-Japanese; anti-German). Diplomatic COMINT was for the Navy, unlike the Army, a sideline.

46. This was essentially an IIC gathering, though the term was not yet in use. The source for this meeting is Memorandum for the director, Tamm to J. Edgar Hoover, 5 July 1940, NSAHC. A copy of this memorandum was provided to the writer in 1975 by FBI liaison after its existence was made known to the writer by CIA historian Thomas Troy.

47. The SIS accomplished this in Washington during 1940 (or earlier) and 1941 as follows: Each morning an officer visited the RCA office, and there he used a special camera, lights, and copystand to photograph telegrams

of interest. He then took the film to SIS, where it was developed and copies were quickly distributed to the cryptanalysts. Interview of Frank B. Rowlett by Vincent Wilson and Henry Schorreck, NSAHC.

48. August 1940 is the date suggested by Captain Safford in a memorandum he wrote on 14 Feb. 1946. (vol. 1, *Catalog*). The first solutions to the PURPLE machine were made on 27 Sep. 1940. (See *History of SSA*, vol. 2, 44–45.) I believe the odd-even agreement dates from *after* the 3 Oct. 1940 agreement, but probably soon after, at least by the end of 1940. See discussion of the odd-even agreement in various testimony in *PHA*; also Wohlstetter, 173–75.

49. Rowlett interview, tape #9.

50. Vol. 2.c.(8), *Catalog*.

51. For aids to British cryptanalysis, see H. Montgomery Hyde, *Room 3603* (New York, 1963) and *Cynthia*, (New York, 1965); for Captain Hyde and the exchange of cipher systems with FBI, see letter to the author from the FBI, 26 Jan. 1976.

52. I believe that BSC had access to cables in New York City, though I have found no documentation. One reason for believing this is that President Roosevelt's friend and confidant, Commander Vincent Astor, USN (Ret), was a director of Western Union. Astor engaged in intelligence coordination and operations for the president and was closely allied on a personal basis with William Stephenson, head of BSC. (The foregoing based in part on conversations by the author with CIA historian Thomas Troy.)

53. Memorandum from Lieutenant Commander A. D. Kramer to OP-20-G, 8 June 1942, subject: Cryptanalysis, FBI Activities, and Liaison with the British (classified), NSAHC, in FBI/Coast Guard general file. This document, hereafter cited as Kramer Memorandum of 8 June 1942, is an exceptionally important historical document covering a wide range of USN-British intelligence relations.

54. Aide-Memoire Lothian to Roosevelt, 8 July 1940, ACSI #2, NSAHC.

55. Memorandum from Strong to Chief of Staff, 19 July 1940, ACSI #2, NSAHC.

56. Ibid; also, memorandum from Henry L. Stimson, secretary of war, to secretary of state, 22 July 1940, ACSI #2, NSAHC.

57. Vernon Davis, *The History of the Joint Chiefs of Staff in World War II*, vol. 1; *Origin of the Joint and Combined Chiefs of Staff* (Washington, DC, Historical Division JCS, 1972), 99–100.

58. Paraphrased Cable, Raymond E. Lee (for Strong) to War Department, 23 Aug. 1940, ACSI #45, NSAHC.

59. General Miles had been Lee's predecessor as Army attaché in London. Both Miles and Lee were found wanting as ACS, G-2. Their selection is a strong indictment of General Marshall's knowledge of and interest in intelligence. This subject is a recurring theme of this study.

60. Memorandum from Patterson to chiefs of arms and services and G-2, 29 Aug. 1940, subject: Information to be Obtained from Abroad, ACSI #45, NSAHC.

61. ACSI #45, NSAHC.

62. Kramer memorandum of 8 June 1942.

63. Letter from Colonel Eastman to General Mauborgne, 5 Sept. 1940, ACSI #45, NSAHC.

64. ACSI #45, NSAHC.

65. Memorandum from ACS, G-2 to chief of staff, 9 Sept. 1940, subject: Directive to G-2 Covering Interchange of Secret Technical Information With Representatives of the British Government, ACSI #45, NSAHC.

66. Memorandum from Miles to Regnier, 4 Oct. 1940, subject: Codes and Ciphers, ACSI #45 (classified), NSAHC.

67. As Colonel Alfred McCormack of the Military Intelligence Service would learn in 1943, the British had been reading U.S. State Department traffic at least until the U.S. entered the war. (Classified memorandum from McCormack to Colonel Carter W. Clarke, 15 June 1943, ACSI #40, NSAHC.)

68. The travel orders are in ACSI #45. There is no mention in these orders of the nature of their mission.

69. Vernon Davis, vol. 1, 108.

70. While I have not found specific documentation on this mission, the Navy's participation was certainly approved and ordered by President Roosevelt. The U.S. party sailed from Annapolis, Maryland.

71. Letter to the author from Professor Sinkov, 1976, NSAHC.

72. Letter to the author from Professor Sinkov; also *History of SSA*, vol. 2, 11–13; and Sinkov-Rosen memorandum to ACS, G-2, 11 Apr. 1941; and *Report of Cryptographic Mission*, signed by Sinkov and Rosen (not dated but obviously is from 1941), all in ACSI #45. Sir John Dill headed "General Marshall's letter to field marshall dated 23 Dec. 1942" in ACSI #44, NSAHC. It is interesting to note that the basic Sinkov-Rosen documents (to ACS, G-2 and the more technical *Report of Cryptographic Mission*) makes no mention of ENIGMA, so secret was this information. The ENIGMA secret was revealed to the U.S. officers with the approval of Prime Minister Winston Churchill. (background paper for Dill)

73. See, for example, the writings of Charles Beard, Herbert Feis, Harry Elmer Barnes, and William Lange. Beard and Barnes were, unfortunately, of the "Conspiracy Theory" school.

74. Frank Birch, *Naval SIGINT, vol. 5(a), (Japanese)*, GC&CS Histories, 93 ff (classified).

75. Ibid., 95.

76. Ibid., 95–96, and Rudolph Fabian interviews conducted by Captain Packard. Captain Fabian, who places Jeff Dennis at the meeting, suggests the date as Dec. 1940 while the GC&CS has it as Feb. 1941. Unless I have run together separate conferences, I believe the latter date is more likely.

77. Birch, *Naval SIGINT, vol (a)*, 101 (classified).

78. Thomas Troy, *The Coordinator of Information and British Intelligence*, 105 (classified).

79. Ibid.

80. Mr. Troy, upon review of documents in his possession, places Captain Hastings with the JIC (called the "Junior JIC") in Washington in the summer of 1941. This is confirmed in Kramer memorandum of 8 June 1942. Hastings's link to the CSS is apparent in numerous later references. Further, his later organizational placement in Washington was with the British Admiralty delegation, and he was formally identified as the CG&CS representative to the U.S. in 1942.

81. All details of this mission are from the oral history of the late Rear Admiral Arthur S. McCollum, transcript in possession of the U.S. Naval Institute in Annapolis, Dr. Jack Mason, historian, custodian. See 244 ff. (hereafter cited as McCollum Oral History).

82. Ibid. Unfortunately, McCollum did not detail this information for the interviewer, and the author has not seen any USN documents related to his mission. McCollum, born in Japan to missionary parents, was a Japanese linguist and long-time ONI veteran. The assist from Sir Dudley Pound was arranged through a U.S. Naval Reserve officer on duty in London, Lieutenant Commander Paul Hammond. Hammond, a wealthy New York banker, was a peacetime yachting companion of Sir Dudley.

83. Birch, *Naval SIGINT vol. (a)*, 209 (classified); also Kramer memorandum of 8 June 1942.

84. Minutes of Conference, August 16, 1941, ACSI #45, NSAHC. This exchange would be handled by BSC, New York.

85. Historical paper entitled "Cooperation with GC&CS" prepared by Lieutenant McCracken, Signal Corps, 1945(?), ACSI #45, NSAHC.

86. Birch, *Naval SIGINT vol. (a)*, 175 (classified).

87. Roberta Wohlstetter's *Pearl Harbor: Warning and Decision* is by far the best account.

88. See McCollum Oral History; McCollum, T.S. Wilkinson, Kramer, etc., testimony in *PHA*.Special

Chapter 2
The First Year of War

THE IMPACT OF WAR

With the outbreak of war in the Pacific on 7 December 1941, the most important U.S. COMINT facilities became the Navy's Cast unit in Corregidor and the Hawaii unit, soon to be known as Hypo. They were also the most exposed, and Cast had to be evacuated within a few months. The Army would also lose its only station then capable of monitoring Japanese army traffic – MS-6, Fort Mills, Philippine Islands.

MS-6, which had copied Japanese army traffic in 1939–40 (though SIS managed no solutions), had during 1941 worked almost exclusively against Japanese diplomatic communications. These intercepts were laboriously reenciphered, often by the chief of MS-6, Major Joseph Scherr, and then radioed to Washington. Beginning on the afternoon of 8 December, which was 7 December in Hawaii and in the U.S., and within hours after the first Japanese air attacks on Clark Field, the station turned its attention to Japanese tactical nets. There were some immediate successes in identifying Japanese air-ground communications controlled from Formosa.[1] When Major Scherr was assigned to the staff of Brigadier General Spencer Akin, General MacArthur's signal officer, MS-6 was briefly commanded by Lieutenant Harold R. Brown, a former enlisted man with extensive COMINT experience. On Christmas Eve MS-6 was dissolved as an SIS unit and moved to Corregidor, where it was placed under the command of Akin and Scherr. From then until late March 1942, it provided COMINT support for the beleaguered U.S. Army forces in the Philippines: intercept and traffic analysis of Japanese army units, monitoring of Japanese air force circuits for early warning, and rudimentary cryptanalysis. Potentially useful information from Japanese communication service messages was faithfully radioed to the SIS in Washington. General Akin and Lieutenant Colonel Scherr left the Philippines with MacArthur in March. On the 24th, MacArthur, in a message from Australia to Lieutenant General Jonathan Wainwright, his successor in the Philippines, ordered Brown and the COMINT detachment (eleven men) to evacuate to Australia. Most of them eventually reached Australia, where they helped form the nucleus of a new COMINT effort.[2]

The Army's only remaining SIS site in the Pacific was MS-5, Hawaii. This station was operated by twenty-five enlisted men, without an SIS commanding officer, under the administration of the Hawaiian department signal officer. Before the outbreak of war, the mission of MS-5 was diplomatic intercept. With the sudden onset of an emergency, the station was hard pressed and unable to provide significant COMINT support. There was no DF equipment, the command structure was confused, and there was no clear mission. The

Army turned to the Federal Communications Commission's Radio Intelligence Division and continued to depend on it through most of 1942.[3]

The situation was no better in Alaska, where a Japanese invasion seemed more likely. The Army's basic communications within Alaska and between Alaska and the U.S. were good. The cable between Seward and Seattle went into operation on 3 December 1941, providing reliable communications between the Alaskan Command and the Western Defense Command.[4] But there was no COMINT unit in Alaska, and there would be none until a radio intelligence company was sent there in 1943. COMINT support was provided by the RID from its several monitoring stations in Alaska and the Pacific Northwest.[5]

As described in chapter 1, the Navy's COMINT assets in the Pacific were considerable. Because both Cast and Hypo were capable of processing their own traffic – performing traffic analysis, DF, cryptanalysis, and translation – problems of communication with Washington over the now-congested radio facilities at Pearl Harbor and Manila were not as important. At this time, the dispersed nature of Navy COMINT was undoubtedly an advantage. Station B at Guam was lost on 10 December when the island was surrendered to the Japanese. Some COMINT personnel were captured, but the Japanese never learned about their activities. As a result of prewar planning, much material had been destroyed or removed as had some of the key personnel. The COMINT operations building and COMINT materials were burned before the Japanese landed.[6]

Within the U.S., the Navy's facilities were also more advanced than the Army's facilities at the beginning of the war. The main OP-20-G stations were already linked to Washington by teletype. The Army had opened a teletype between the Presidio (MS-2) and Washington on the night of 6 December. Teletype had also been installed between Washington and MS-1, Fort Monmouth/Fort Hancock, but the operators there failed to respond to the SIS attempt to open that link on 6 December.[7]

The outbreak of war, then, disrupted and endangered some COMINT facilities. The extreme inadequacy of Army intercept facilities for the new tasks at hand was apparent.

THE EXPANSION AND REORGANIZATION OF ARMY COMINT DURING 1942

When the war began, the SIS was operating under a new chief, Lieutenant Colonel Rex Minckler, and a new chief signal officer (CSO), Major General Dawson Olmstead. Minckler had replaced the highly regarded Spencer Akin in June 1941, with the latter, as we have seen, going to the Philippines as General MacArthur's signal officer. Minckler, later described as a poor organizer and manager, and as uncooperative with MID, would be replaced in April 1942.[8]

General Olmstead had been General Marshall's personal choice as chief signal officer to replace General Mauborgne, who was pressured to retire in July 1941, six weeks ahead of schedule. Mauborgne confidentially told General Marshall at the time that he did not feel Olmstead was qualified for the task. Mauborgne's choice was Colonel Harry C. Ingles, who in fact replaced Olmstead when the latter was forced out in disgrace in 1943.[9] General Olmstead, unlike General Mauborgne, had very little knowledge of COMINT.[10] About two weeks before Pearl Harbor, Olmstead departed Washington for an inspection tour of Panama in spite of the entreaties of his chief assistant, Colonel Otis K. Sadtler, who believed that war was imminent. He did not return until 16 December, and Colonel Sadtler ran the Signal Corps and SIS during his absence.[11]

Major General Dawson Olmstead, chief signal officer

On 27 December the SIS became a division of the Operations Branch, OCSigO, but a few days later the Army Communications Service was created, and the SIS remained under this element of the OCSigO throughout the war. The Communications Service was first headed by Colonel Sadtler, who was replaced by Brigadier General Frank Stoner during 1942. Stoner remained in this position and was closely involved in high-level policy related to the SIS.

The SIS itself was broadly organized into these units in January 1942:

A	(Administration)	Major Harold G. Hayes
B	(Cryptanalytic)	Major Harold Doud
C	(Cryptographic)	Captain Earle F. Cook
D	(Laboratory)	Major A. J. McGrail
Second Signal Service Company		Captain Robert Schukraft

The COMINT (Cryptanalytic) unit B was divided into:[12]

B-1	(Japanese)	Major Eric Evensson
B-2	(German)	Captain Solomon Kullback
B-3	(Italian)	Captain Abraham Sinkov
B-4	(French)	Lieutenant H. F. Bearce

B-5	(Stenographic)	Miss Louise Prather
B-6	(Traffic)	Captain Robert Schukraft (who also commanded the Second Signal Service – the unit intercepting the traffic)
B-7	(South America)	Lieutenant Larry M. Glodell

Further expansion of this structure was directed by the Military Intelligence Service (MIS) in April 1942. The MIS was created when the War Department was reorganized in March 1942. This action profoundly affected the SIS and military intelligence in general. By this general reorganization, the old War Department arrangement, with chiefs of arms and services existing alongside the General Staff, was swept away. The offices of the chiefs of infantry, cavalry, and field artillery (and others) were abolished. The CSO and OCSigO remained, but they were now made subordinate to a huge new CONUS command, the Services of Supply, soon renamed the Army Service Forces (ASF). Its chief for the duration of the war was Lieutenant General Brehon B. Somervell, a veteran Army engineer. Thus the Signal Corps lost its direct access to the chief of staff, and the SIS was placed under yet another layer of control.

The MID remained as G-2 on the Army General Staff. But because of the sentiment within the Army's reorganization committee (which was chaired by General Joseph T. McNarney) that the General Staff should be limited in size and not be an operational organization, a curious structure was created. Henceforth, MID would be a small group performing purely staff functions. Its operational arm would be the Military Intelligence Service, a theoretically independent War Department Agency which, however, would report to ACS, G-2.

The first chief of MIS was Colonel Hayes A. Kroner of the old MID. Kroner also had the title of deputy ACS, G-2.[13] By the end of April 1942, the MIS would consist of 342 officers and 1,005 civilians and enlisted personnel.[14] The MIS charter, contained in War Department Circular Number 59, dated 2 March 1942, stated that "the Military Intelligence Service, under the direction of the assistant chief of staff, Military Intelligence Division, War Department General Staff, will operate and administer the service of collection, compilation, and dissemination of military intelligence."[15] In practice, the MIS and MID continued to act as one until the summer of 1944, when another attempt was made to separate staff from operations. The MIS charter was a clear basis for its control of SIS (SIS was not, of course, mentioned in circular 59 because it was so secret an organization), as would soon be made clear.

The post-Pearl Harbor changes resulted in the departure of General Miles as ACS, G-2. He was sent to Latin America on an inspection tour in January, and when he returned he had, in effect, lost his job. The new G-2 was Brigadier General Raymond Lee, late of attaché duty in London. His tour was very brief and unsuccessful, and he was replaced by sixty-two-year-old Major General George V. Strong, an officer of towering reputation in the Army.[16]

There now entered on the scene two men who would guide Army COMINT policy throughout the war: Carter W. Clarke and Alfred McCormack. Mr. McCormack was the law partner of John J. McCloy, who had recently been appointed assistant secretary of war. In December 1941 Mr. McCormack came to Washington and asked McCloy for the toughest assignment the latter had.[17] At about the same time, Secretary of War Henry Stimson came to the conclusion, in the light of Pearl Harbor, that Army COMINT was inadequate. He asked Assistant Secretary McCloy to suggest someone, preferably a lawyer experienced in handling complicated matters, who could establish an organization to properly deal with COMINT. McCloy offered the job to McCormack. The latter then received his charge from Mr. Stimson: study the problem and make recommendations on how to expand Army COMINT and make it usable.[18]

Mr. McCormack (commissioned as a colonel a few months later) went to work in January 1942. He looked into SIS's production of COMINT and its handling within MID. While a new subelement had been established in the Far East section of MID to specifically study COMINT, McCormack found that the procedures were much as before as the responsible officer would ". . . take what looked interesting and pass it along in paraphrased form without any attempt either to check or evaluate the information or to supplement it by collateral intelligence."[19]

McCormack was a hard taskmaster, and he summarily dismissed from his presence several officers who had been assigned to aid him in his study.[20] Ultimately he came into contact with Colonel Carter W. Clarke, chief of the Safeguarding Military Information (SMI) section of MID. Clarke was a regular officer with twenty-five years in the Army, much of it spent in intelligence work.[21] By March 1942 Colonel Clarke had assumed a preeminent position in Army COMINT management, although the final definition of his role would not come until May.

Carter W. Clarke, wartime chief of special branch (1954 photograph)

By March McCormack had concluded that a very large expansion of Army COMINT was needed and that this could best be accomplished by placing it under the operational control of G-2.[22] General Strong agreed with this view. As a step in that direction, the Special Service Branch, soon renamed the Special Branch, was created in mid-May 1942. Colonel

Clarke was appointed as its chief, and McCormack became his deputy. Clarke was appointed "the authorized representative of the assistant chief of staff, G-2, for the purpose of supervising all signal intelligence activities of the War Department."[23] His responsibilities were to include liaison with other government agencies involved in COMINT, preparation of COMINT directives to the CSO, and the appropriate supervision to insure their accomplishment. The functions of the Special Branch included the following:

1. analysis of COMINT received from SIS

2. dissemination of COMINT within the War Department (and to other agencies)

3. security of COMINT[24]

During the first year of its existence, the Special Branch was divided into Headquarters (Clarke, McCormack), Area Sections (the research desks), and Reports Section. The personnel buildup was slow – there were thirty-eight officers and civilians by July 1942, and twenty-eight officers and fifty-five civilians by March 1943.[25] Colonel McCormack initially concentrated on recruiting analysts while Colonel Clarke worked with SIS on expansion of their facilities and personnel. The product of the Special Branch was the daily MAGIC Summary, an analysis of key SIS translations. Special studies were also prepared. Recipients of this product, which was finished intelligence, included the secretary of war, the chief of staff, key officers of the General Staff (such as in the Operations Division), ONI, and State Department.

In June 1942 General Strong made an effort to bring these activities to a logical (to MID) conclusion. He recommended to General Marshall that the MIS should have complete control of Army COMINT and cryptography, an arrangement that had existed until 1929 when Army regulations were changed.[26] Strong reasoned that the daily operating decisions of the SIS were intelligence decisions that ought to be under his control but that at present "... G-2 has only a limited control over this extremely important source of intelligence, while the officers of the Signal Corps are burdened with decisions requiring the training and information that they do not have."[27]

The Strong proposal was rejected. As MIS would later learn, Strong's proposal was favored by Colonel Frank Bullock, the new chief of SIS; by Lieutenant Colonel Minckler, his predecessor; and by Mr. Friedman and other SIS officers. The transfer of authority was strongly opposed by General Olmstead and General Stoner. Because of that opposition, the SIS committee studying the Strong proposal reported against the transfer of authority.[28] Nonetheless, the preeminence of Colonel Clarke and the MIS was established. Evaluation, dissemination, and security of COMINT would be a function of intelligence rather than signals.[29]

Meanwhile the expansion of SIS had begun. In late March 1942 important discussions were held between Clarke, Stoner, and SIS officers. Clarke advised SIS that new priorities would be forthcoming and that highest priority was to be given to the army and air force traffic of Germany, Japan, Russia, and Italy.[30] In addition, large intercept stations were to be established near Washington and on the West Coast.

This was formalized (and altered) in an important directive of 18 April 1942 from MIS to the CSO.[31] The immediate expansion of SIS was directed. A large, permanent intercept station was to be built near Washington to cover European traffic, and a similar station was to be built on the West Coast to cover the Pacific and Asia. The SIS was to consider moving its headquarters out of Washington for better security from enemy agents and possible bombing. Secondary intercept stations were to be in Alaska and Ireland or Iceland. The SIS priorities in intercept and processing were to be in this order:

1. The armies and air forces of Germany, Japan, Italy

2. Japanese, German, and Italian military attachés

3. Axis diplomatic traffic

4. German administrative radio nets

5. Vichy traffic

6. Other diplomatic traffic between Tokyo and Latin America, Sweden, Vichy France, Bangkok, Lisbon, Madrid, and Moscow

7. Traffic between Berlin and Latin America, Lisbon, and Madrid

8. Vatican traffic

The SIS could vary these priorities, on their own initiative when conditions warranted, but MIS was to be notified immediately.

The SIS was to fully process intercept and furnish translated material to MIS. SIS collaboration with the British was authorized for exchange of intercept, exchange of methods of solution, and assignment of liaison personnel. The existing arrangements for obtaining traffic from the FCC, Navy, and Coast Guard were to be continued. And finally, the SIS was to procure mobile DF equipment for the field forces, leaving long-range, fixed DF equipment to the other services (i.e., Navy, Coast Guard, and FCC).

Through the efforts of Colonel Clarke and Colonel Bullock, the SIS obtained the buildings and grounds of the Arlington Hall Junior College in Arlington, Virginia. SIS headquarters moved there in July 1942. At the same time, a farm was purchased near Manassas, Virginia, for use as the primary monitoring station for the East Coast. By June 1943 there would be 53 officers and 1,627 enlisted men of the Second Signal Service Battalion (formerly company) at Vint Hill Farm Station (VHFS).[32] Two Rock Ranch near Petaluma, California – forty miles north of San Francisco – became the primary monitoring station for the West Coast. Two Rock, purchased by the War Department in August 1942, was operational in January 1943.[33] VHFS became the new MS-1, replacing Fort Hunt, Virginia (formerly MS-7), and Fort Monmouth/Fort Hancock (formerly MS-1).

Two Rock Ranch became MS-2, replacing the SIS site at the Presidio (the former MS-2). Two Rock would remain much smaller than VHFS, but it became the SIS's largest single source of Japanese army traffic.

Aerial view of Arlington Hall Station, 1945

Coexisting with the intercept service of the SIS's Second Signal Service Battalion were the signal radio intelligence (SRI) companies. Under Army doctrine at the beginning of the war, SRI companies were organic to general headquarters or numbered armies, while radio platoons (intelligence) were to be assigned to division.[34] There were various changes in these procedures dictated by the existing organizational structures in the different theaters. As an example, radio intelligence companies, known as signal service companies (SSC), were assigned to each corps in the European theater from D-Day on. The purpose of the SRI (and SSCs) was to provide tactical COMINT for the field commanders through interception and analysis of lower-level enemy field communications. These involved enemy ground forces' tactical Morse traffic, air-to-ground voice, and Morse. The SRI company might perform DF, TA, lower-level CA, and translation, to give the army (or corps) commander intelligence from the tactical signals of his opposite number in the field. The SRIs were under the command of the appropriate commanding general; this authority was exercised through the theater (as General Akin in Southwest Pacific Area – SWPA), army or corps signal officer, and G-2 officer.

In practice there were many variations leading to administrative confusion (at least for the War Department in Washington). For instance, the West Coast SRIs (Western Defense Command), especially prior to the activation of the new MS-2 at Two Rock Ranch, were intercepting high-level Japanese army communications and sending them to SIS for processing. This was not tactical COMINT. The SIS station in Hawaii, MS-5, was ultimately manned by an SRI company rather than by Second Signal Service personnel. And in the SWPA the SRIs intercepted what Japanese signals they could, at any level (except diplomatic).

This two-tiered intercept system continued throughout the war: one level under the SIS, the other under field/theater commanders. However, the MIS did send directives to the SRIs, via the commanding generals, at various times during the war. The first group of directives, prepared by Colonel Clarke, was sent out on 31 March 1942.[35] While these directives were not entirely practical and were replaced within a year, they are listed here to give some idea of the early deployment of SRIs:

Major Command and SRI Company	Intercept Assignment
Western Defense Command:	Japanese army stations
102nd (The Presidio) and 125th (Fort Lewis)	
Third Army:	Axis espionage and Mexican army stations
122nd and 124th, Fort Sam Houston, Texas	
Caribbean Defense Command:	Axis espionage stations
120th (Trinidad and Panama)	
Hawaiian Department:	Japanese army stations
101st (not there for several months)	
Eastern Defense Command:	
Section of Twenty-first Signal Service Company (Newfoundland)	German army and air force stations
Detachment of 122nd (Northern Ireland)	German army and air force stations
Detachment of 122nd (Fort Dix, New Jersey)	Axis espionage stations
123rd (Fort Benning, Georgia)	Axis espionage stations
121st (staging for Iceland)	German army and air force stations
Also: Detachment of 121st (under orders for Australia)	Japanese army stations

In each case, the CSO (in Washington) was authorized to deal directly with the above units regarding circuits to be covered, frequencies, form of copying material, and submission of traffic. Copies of all intercept were to be forwarded by mail to SIS.

At the same time, the SIS and MIS assigned monitoring station numbers to all sources of traffic. This was done to keep better track of the (theoretically) multitudinous sources of traffic over and above that of the SIS/Second Signal Service. As an example, the Western Defense Command traffic (i.e., the 102nd and 125th SRIs) was known as MS-15; traffic from the FCC's RID was known as MS-91.[36]

SIS underwent various name changes through the summer of 1942. On 22 June it was briefly renamed the Signal Intelligence Service Division and three weeks later the Signal Security Division (SSD).[37] During the next year it would be called the Signal Security Service (SSS) and finally the Signal Security Agency (SSA).[38]

Until November 1942 Army combat operations were restricted to the Southwest Pacific Area. MacArthur and his headquarters party, which included COMINT experts Major Joseph Scherr and Brigadier General Spencer Akin, reached Australia from the Philippines on 17 March 1942. On 1 April 1942 General MacArthur radioed the War Department urgently requesting the assignment of COMINT and cryptographic personnel. He requested twelve persons qualified in cryptanalysis and translation. He noted that the delay in sending intercepts to Washington (versus having his own CA people) was a problem.[39] Colonel Clarke drafted a reply that was radioed on 3 April: eighteen officers and enlisted men with appropriate qualifications would depart by air for MacArthur's headquarters as soon as possible. The message referred to "SIS at your headquarters," a clear statement that MacArthur would have his own COMINT center.[40] The advance party, consisting of Captains Abraham Sinkov and Hugh Erskine, arrived at MacArthur's headquarters in Melbourne during April. More Washington SIS personnel would follow.[41] Interestingly, Sinkov and Erskine received no instructions from the ACS, G-2 or MIS. It was clear to them that they would be working for General Akin only.[42]

MacArthur's COMINT charter had actually been radioed to him on 30 March, perhaps prompting his request for personnel. Like the directives to the SRI companies (detailed above), it was general. However, it gave General MacArthur the authority to assign his own intercept directives. Still, the CSO was authorized to communicate with MacArthur's SRI company on technical matters.[43]

The result of this – and actions within the theater – was the creation of the Central Bureau, later called Central Bureau Brisbane (CBB), on 6 April 1942. Planning for this organization had begun under Scherr and Akin as soon as they arrived in Australia. CBB was an Allied COMINT organization consisting of U.S. Army, Royal Australian Air Force (RAAF), and Australian army personnel. All intercept was accomplished by Australian units until the end of 1942, when the U.S. Army's 126th SRI Company began operations. General Akin retained the title of director CBB, while day-to-day operations were under a three-man board of deputy directors, one of whom was Captain (later Colonel) Sinkov. Sinkov also headed the U.S. Army's 837th Signal Service Detachment, the administrative unit for the SIS personnel in CBB.[44] The development of CBB will be described in greater detail in chapter 3.

COMINT support for the European theater was slower in development. The need was less immediate, and there was an elaborate British COMINT organization far beyond anything that existed in the Pacific. The first U.S. Army headquarters in the European theater was the U.S. Army Forces British Isles, created in January 1942 and redesignated European Theater of Operations U.S. Army (ETOUSA) on 3 June. A platoon of the 122nd

SRI Company went to Ireland in the spring of 1942 and made attempts to intercept German army traffic in mid-May.[45] In June 1942 Lieutenant Colonel George Bicher, a Signal Corps veteran with extensive training and experience with SIS, was named director of the Signal Intelligence Division, Signal Section, Hq ETOUSA. He was also director of SIS ETOUSA.[46] Initially he had operational control of the SRI companies arriving in the U.K., which meant he was charged with their training. He maintained contact with G-2 ETOUSA and the Government Code and Cipher School. By March 1943 his staff consisted of only thirty-four officers and enlisted men. As a member of his staff would later recall, SIS ETOUSA personnel occupied themselves learning all they could from the British about the German army field code, German communications technique, and practical aspects of field intercept. This in turn was passed on to the SRI personnel.[47]

George Bicher, director, Signal Intelligence Division, Signal Section, HQ ETOUSA

When the U.S. Army did go into combat in North Africa in November 1942, the Army's field COMINT came under other organizational structures activated specifically for this campaign. At AFHQ there was a "Y northwest Africa Committee" under SIS veteran Lieutenant Colonel Harold G. Hayes. The U.S. Army COMINT units in its sphere were the 122nd and 128th Signal Radio Intelligence (SRI) companies. Subsequently, 849th SIS was created to provide U.S. SRI companies in North Africa with better field processing capability. The 849th was activated at Ft. Devens, Massachusetts, on 2 December 1942 with a strength of 16 officers and 102 enlisted men; it arrived in Algiers on 1 February 1943.[48]

Another special unit was Signal Intelligence Detachment 9251-A, with eighty-nine officers and men. This unit was trained at Vint Hill, Arlington Hall, and ETOUSA. When it arrived in Algiers on 20 February 1943, it provided personnel for the intelligence branch of the 849th. With the arrival of the 123rd and 117th SRI companies in early 1943, there were four SRI companies in North Africa operating under the 849th.[49]

Army COMINT was now very much in combat, providing direct support to commanders through theater G-2 channels. This was pure tactical COMINT derived from the communications of German combat units operating in the theater. Once (and if) the units received special training at Arlington Hall or Vint Hill, the SIS had no further role until traffic was received, and that did not always happen. (Nor did all units receive SIS training.) The MIS played little part in the operations of the SRIs other than to issue broad intercept directives from time to time. It is doubtful if the MIS had much information about what went on at SIS ETOUSA or with the 849th in North Africa.

Cryptographic and security personnel, 849th SIS

NAVY COMINT REORGANIZATION AND EXPANSION IN WASHINGTON DURING 1942

On the night of 7 December 1941, Assistant Secretary of State A. A. Berle Jr., wrote in his diary that one job he would not want at that moment was director of naval intelligence.[50] Actually Admiral T. S. Wilkinson, the DNI, survived the Pearl Harbor debacle and remained on the job until July 1942, when he went to sea. He served in important combat roles throughout the war. ONI, however, had by that time begun a steady decline.

In OP-20 and OP-20-G, major changes were afoot by the second month of the war. On 23 January 1942, Captain Laurance Safford, the long-time head of OP-20-G, proposed a major reorganization in a memorandum to the director of naval communications, Admiral Leigh Noyes. Safford suggested the creation of OP-20-Q, a cryptographic division, under himself, while OP-20-G would be limited to communications intelligence. He suggested that Lieutenant Commander Welker assume control of OP-20-G.[51] The reason for Safford's action is not clear. He had recently been promoted to captain, and, at his request, had been placed on engineer duty only, a move that would allow him to remain at his specialty rather than return to sea duty. Possibly Safford was forced out; that was the contemporary view. As Commander Arthur McCollum described the situation, the CNO's staff was having a "nervous breakdown" in the wake of Pearl Harbor, and Safford, an excitable person himself, had to go.[52] Perhaps Safford knew that he would be replaced and preempted his relief with a suggestion that would still leave him an important activity.[53]

Safford's suggestions were circulated for comments in OP-20/OP-20-G. The result was a new organization, considerably different from what Safford had envisioned. On 12 February 1942, Commander Joseph R. Redman, the assistant DNC, directed the following realignment in OP-20:[54]

OP-20-G	Radio Intelligence	Commander John R. Redman
OP-20-K	Communications Security (COMSEC)	Lieutenant Commander Densford
OP-20-Q	Cryptography	Captain Safford

Commander John R. Redman, the brother of Joseph Redman, was an experienced communications officer, without any prior involvement in Navy COMINT. He got the job because he was available, because of political maneuvering, and undoubtedly because he was the brother of the assistant director of naval communications (ADNC). Prior to Pearl Harbor, he had been in Washington for several years serving as the Navy Department's representative to the various U.S. radio frequency allotment committees. He was then selected for sea duty. Soon after Pearl Harbor, the new vice chief of naval operations (VCNO), Vice Admiral Frederic J. Horne, cancelled those orders so that Redman could remain at OP-20 to prepare directives on radio authentication (a speciality of his). When

John Redman found that Admiral Noyes was not acting on these proposed directives, he (Redman) reluctantly went to Admiral Horne to discuss the situation.⁵⁵ On 24 February, Noyes was relieved as DNC and replaced by Joseph R. Redman.⁵⁶

Commander Joseph N. Wenger, who had been serving on the DNC's staff, was selected as the executive officer (OP-20-GA) for John Redman. Wenger was an experienced COMINT officer with special expertise in traffic analysis. Wenger remained in OP-20-G throughout the war, becoming its head in late 1944. He was the moving force within the organization and the person most responsible for guiding its administration and interservice relationships.

Rear Admiral Joseph Redman, director, naval communications

The 12 February memorandum that announced the cryptologic changes in OP-20 contained mission statements for each of the new sections. OP-20-G was to have the following major responsibilities:

1. General operational control and coordination of intercept and monitor stations, DF nets, and decrypting units
2. TA
3. CA and decryption
4. Translation of decrypts
5. Correlation and interpretation of radio intelligence

This was a first step in clarifying the expanding role of OP-20-G. Of special interest was the command-and-control feature: there was to be a general operational control and coordination of all naval COMINT units, both for intercept and processing. And OP-20-G assumed the function of analyzing its own product, a situation far different from that in the Army. This was, however, a somewhat unilateral definition of responsibilities, for ONI and commander in chief U.S. Fleet (COMINCH) also "correlated and interpreted" COMINT.

The Navy, like the Army, underwent a general reorganization in the first months of war. In late December 1941, Admiral Ernest J. King was appointed COMINCH, and on 18 March 1942 he also became chief of naval operations (CNO), replacing Admiral Harold R. Stark. With these hitherto separate positions combined under one person, other changes followed. The COMINCH staff (with the designator F, e.g., F-1 was the plans division) was responsible for combat operations. The CNO staff (represented by the OP symbol, as in OP-20, communications and OP-16, ONI) was charged with broad support activities.[57]

This general reorganization worked well, but there were problems for the intelligence organizations because COMINCH had its own intelligence staff (F-11) under the plans division (F-1). This intelligence staff also was in charge of F-35, the operational information section of the operations division (F-3). These sections, as we will see, were consolidated in 1943.[58] But F-11/35 did not replace ONI (OP-16), the Navy's traditional intelligence organization, and they were both served by OP-20-G, which, as noted above, also evaluated its own product. The key figure in all of this would be Admiral Horne, the VCNO.[59]

OP-20-G, like the Army's SIS, expanded rapidly during 1942. In April 1942 the personnel strength in Washington was 475; by mid-June it was 750.[60] By the end of the year, there were well over 1,000 people in 20-G, and the organization was then relocated to a former girls' school on Nebraska Avenue in Washington.

The most important subdivisions of OP-20-G during 1942 were as follows:

GI, combat intelligence	Commander Sam Bertolet
GL, collateral information	Commander A. D. Kramer
GT, traffic analysis	(Various)
GX, intercept and DF control	Commander Welker
GY, cryptanalysis and decryption	Lieutenant Commander L. W. Parke
GZ, translation and code recovery	Commander A. D. Kramer

GY, the heart of the organization, included a cadre of experienced COMINT officers such as Lieutenant Commander Ford, who headed the JN-25 effort; Lieutenant Currier (who had been on the prewar PURPLE machine mission to GC&CS); Mrs. Agnes Driscoll, who worked German systems; and Lieutenant Frank Raven, a general troubleshooter. Unlike the SIS, which lacked the traffic of the Axis military forces, OP-20-G and the Pacific centers had an overwhelming amount of intercept to attack: Japanese naval and merchant marine, German U-boat, Vichy French naval, Portuguese and Spanish naval. There was also the diplomatic and attaché traffic.

While this history is not of COMINT operations and exploitation, a brief summary follows of OP-20-G's successes by the end of 1942, by way of illustrating the very advanced nature of the U.S. Navy's primary COMINT efforts:

German naval:[61] By the beginning of the war, German U-boat circuits were known and were being covered by East Coast intercept stations, Cheltenham, Maryland (Station M), being the primary site until replaced by Chatham, Massachusetts (Station C), in January 1943. U-boat traffic (ENIGMA) was readable – intermittently – beginning in December 1942.

Japanese naval:[62] There were numerous Japanese naval (JN) systems. The merchant shipping code (known first as N-L and later as JN-50) became readable in 1939. JN-25, the most important system, became readable in early 1942. By the end of 1942, there were 299 OP-20-G personnel in Washington working JN-25. Japanese naval attaché traffic was readable during (and before) 1942.

In all of their cryptanalytic efforts, OP-20-G had been aided by a technique not available to SIS: clandestine access to cryptographic materials through missions undertaken by ONI agents, especially in New York City and San Francisco. The SIS had no personnel to undertake such operations, nor did the prewar MID.[63]

The subsection of OP-20-G responsible for distribution of COMINT was GC (communications). A few officers from this then small element delivered naval COMINT summaries, written by GI (Combat Intelligence), twice daily to COMINCH and ONI. They delivered MAGIC (diplomatic) summaries to the DNC, the White House, the secretary of the navy, COMINCH, and ONI.[64]

Outside Washington, COMINT items were dispatched in a variety of ways. Intelligence from decryption and traffic analysis was sent to the collective address "COMB," which comprised FRUPAC (Fleet Radio Unit Pacific in Hawaii); the Pacific commands; Fleet Radio Unit Melbourne (FRUMEL – the COMINT unit in Melbourne, Australia, composed of Cast evacuees); and COMINCH and OPNAV (CNO) in Washington. Technical information went out on the TUNA collective address, which included FRUPAC and FRUMEL. These items went out by radio (except for the local, i.e., OPNAV and COMINCH, addressees) from the Navy Department's radio central (OP-19). Not until 1943 would OP-20-G (GC) have its own communications.[65]

With the loss of the Philippines, accurately foretold by Commander Wenger in January 1942, the Navy's West Coast intercept stations became more important. Because of Wenger's correct appreciation of the probable course of events, West Coast intercept of Japanese naval traffic began in earnest during March.[66] This, combined with FRUPAC's intercept and processing, seems to have met the Navy's needs from March until May while the Philippine unit was reforming in Australia.

In late June 1942, Navy COMINT policy was reevaluated by Admiral Horne. According to Commander McCollum, this came about after discussions between Admiral Horne and the Redman brothers did not result in agreement as to how COMINT operations were to be directed. Joseph Redman had opined that a division of authority between ONI and OP-20-G was unworkable, though cooperation between the two elements had been going on for a number of years. Redman wanted all or nothing. At a conference attended by Joseph and John Redman, Admiral Wilkinson, Admiral Schuermann (a future DNI) and McCollum, Horne announced that henceforth ONI would no longer have any control over COMINT policy. COMINT would be entirely under the control of naval communications.[67]

However, ONI maintained its evaluative function for the time. In a COMINCH directive of 6 August 1942, the VCNO was advised that ONI would be "... responsible for early evaluation of a subject traffic with a view to correcting, expanding, amplifying, and effecting other necessary treatment thereof, and for dissemination, when deemed necessary by the vice chief of naval operations, of these results to the addressees who were former recipients of the unevaluated information."[68]

In another measure taken during the summer of 1942 to establish principles governing Navy COMINT, Admiral King directed that COMINT could be passed to subordinate commanders (that is, those commanders under the commanders in chief Atlantic and Pacific, and commander Southwest Pacific Force) only in the form of operational directives. "Every effort must be made to avoid indicating any correlation between the source of intelligence and the outcome of operations."[69] These rather basic standards amounted to a paraphrase of the long-standing British rules governing COMINT. More elaborate regulations would follow.

In October Captain Earl E. Stone replaced John Redman as head of OP-20-G and Captain Carl Holden replaced Joseph Redman as DNC. During July Admiral Wilkinson returned to sea duty and was replaced by Rear Admiral Harold C. Train. Captain Stone's title was upgraded to that of assistant director of naval communications for communications intelligence.[70] These developments will be further traced in a following section of this chapter.

THE ARMY-NAVY-FBI COMINT AGREEMENTS, MARCH–JULY 1942

By mid-1942 the Army, Navy, and FBI had reached an understanding concerning the division of COMINT effort and dissemination of product. These basic wartime agreements were reached in a roundabout fashion, and, regrettably, there is reason to believe that the motives behind these negotiations were not entirely those of operational efficiency. This story will be described in great detail, because all the U.S. COMINT agencies of the time were involved in this complex development of policy. Ultimately the Joint Chiefs of Staff (JCS) and the president were called upon to render decisions.

Early in the war there were efforts to coordinate and consolidate U.S. COMINT, especially intercept operations. In February 1942 Commander Wenger advised the director of naval communications that "... there is a movement under way to consolidate all of the various monitoring activities under a single head. ..."[71] This move seems to have originated with the FCC's intercept organization, the RID. Wenger suggested to the DNC that coordination was most desirable but consolidation was not, because the Navy had intercept problems peculiar to the communications of foreign navies. This required special (i.e., naval) background and training for intercept personnel. Wenger saw no reason to alter the existing procedure: the Navy would continue to work foreign naval traffic, the Army foreign military traffic, and they would divide the diplomatic traffic because of mutual interest. He thought that other foreign communications, such as espionage traffic and propaganda broadcasts, could be left to the FBI and FCC.

Pressure for consolidation was also coming from the British. Captain Edward Hastings, their COMINT representative in Washington (see chapter 1), was busily establishing good relations with the Army and Navy COMINT organizations, the FCC, Coast Guard, ONI, State Department, MID, and FBI. He was in the pipeline of U.S.-British COMINT exchange.[72] His major objective, thought Commander Kramer, who was his point of contact in OP-20-G, was to bring about a combined U.S. COMINT organization. Kramer also believed that the FCC and FBI were most receptive to his ideas.[73]

Captain Hastings's closest contact in the U.S. COMINT community was with the Coast Guard unit. In March 1942, this unit was merged into OP-20-G, where its mission remained the same: interception and processing of clandestine radio traffic.[74] For some time, Hastings had been receiving intercept from the USCG. In early March, Captain Hastings, seeking assurance that the British would continue to receive the USCG product, sent representatives to discuss the matter with Commander John Redman. Commander Redman invited Kramer to the meeting. Kramer suggested to Redman that the first step in formalizing this collaboration should be a meeting of the U.S. agencies working the clandestine problem. Kramer proposed that the State Department chair this coordination meeting. In the meantime British-USCG exchange continued.

On 28 March 1942, DNI Admiral Wilkinson wrote Assistant Secretary of State A. A. Berle proposing an agreement between the COMINT agencies involved in clandestine intercept in the Western Hemisphere.[75] Admiral Wilkinson noted that a special problem to be considered would be how to prosecute espionage agents and still protect COMINT.

On 2 April a meeting was held in Mr. Berle's office. Among those present were Major General Strong, ACS, G-2; Commander John Redman; Chairman James Fly of the FCC; and Mr. D. M. Ladd of the FBI.[76] The conferees agreed that enemy clandestine radio stations, whose traffic was being exploited by the U.S., should not be seized unless there was an immediate threat to shipping, and that such action would require the approval of the War and Navy Departments.[77]

Mr. Fly then suggested the consolidation of the various U.S. cryptanalytic organizations.[78] He offered the opinion that there was duplication of effort and incomplete coverage under existing arrangements. John Redman agreed and suggested as a remedy the centralization of the clandestine problem within the USCG COMINT unit. He said that most intelligence on that problem was already coming from the Coast Guard. Mr. Ladd said that the FBI could not agree to dropping its own cryptanalytic capability. Following more discussion, Berle recommended that the "Intelligence Committee" be asked to secure an executive order from the president that would prevent the establishment of any more cryptanalytic organizations and provide for better coordination among the existing ones. With that, the meeting was adjourned.

This extraordinary meeting had touched on a number of different areas, and one suspects that those in attendance were not on entirely common ground. Fly seems to have been advancing the notion of total centralization, while Redman, at least, wished to deal only with the clandestine problem. For whatever reason, cryptanalysis alone, rather than the total cycle of intercept, cryptanalysis, translation, and exploitation, was at issue. And the matter of dealing with the British was not discussed.

However, when the IIC met on 8 April 1942 in J. Edgar Hoover's office, Mr. Hoover requested a special conference to discuss the complete problem – interception, processing, dissemination, and "action."[79] The IIC then appointed a committee to carry out this suggestion. The designees were D. M. Ladd for the FBI, Colonel John T. Bissell for MIS (Counterintelligence Group), Commander John Redman for the DNC, and Lieutenant Commander A. D. Kramer for ONI. The committee was to determine if the Army, Navy (including USCG), and FBI could handle the entire COMINT problem to the exclusion of the COI, FCC, ". . . and other agencies yet unborn."

Ironically, the day before this IIC meeting, Louis De LaFleur, the FCC's monitoring officer in New York City, had written Colonel John C. Moore, the signal officer for the Army's Eastern Defense Command, suggesting the establishment in Washington, D.C., of a radio intelligence center, much like that recently established in San Francisco.[80] De LaFleur noted that arrangements were being made for a teletype connection between the FCC, G-2, and ONI ". . . for instantaneous exchange of radio intelligence information." The San Francisco radio intelligence center had been established at the beginning of 1942 in response to an urgent request from General John De Witt, commander of the Western Defense Command. Its purpose was to locate possible Japanese clandestine transmitters in California and the Pacific Northwest and to obtain bearings on enemy radio transmissions in the Pacific.[81]

The newly formed COMINT committee met on 21 April 1942 at the FBI.[82] In attendance were Colonel John T. Bissell and Colonel Carter W. Clarke from the War Department; Commander John Redman, Commander Joseph Wenger, and Lieutenant Commander A. D. Kramer from the Navy; and D. M. Ladd and E. P. Coffey from the FBI. The committee discussed coordination and cooperation in cryptanalysis and other processing. There was agreement that some type of coordination was needed to preserve secrecy, to make the best use of the small number of specially trained people available in the field, and to confine the work to those agencies with the most experience, i.e., Army, Navy, FBI. The committee concluded, rather strangely, that this type of effort was ". . . definitely investigative intelligence, and the investigative jurisdiction in national defense matters rests with these agencies."[83]

The committee drafted a proposed executive order that directed the creation of a communications intelligence committee as a subcommittee of the IIC. This committee would be empowered to divide the work, prevent duplication, and work out policy matters. It would also serve the JIC. The draft executive order further directed that cryptanalysis be controlled and undertaken by the Army, Navy (including USCG), and FBI.

This draft executive order seems not to have reached President Roosevelt. Instead, the study of the problem continued. The Army's SIS, previously not involved in these negotiations (the SIS was not on the IIC), entered the picture. At a 25 May 1942 meeting of the committee, the War Department was represented not only by Lieutenant Colonel Willard Holbrook of MID but also by Colonel Frank Bullock, chief of SIS, and William F. Friedman, his civilian assistant. Navy and FBI attendance was the same as at the 21 April meeting.[84] The purpose of this meeting was to study and make recommendations about processing and dissemination. Processing was defined as sorting, preparation, and distribution of raw material, decryption or cryptanalysis, traffic analysis, translation and correlation, and preparation for dissemination. Intercept was not discussed. The committee made these general recommendations regarding dissemination of COMINT:

Nature of COMINT	Recipients
Diplomatic	War Department, Navy, State, President
Enemy naval	Navy
Enemy military	War Department
Western Hemisphere clandestine	War Department, Navy, State
International clandestine (Other than Western Hemisphere)	War Department, Navy, State

The COI was briefly considered as a proper recipient of international clandestine COMINT but then was rejected in favor of the State Department. The committee also issued a survey of existing U.S. cryptanalytic organizations.[85] The survey was a brief historical outline of the development of the COMINT components of the Army, Navy, Coast Guard, and FBI, together with a speculative outline of the cryptanalytic units of the FCC and Censorship Office. There was an extensive accounting of each organization's manpower (excluding intercept operators and COMSEC personnel) in Washington and in the field. The agencies described their own current cryptanalytic undertakings and internal handling as follows:

War Department: This department was working on enemy military, attaché, and weather systems, enemy diplomatic, enemy commercial, and potential enemy diplomatic and commercial. Results were to be furnished to MID.

Navy Department: This department was working on enemy naval (including air and weather), enemy diplomatic, enemy clandestine, and potential enemy naval and diplomatic. The results were to be furnished to forces afloat, COMINCH, ONI, and State Department. ONI would distribute clandestine COMINT.

FBI: This department was working on enemy diplomatic, commercial, clandestine/espionage, shore-to-ship communications, and criminal communications.

These efforts to bring about more orderly cooperation now hit an unexpected snag. On 5 June, at the weekly communications intelligence meeting between the Coast Guard COMINT unit and Captain Hastings, the latter announced that he would be dealing solely with the FBI in the future. Any collaboration with the USCG would have to be through the bureau. While this sudden shift by Captain Hastings would prove to be temporary and USCG-British cooperation would soon be cordial again, there seems little doubt that this incident further poisoned the atmosphere between the wary services. The Navy was concerned about the FBI because of the latter's alleged security violations and disregard of basic rules on the uses of COMINT, as well as the FBI's stated position that if prosecution of enemy agents required the presentation of COMINT in court, then that would be done. Yet another problem was FBI interference in ONI covert activities in New York City wherein the FBI allegedly took advantage of a too-cooperative ONI officer and then invited the BSC to become involved.[86]

In addition, there was some sentiment within OP-20-G to force the FBI out of the COMINT picture (except for purely domestic matters) and to restrict the field to the Army and Navy. U.S. intelligence relations with the British were also to be reconsidered.[87] Commander John Redman, in a tentative memorandum for Admiral Horne, took a stronger stand.[88] Redman suggested that all U.S. cryptanalysis be performed only by the Army and Navy, except that the FBI have this responsibility for criminal communications (i.e., gambling cases). Redman noted that the FBI had been accepted as a partner in COMINT only to avoid an impasse and ". . . to get the matter out of the hands of that committee."[89] He further suggested that an intercept committee be established consisting of the various organizations performing that function, but that all resulting traffic go solely to the Army and Navy, who, after processing, would furnish the results in accordance with the 25 May dissemination formula.[90]

On 17 June the IIC reconsidered the committee's 25 May report and directed the establishment of an allocation committee to make a specific division of the cryptanalytic tasks at hand.[91] The reason for appointing a "new" committee is uncertain. The membership was the same, though the objective was not confined to allocation.

At the same time, results of the 25 May report were distilled for the JCS by the Joint Intelligence Committee (JIC). The JIC stated that the informal committee composed of "FBI, MIS, and ONI" [sic] had studied the cryptanalytic situation and concluded that the three services could handle all COMINT processing. The JIC advised that specific allocation of the work would be made. The JCS was asked to obtain presidential approval of these arrangements especially because other cryptanalytic units existed – in Censorship, FCC, and COI.[92]

The following week the most significant negotiations were undertaken. Commander John Redman proposed to the DNC and to Admiral Horne that the Navy drop its diplomatic COMINT effort in favor of the Army. There were a number of practical reasons for this. While OP-20-G and the SIS had effectively cooperated in this area for two years, "this procedure . . . is not conducive to efficiency."[93] Indeed it was not, for the 1940 procedures including division of circuits covered and alternate day processing of traffic were still in effect. Redman felt that the Navy had more Japanese naval traffic to work than it could handle while the Army had little else to work except diplomatic traffic. The Army was most willing to assume responsibility for all diplomatic coverage and processing and would continue to furnish full results to the Navy. The Navy would make its own internal dissemination of diplomatic COMINT and would continue to distribute it to the president. The thirty-eight OP-20-G personnel working the diplomatic problem would be shifted to Japanese naval problems. In all this, Redman had obtained the concurrence of the DNI. Redman also suggested that there should be an agreement with SIS allowing the return of Army-Navy division of diplomatic work at any time, but especially at the end of the war.

Commander Wenger would recall a year later, when reviewing Army-Navy relations, that it had been his idea, as far back as February 1942, to give the Army all diplomatic work, but that this would not necessarily be a permanent arrangement.[94] While the Army's complete takeover of the diplomatic problem would be formalized a few days after the Redman memorandum to Admiral Horne, there seems never to have been any agreement as to when, or if, the Navy could reenter the picture. The diplomatic COMINT records of the Navy were given to the SIS for safekeeping, and OP-20-G turned its main attention to foreign naval problems.[95]

On 30 June the "new" Allocation Committee met and agreed on this division of cryptanalytic responsibility.[96]

Type	Responsible Agency
Diplomatic	Army
Enemy naval operations	Navy

Enemy military operations	Army
Western Hemisphere clandestine	FBI and Navy
International clandestine (i.e., other than Western Hemisphere)	Navy
Army weather	Army
Navy weather	Navy
Domestic criminal	FBI
Voice broadcast	FBI
Cover text communications	FBI
Trade codes	To be assigned by committee

The report that included the above assignments was signed by the following:

War Department – Colonel Carter W. Clarke, Colonel Frank W. Bullock, and William F. Friedman; Navy Department – Commander John R. Redman, Lieutenant Commander A. D. Kramer, Commander J. N. Wenger, and Lieutenant Commander Leonard T. Jones; FBI – E. P. Coffey and D. M. Ladd.

One of the committee's recommendations was that a standing committee should be created representing the technical organizations, with membership to consist of the chief of SIS, officer in charge of OP-20-G, and chief of the FBI Technical Laboratory. It was hoped that this standing committee would meet often to exchange information, discuss pooling of resources, and eliminate duplication.

Thus the basic wartime agreements as to production and dissemination' of COMINT had been reached. The shortcomings of these agreements are rather obvious. The division of Western Hemisphere clandestine cryptanalysis between the Navy (USCG unit) and FBI was meaningless without specific arrangements. Such arrangements would never be made, and a shameful antagonism between OP-20-G/ONI and the FBI would grow until cooperation of any type almost ceased. The complete disregard of the committee(s) for the work of the RID was equally unfortunate. The Navy especially would work to dismember the RID, the organization that would remain almost the sole source of traffic for the FBI's cryptanalytic program.

Finally, in July 1942 the matter of allocation of COMINT tasks was brought before the president by the JCS with this recommendation: "As the Army, Navy, and the Federal Bureau of Investigation now have large organizations well-equipped and capable of handling the processing of all the raw material currently intercepted, the Joint Chiefs of Staff recommend that these activities be limited to the three agencies mentioned." The president was further advised that the services had reached an agreement on allocation.[97]

On 8 July President Roosevelt issued a brief, and informal, directive to the director of the budget.[98] He stated his agreement with the Chiefs of Staff and concluded, "Will you please have the proper instructions issued discontinuing the cryptanalytical units in the offices of the Director of Censorship, the Federal Communications Commission, and the Strategic Services. If you are aware of any other agencies having services of this character, will you please have them discontinued also."

This directive did not concern intercept or other COMINT activities short of cryptanalysis. The FCC had never engaged in organized cryptanalytic operations. RID chief George Sterling had personally instructed a few of his people in cryptanalysis, and they were able to read certain elementary German agent systems. The RID notified the director of the budget that its cryptanalytic effort was merely an aid in identifying traffic. This met with no objection.[99]

Censorship's small cryptanalytic unit, which by mid-1942 was reading some minor diplomatic systems, actually seems to have expanded during the war. However, this was in regard to its work on "open codes" rather than on the formal systems of foreign governments.

There was a strong protest from William Donovan of the OSS, based more on the denial of access to COMINT than on the prohibition against cryptanalysis. As we have seen, OSS had no access to COMINT under the 25 May 1942 agreement. In October Donovan directed two angry memorandums to the JIC (of which he was a member), then chaired by General Strong.[100] Donovan reminded General Strong and the JIC that he had agreed to desist from cryptanalytic work because he assumed that ". . . the proceeds resulting from the decoding by the Armed Forces would be made available to (the OSS)." As the JCS had charged the OSS with operating a secret "espionage service," it seemed unreasonable to withhold any intelligence material, particularly where it might aid and protect OSS agents on dangerous assignments. The OSS also had an intelligence research and analysis mission to perform that would be enhanced by access to COMINT. Donovan strongly questioned the real motives for the military's denial of COMINT to OSS: was it because the "loyalty, discretion, or intelligence of OSS" was being questioned?

The reply from the Joint Chiefs was slow in coming. The JCS study group recommended continued Army-Navy control of COMINT dissemination and failed to make a clear recommendation about OSS access. On 19 January 1943 the JCS ruled that existing JCS/JIC operating procedures already called for free interchange of information between MIS, ONI, and OSS. Further, the Army and Navy representatives on the OSS staff could obtain for OSS whatever information was needed in accordance with the existing procedures.[101]

The rivalry between the OSS and the services continued through the war, in spite of the OSS's alleged integration into the military structure by being placed under the Joint Chiefs of Staff. As late as 1945, only a few months before the victory over Germany, the

OSS in Europe was still barred from receiving highest-level COMINT (ULTRA), although it was receiving and exploiting COMINT related to the German intelligence services. The OSS relationship with the Army, Navy, FBI, and British is too complicated for further discussion here. Suffice to say at this point that while the OSS mission was ever-changing, and it became the premier U.S. agency involved in espionage and irregular warfare, it never became a total recipient of COMINT.[102]

The standing committee composed of Army, Navy, and FBI COMINT representatives seems to have met only a few times. The first meeting, held on 25 August 1942, was a stormy one.[103] Mr. E. P. Coffey, the FBI representative, advanced the view that the bureau had a definite interest in diplomatic traffic related to the Western Hemisphere. He noted that the FBI had useful intelligence contacts in Latin America who could be helpful in diplomatic COMINT. Coffey seems to have gotten no commitments from the Army. Coffey also raised the point of the assignment of both the Navy (USCG unit) and FBI to the Western Hemisphere clandestine problem. He opined that there was duplication of effort. He and Commander Jones then agreed that each service would continue to work systems each had solved but to consult with one another before beginning work on a new system. Coffey agreed to furnish a list of FBI-solved systems (this was never done). Coffey was also troubled about the dissemination of clandestine COMINT by the Navy. He was told that dissemination was to be done by ONI rather than OP-20-G (or the USCG units).

On the still unresolved question of trade codes, there was some agreement. The Navy would handle the enciphered trade codes of Japan, Germany, and Italy, and the FBI those of Spain, France, and Portugal.

The greatest problem before the committee was, according to Commander Wenger, the FBI's insistence on learning about specific cryptanalytic results from systems that were solely the responsibility of the Navy (or Army). He explained that this violated the long-followed Army-Navy procedure. Coffey disagreed with Wenger. He said that if the FBI submitted material in an unsolved system to the Navy, then the latter must inform the FBI of the cryptanalytic results. Otherwise, the FBI would be compelled to attempt all its own cryptanalysis. Not surprisingly, the Army representatives backed the Navy position. There was no resolution, though Coffey expressed the hope that decisions could be made case-by-case and that a ". . . workable arrangement could, no doubt, be effected." No agreement was ever reached.

The committee met again on 4 September.[104] Some further arrangements were made concerning trade codes. A few minor agreements were made, and the committee adopted a new name: Cryptanalysis Coordinating Subcommittee of the Joint Intelligence Committee. The tie-in with the JIC was an interesting attempt to place COMINT policy within the JCS structure.

There was no further development of this concept. The subcommittee members agreed to meet only "as needed." The Army and Navy, satisfied for the time with their own arrangements, saw no need for further formalization, particularly when their unwanted partner, the FBI, was a relatively minor participant in COMINT production.[105]

In all of these agreements, as noted before, the FCC's RID was ignored. The RID continued its vast intercept operations, sending the results to the FBI, Army, Navy and British, as well as to the State Department Board of Economic Warfare (plaintext economic traffic). There was an unremitting effort by the Navy to downgrade the RID's work and to force it out of business.[106] Although the RID turned out a good and useful product, the Navy, especially, resented the existence of a large, well-trained and equipped *civilian* COMINT organization. That RID in no way infringed upon Op-20-G or SIS operations is extremely well documented, as is the fact that RID responded to numerous specific requests from all services.[107] One shortcoming of RID, shared with the FBI, must be noted. The organization allowed, and perhaps sought, publicity regarding some of its operations. This did not inspire Army or Navy confidence.

U.S.-BRITISH COMINT AGREEMENTS IN WASHINGTON – 1942

The U.S.-British COMINT relationship prior to Pearl Harbor was described in chapter 1. During the first year of war, the U.S. Navy reached specific agreements with the Government Code & Cipher School that were the basis for cooperation well into 1944, when they were expanded. The Army was slower to reach major understandings with our ally. The Army was well behind the Navy in all phases of COMINT, so internal expansion and reorganization were the first order of business. Also the Army's understanding of the full potential of cooperation with the British was slow to develop, perhaps because the Army's COMINT policy group – the MIS Special Branch – was rather overwhelmed by the analytic work to be done with U.S. material alone.

British intelligence, including COMINT, was more centralized than U.S. intelligence. This continually placed the U.S., especially the Army, at a disadvantage in dealing with the British. U.S. officers were aware of this problem, which ultimately acted as a spur toward greater cooperation between the Army and Navy. It may be well to outline briefly the nature of British intelligence as it existed in 1942.

Counterintelligence in Britain and the Empire was centralized in the Security Service, known during the war as MI-5. Through most of the war, MI-5, under the direction of David Petrie, supervised the XX committee, which controlled double-agent operations initiated by the regular capture of German agents attempting to infiltrate the U.K. COMINT was the major reason these agents were seized and doubled.

Secret intelligence and counterintelligence outside Britain and the empire were under the Secret Service, also known as the Secret Intelligence Service or MI-6. The Chief of the Secret Service (CSS) was Brigadier (later Major General) Stuart Menzies. Within the Service he was known as "C." He played a significant role in U.S.-British COMINT relations because he was also director – later director general of the Government Code and Cipher School, the centralized all-service COMINT organization of Great Britain. Actual day-to-day control of GC&CS was under Commander A. G. Denniston, who later shared this function with Commander Edward Travis (the smaller share remained with Denniston).

From 1942 until 1945 GC&CS was divided into two broad groups: civil (under Denniston) and services (under Travis). The civil organization, often called Berkeley Street, after its main location in London, was concerned with foreign diplomatic, economic, and certain espionage COMINT. The services organization, usually called Bletchley Park, was concerned with COMINT related to foreign military, air, and naval activity. Supporting GC&CS (both Bletchley Park and Berkeley Street) was a vast intercept or "Y" organization composed of army, navy, air force, and civilian stations.

But there was another British COMINT organization not directly under GC&CS. This was the Radio Security Service (RSS), the British counterpart to the FCC's radio intelligence division. The RSS covered foreign clandestine links worldwide, but the actual cryptanalysis was performed by GC&CS. The RSS was under Section V of MI-6; thus it too was under Stuart Menzies, the CSS.

As previously stated, BSC, in New York City, was an arm of MI-6; it had an important role in British-U.S. COMINT relations, especially as the conduit for traffic exchange.

From March 1941 to October 1943 the British COMINT organization was controlled in this fashion:[108]

Chiefs of Staff

The Y Board

    Chairman: the CSS

    Members: The Army, Navy, RAF directors of intelligence, chairman of the Y Committee, representative of home forces

    Function: To retain functions of the former Main Committee and to coordinate intercept and cryptanalysis.

The Y Committee

    Chairman: A senior military officer

    Members: Heads of the Army, Navy, and RAF/Y organizations, representatives of cable censorship (foreign Office) and the RSS, deputy head of GC&CS, representatives of home forces, Admiralty, War Office, and MI-6

    Functions: general control, study

Various Subcommittees

To deal with this impressive organizational structure, the U.S. had the COMINT "committee(s)" of the JIC. The JIC was never charged with important foreign liaison (certainly not in COMINT); therefore, each service represented itself in dealing with the British.

The SIS and GC&CS had agreed to exchange traffic prior to Pearl Harbor. Details of actual exchange in the prewar period are sketchy. However, on 14 December 1941 the SIS responded favorably to a British proposal for exchange of traffic in GEC, a principal German diplomatic system.[109]

In April 1942, the MIS authorized the SIS to exchange traffic and methods of solution with the British and to exchange liaison officers (see Section 2 of this chapter). During that period two British COMINT missions came to the U.S. – the Sandwith group to visit OP-20-G and the Canadian COMINT organization, and Lieutenant Colonel John Tiltman to visit SIS.[110] Lieutenant Colonel Tiltman was in Washington from 26 March until 26 April 1942. He was to effect ". . . a complete interchange of all technical knowledge and in particular to hand over to SIS all our technical documents." There may have been some discussion of ENIGMA, though there could not have been sufficient material from Tiltman to allow the SIS to work that high-level problem (for one thing, the SIS lacked German military traffic). Tiltman also continued the theme advanced to the SIS before the war by Commander Denniston – that the U.S. Army should concentrate on anti-Japanese COMINT, leaving German and Italian COMINT to the British.[111]

This visit was promptly returned by SIS. In May Major Solomon Kullback, Chief of B-2 (German cryptanalysis) at SIS and Captain Harold McD. Brown, also of SIS, went to Bletchley Park. They remained there into July. Kullback studied the organizational structure of GC&CS and obtained considerable information about its work. He brought back to SIS information on various French, Italian, German, and Japanese systems, including the wiring for the German intelligence agents' ENIGMA machine, along with some of its traffic and keys. Kullback also studied the scanning machinery used by GC&CS in handling military ENIGMA traffic.[112]

Solomon Kullback, chief B-2, SIS

Upon his return to Washington, Major Kullback recommended that

1. An experienced SIS officer be assigned to Hut 3 (intelligence production) at Bletchley;

2. A junior SIS cryptanalyst be assigned to Bletchley to work on machine traffic (ENIGMA) because "we cannot intercept much of this material and it will be some time before we are in a position to have the necessary background of information and experience and machinery to do the job here";

3. SIS Washington contact with Britain be through SIS-ETOUSA.

In late 1942 Captain Roy D. Johnson of SIS went to Bletchley to continue Kullback's studies, and he became the first permanent liaison officer there.[113]

In the meantime, Captain Hastings, the erstwhile British intelligence liaison officer in Washington, was specifically appointed by Commander Travis as the GC&CS representative in Washington on matters of policy. Major Stevens, who had been at SIS since the end of 1941, was assigned to Hastings.[114]

A curious high-level exchange occurred during the summer of 1942. On 9 July President Roosevelt wrote General Marshall:[115]

> Some time ago the prime minister stated that our cipher experts of the United States and British navies were in close touch but that he was under the impression that there was not a similar intimate interchange between our two armies. I wonder if you could take this up with General Dill and let me know.

The result of this rather informal presidential inquiry was in the bureaucratic form, predictable but unfortunate. General Marshall turned to General Strong, ACS, G-2, for comment. Strong told Marshall that there had been an exchange of technical cryptanalytic information for over a year and that it was satisfactory. If U.S. Navy-British exchange seemed more advanced, it was because there had been a greater need.[116] Two days later General Marshall replied to the president, essentially advancing General Strong's view (General Marshall also stated that he had discussed the matter with Sir John Dill).[117]

What Strong – and Marshall – stated was correct. But they missed a marvelous opportunity to explain to the president that the War Department was not receiving highest-level COMINT from the British, nor was the Army receiving sufficient information about ENIGMA to begin its own military COMINT program. Indeed, this situation would erupt several months later, causing an exceptionally fierce struggle between the War Department and Field Marshall Dill. Had the matter been presented to the president at the time when the latter (and the prime minister) had sought information on the subject, Army COMINT might have gained sources and methods that were to be denied for more than a year.

Meanwhile, the SIS-GC&CS traffic exchange was in operation via BSC in New York City. This method of exchange came to be used by all the COMINT services. Traffic went from Washington to BSC by mail, radio, or landline teletype. From New York the traffic went to the U.K. via the transatlantic cable, by air or ship, or sometimes by radioteletype from Montreal. Traffic from GC&CS reversed this procedure. It bears repeating at this point that this SIS-GC&CS traffic exchange, until well into 1943, involved foreign diplomatic, economic, and intelligence service communications, rather than military communications.

The USN-British arrangements regarding anti-Japanese COMINT up to Pearl Harbor have already been described in some detail. In February 1942 the British Y Board sent a COMINT mission to the U.S. headed by Captain H. R. Sandwith, R.N. All the British armed services, and the foreign office, were represented. The Sandwith mission was charged with studying U.S. and Canadian COMINT services.[118]

A conference was held in Washington, 6–17 April 1942, and a detailed report was written. The most significant recommendation was for the creation of an Anglo-American Y Committee; however, this committee was never created. There were numerous technical recommendations, as well as recommendations on the exchange of traffic. Among the latter, these were of special interest:

1. JN-25 material was to be sent to Washington for processing, but not to London (this did not apply to Hawaii or Melbourne);

2. German naval traffic, including U-boat traffic, was to be left for future resolution;

3. German military and air traffic was to go only to London, except that some would be mailed to Washington for training purposes.

Perhaps the Sandwith mission and resulting conference were most notable as an early effort to deal with technical intercept details. The British also had a chance to learn more about their U.S. counterparts. Captain Sandwith made a number of interesting observations concerning U.S. problems with duplication.[119] As he saw it, the FCC had the largest U.S. intercept operation, and their activities should be coordinated with those of the Army, Navy, (and Coast Guard). The U.S. also needed a coordinating group similar to that of the British Y Board or Y Committee. As we have seen, this was a recurrent theme.

The matter of German U-boat and other German naval traffic was never really covered by a separate comprehensive USN-British agreement. It was certainly under continuous discussion, and notable cooperation did result. During 1942 OP-20-G simply undertook its own solution of ENIGMA enciphered traffic and construction of bombes. The turning point seems to have been reached in September 1942 when, after conversations with Commander Wenger of OP-20-G, Captain Hastings notified London that the U.S. Navy was commencing work on U-boat traffic as the British had "lost" U-boat traffic since January.[120] Of course, OP-20-G had been working on this traffic before September 1942.

Prompted by the Hastings message, Commander Travis and Mr. Frank Birch of the naval section at GC&CS visited Washington in late September to formalize a naval COMINT agreement with OP-20-G. The result was the Holden Agreement of 2 October 1942.[121] This agreement was in the form of a memorandum from Captain Carl Holden, DNC, to Commander Travis. Very important understandings were reached:

1. The British would cease their Far East Japanese naval cryptanalytic effort (then centered at Kilindini, East Africa), leaving this effort to OP-20-G. This unit, however, would "read traffic from recoveries supplied by other units."

2. The British-U.S. naval COMINT unit at Melbourne would become a U.S.-controlled operation (i.e., FRUMEL).[122]

3. OP-20-G would be responsible for ". . . passing naval recoveries and pertinent naval information to the Admiralty (GC&CS) for transmittal to the commander in chief, Eastern Fleet and Kilindini."

4. OP-20-G was to pass all Japanese raw traffic to GC&CS and "to pass to the Admiralty (GC&CS) (a) radio intelligence from Japanese naval communications, indicating major strategic moves in any area and details bearing upon operations in the Indian Ocean area; (b) all Japanese naval code and cipher key recoveries."

5. The British agreed in principle to collaborate with OP-20-G on German U-boat and other naval cryptanalysis. The British recognized the U.S. desire "to attack submarine and naval problems."

In summary, then, the Japanese navy was a U.S. Navy COMINT responsibility while the Atlantic was to be dealt with cooperatively. According to Mr. Birch, the arrangement was by no means satisfactory to the British, as they now seemed dependent on the U.S. Navy for intelligence support for the Royal Navy's Eastern Fleet. Subsequent USN-British agreements only reaffirmed the basic intent of the Holden Agreement.[123]

The OP-20-G/Royal Canadian Navy (RCN) COMINT relationship was well established by late 1942. The RCN "Y" Service was involved in a wide range of activities, including interception of German and Japanese naval traffic and DF. The USN-RCN effort involved OP-20-G operation of stations in Canada and integration of both countries' naval DF networks, particularly regarding German U-boats.[124]

A direct relationship between the FCC and the British was proposed in April 1942. On 16 April Captain Drake, of the office of the Canadian director of military operations and intelligence, met with S. W. Norman, temporary chief of RID.[125] Drake advised that Captain Kenneth J. Maidment of BSC, New York, was interested in direct contact with the FCC. There had been FCC contact with the British earlier, through Captain Hastings and the FBI. But Captain Drake proposed an FCC-BSC teletype link for exchange of technical data about German clandestine stations. Chairman Fly, after consulting with the State Department, approved the proposal. The BSC took no further action for some months, possibly because the FBI held that all BSC contact with U.S. agencies should be through the bureau.[126] During August, Mr. E. P. Coffey of the FBI Technical Laboratory contacted RID to suggest a meeting of representatives of the RID, FBI, BSC, and USCG, to discuss clandestine traffic.[127] The meeting would be limited to a discussion of callsigns, frequencies, schedules, traffic characteristics, and locations of stations. Intelligence product and policy were not to be considered.

The Army notified the FBI of its interest and was added to the conference. The first meeting was held on 25 August 1942 with the following in attendance: Captain Maidment and B. de Bayly, assistant director of communications, BSC; Major Robert Schukraft, SIS; Lieutenant Commander L. T. Jones, USCG (OP-20-G); Albert MacIntosh, RID; and E. P. Coffey, P. A. Napier, and R. E. Thornton, FBI.

These representatives agreed that they did not constitute an "official" committee and that "discussion of policy matters was outlawed."[128] Whatever the status of this unofficial committee, it met every Tuesday for almost a year. Major Telford Taylor of the MIS Special Branch also became a participant sometime later in 1942.

In the opinion of George Sterling of RID, there was less than full cooperation among members of the committee, and the Army especially tended to block the flow of information. On 4 August 1943 the committee dissolved, after the Army and USCG representatives withdrew. Only the RID and FBI remained, and they, too, agreed to dissolution. This in no way hindered the excellent BSC-RID association that had begun independent of the unofficial committee, in about October 1942. As Captain Maidment told Mr. Sterling, the British RSS considered the RID to be its direct counterpart in the U.S.[129] Until the end of the war, there was continuous RID-BSC exchange of intercept and technical information under the good offices of George Sterling and Al MacIntosh for RID and Kenneth Maidment (and later Captain J. Lakin) for BSC.[130]

The unofficial committee did serve to reopen British intelligence contact in the U.S. with agencies other than the FBI (see the Captain Hastings affair in "The Army-Navy-FBI COMINT Agreements" section of this chapter). Individual British-U.S. agency contacts would continue through the war, often on a friendlier basis than among the U.S. agencies themselves. And there were special channels, too. In London the FBI representative, Mr. Cimperton, obtained COMINT for bureau use directly from the British. This did not please the Army or Navy and was instrumental in creating further squabbles between the Navy and FBI, as will be noted below.[131]

NAVY COMINT IN THE PACIFIC

During the first year of the war, there were three administrative and organizational highlights in naval COMINT in the Pacific: the establishment of FRUMEL as a U.S.-controlled joint operation, the establishment of the Intelligence Center Pacific Ocean Area

(ICPOA) in Hawaii, and the power struggle at FRUPAC and the replacement of Commander Rochefort. These will be treated in summary form here; a detailed account of FRUMEL, FRUPAC, and ICPOA belongs in the operational history.

When the former Cast unit relocated in Australia, after a portion of the group briefly operated in the Netherlands East Indies, it was within a joint-service group of Royal Australian Navy, British, and U.S. personnel, each national group under its own chief. The Holden Agreement placed FRUMEL under U.S. command, allowing the U.S. to retain such British-Australian personnel as desired and to request additional personnel from Kilindini. FRUMEL thus came under the command of Lieutenant Commander Rudolph Fabian, who remained in that position until December 1943. FRUMEL was initially served by one Australian navy intercept station located near Melbourne. There were U.S. Navy personnel at this station, and a second station manned mainly by U.S. personnel was later opened near Darwin.[132] A large DF net was also developed. The processing was done at FRUMEL by the multinational group working as a team.

The purpose of FRUMEL was intelligence support for "General MacArthur's Navy," i.e., U.S. naval forces in the southern Pacific area. FRUMEL was under the military control of commander, Southwest Pacific Force, and its successor organization, the Seventh Fleet. Admiral Carpender commanded these forces for much of the war. The command relationship as seen in the field is aptly summarized by Commander Fabian. "It [FRUMEL] received technical support and guidance from OP-20-G, but that guidance in no way detracted from our local responsibility to the fleet commander, the same as [had been] true for Cast unit."[133] Of course, this was not seen exactly the same way by OP-20-G, which was at pains then and later to make it clearly known that FRUMEL was a field arm of OP-20-G in Washington. FRUMEL directly served General MacArthur, who received briefings on its product from Admiral Carpender and the latter's intelligence officer (by late 1942), Commander Arthur McCollum, the ONI veteran. Commander Fabian also seems to have personally made presentations to the general.[134]

In all this, Commander Fabian's work was eased by having Washington support. He was held in high regard by the Redman brothers and escaped the drastic Redman-Horne-inspired changes that swept away Safford, Rochefort, and ONI's authority in COMINT matters.[135]

In Hawaii Admiral Nimitz, as commander in chief Pacific (CINCPAC), received his COMINT support from FRUPAC, which was still under the command of Commander Joseph Rochefort. Rochefort doubtless viewed his role as did Fabian: regardless of chain of command, his first duty was to CINCPAC.

In an attempt to bring about some centralization of intelligence analysis for Admiral Nimitz's command, both ONI and the Marine Corps advanced the idea, in the spring of 1942, for the creation of a joint intelligence center. From this concept came ICPOA, and later in 1943, the Joint Intelligence Center Pacific Ocean Area (JICPOA).

In April 1942 Commander McCollum, who was still at ONI, was sent to CINCPAC to discuss plans then being formulated in the office of the Commandant of the Marine Corps and ONI. The plan was to establish the intelligence center at Pearl Harbor with a rather large staff. The center would receive and interpret all types of intelligence bearing on CINCPAC's sphere of operations. Admiral Nimitz liked the idea but, disliking large staffs, was somewhat resistant on personnel grounds. There followed a great deal of correspondence between Pearl Harbor and Washington. ICPOA was, however, created, with Commander Hillenkoetter from ONI as officer in charge. ICPOA was detached from the CINCPAC staff and placed under the command of the Fourteenth Naval District (Pearl Harbor).[136] The ICPOA concept was warmly received by Rochefort, if less so by Nimitz's fleet intelligence officer, Captain Edwin Layton.[137]

The upshot of all this was an elaborate organization, ultimately placed under Brigadier General Joseph Twitty, in September 1943, as the JICPOA. ICPOA/JICPOA never controlled FRUPAC or other Navy or Army COMINT operations, but used COMINT in a closely controlled way, initially via Commander Layton, the fleet intelligence officer.[138]

FRUPAC became an ever larger center charged as before with a full range of COMINT functions, from intercept to cryptanalysis, decryption to translation. The analysis and dissemination of its product at CINCPAC and Combat Information Center (CIC) were done by a very small number of people. In mid-1943 CIC had only ten people.[139] Commander Layton's staff was also small. Thus the complex arrangement, at least until later in the war, involved rather few people outside FRUPAC itself. Though COMINT was the most valuable secret source available to CINCPAC, the great majority of the ICPOA/JICPOA staff was involved with maps and charts, air reconnaissance photos, POW reports, action reports, and the like.

Lieutenant Commander Luther L. L. Dilley, USN
Cryptanalysis Section, FRUPAC

By the time the center was fully operational, Commander Rochefort had been relieved by Washington and was replaced by Commander Goggins, in one of the sorriest episodes in the annals of U.S. intelligence. As Admiral Nimitz observed, ". . . Rochefort's sin was probably one of doing too much rather than too little – a hard thing for which to condemn a man."[140] Full details of this affair belong in the operational history, but it must be touched on insofar as it reveals the attitudes toward COMINT policy of Admirals Horne and Nimitz and the Redman brothers.

Within two weeks after the U.S. victory at Midway, due in large measure to the work of FRUPAC (and FRUMEL too), the Redman brothers and Admiral Horne had determined to review the naval COMINT picture. One result was the downgrading of ONI described in the "Navy COMINT Reorganization and Expansion in Washington during 1942" section of this chapter. On 30 June 1942, Joseph Redman, DNC, sent Admiral Horne a lengthy and important analysis of COMINT.[141] His theme was that technical people, i.e., communicators, should totally control COMINT. Redman noted that in theory all intelligence should be under a single director, but that this was not necessarily practical because ONI and noncommunications people ". . . just don't speak our language." Most phases of COMINT, he wrote, require communications skills, and the emerging techniques made even greater demands on skilled communications personnel. Among these techniques were TINA (identifying enemy radio operators by their manual technique), RFP (radio fingerprinting to identify enemy transmitters), and the use of ionospheric data to measure distance to enemy transmitters. Thus COMINT must be under naval communications. Redman then described the existing command situation and bluntly observed that the key center, FRUPAC, was under command of a weak administrator who was merely an "ex-Japanese language student" and who had this command solely on the basis of seniority. Neither this person (Rochefort – whom Redman never names in the memorandum) nor the fleet intelligence officer (Layton) had any communications training. Therefore, Redman concluded that a change of command must be made. Rochefort was replaced, and he was denied the decorations recommended by Admiral Nimitz for his role in the victory at Midway.

Following this, there was an unfriendly exchange of correspondence between Admiral Nimitz and Admirals King and Horne. On 28 October Admiral King wrote Admiral Nimitz that he had heard "unofficially" from sources in Washington and Hawaii that the intelligence center had not functioned well because of the resistance of Rochefort and Layton. This is why Rochefort had been replaced by Goggins. Admiral Nimitz replied two weeks later praising Layton and the departed Rochefort. A long letter from Admiral Horne followed in which he laboriously explained the nature and organization of naval COMINT. Horne explained that all COMINT was under him through his authority over the DNC, and that the Washington unit (OP-20-G) exercised ". . . control as necessary over the units at Pearl Harbor and Melbourne in order to coordinate all efforts for the maximum efficiency of the entire organization." Nonetheless, these field units supported the fleet commanders, and these commanders could divert the local COMINT units to special tasks when required. Horne closed with the observation that "the operation of this organization in no way comes under ONI...."[142]

Admiral Chester W. Nimitz, CINCPAC

Admiral Nimitz replied to Admiral Horne on 8 December. He made it clear that he understood naval COMINT requirements, as he had formerly been chief of the Bureau of Personnel, where he had worked to insure adequate manpower for OP-20-G. He then made it known that the local COMINT unit (FRUPAC) could not automatically bypass him in dealing with Washington. He had found that his communications officer held a private cipher system which he (Nimitz) did not hold, for the purpose of direct communication with the DNC and OP-20-G. This he found intolerable, and henceforth messages to OP-20-G or DNC would be cleared through him, an interesting development because his new communications officer was none other than John Redman, who in October had been replaced as head of OP-20-G by Captain Earl E. Stone.

GROWTH OF U.S. NAVAL COMINT IN THE PACIFIC

Intercept Site	Number of Radio Receivers
December 1941	
Bainbridge Island, Washington	13
Hilia, Territory of Hawaii	21
Guam	9
Corregidor	25
Total	**68**
December 1943	
Bainbridge Island	120
Imperial Beach, California	75
Wahiawa, Territory of Hawaii	200
Australia	50
Total	**445**
August 1945	
Bainbridge Island	142
Imperial Beach	67
Skaggs Island, California	48
Admiralty Islands	105
Wahiawa, Territory of Hawaii	183
Guam	160
Australia	58
Iwo Jima	12
Total	**775**

There was also an expansion of radio intercept teams afloat: from 1 operator and 1 receiver in December 1941 to 8 intercept teams and 120 receivers by the end of the war.[143]

Notes

1. *Reminiscences of Lieutenant Colonel Harold R. Brown*, OCSigO, 4 August 1945 (classified).

2. Ibid. At least one became a prisoner of the Japanese, and one or two others became guerrillas.

3. Interview of George S. Sterling by the author; also Sterling article in *Studies in Intelligence*; and George R. Thompson, Dixie R. Harris, Pauline M. Oakes, Dulaney Territt, *The Signal Corps: The Test (Dec 1941 to July 1943)*, (OCMH), 298.

4. *The Test*, 123-125.

5. Sterling interview; also Sterling article. See also box 27, RG 173 for wealth of material about RID operations in Alaska in support of the Army.

6. Captain Harold Joslin, *Cryptologic Spectrum*, Spring 1974 (FOUO). Joslin was an operator at Station B and was captured. See Wenger file "Historical Review" manuscript, 13-16, for number of receivers, NSAH.

7. Rowlett interview.

8. Memorandum from Colonel Carter W. Clarke, assistant chief MIS to Major General Clayton Bissell, 1 December 1944, ACSI #49, NSAH; also letter to the author by Carter Clarke, 1976.

9. General Mauborgne had been personally involved in COMINT since 1917. His early retirement was allegedly prompted by problems concerning Air Corps communications. See *The Emergency*, 271-273, for a discussion of the reasons for Mauborgne's early retirement; also PHA, Part 3, 1279. For Mauborgne's opinion of Olmstead, Memorandum from General Marshall to General Moore, 31 July 1941, Folder B/F25 (Directives – the Deputy Chief of Staff 1941-41), Marshall Library. For Olmstead's subsequent removal, see chapter 3 of this study.

10. Rowlett interviews; also Friedman testimony, *PHA*.

11. Sadtler testimony, *PHA*.

12. These various organizational developments are in *SSA History*, vol. 1, 76-78; vol. 2, 4 ff.

13. For the reorganization of 9 March 1942, see Otto L. Nelson Jr., *National Security and the General Staff*, (Washington, 1946), and James E. Hewes Jr., *From Root to McNamara: Army Organization and Administration, 1900-1963*, (Washington, D.C., CMH, 1975). For the creation of MIS, see Nelson as well as part five of Bruce W. Bidwell, *History of the Military Intelligence Division, Department of the Army General Staff,* manuscript on file at CMH, Washington, D.C. Nelson as a colonel and general officer was on the General Staff 1942-45 and was often involved in MIS and SIS matters.

14. Nelson, 390.

15. Circular 59 quoted in Nelson, 371 ff. See also Bidwell, part five, 3 ff.

16. Colonel Paul M. Robinett, *Part of the Story 1941-42*, 333; 349-50; 374. This is the wartime diary of Colonel Robinett, an experienced intelligence officer. A typescript of the diary is at the Marshall Library. For a summary of General Strong's long career, see *Time* magazine, 29 July 1940. He had fought Indians and Moros early in the century, directed important operations in France in World War I, was an Army judge advocate, and had numerous assignments in international affairs (see chapter 1 for his prewar COMINT role).

17. Letter to the author by Carter W. Clarke.

18. Memorandum from McCormack to Carter W. Clarke, 15 April 1943, subject: Origin and Functions of the MIS Special Branch (classified), ACSI #2, NSAH. (Hereafter cited as McCormack Memorandum, Origin and

Functions). See also Henry L. Stimson's autobiography (written with the assistance of McGeorge Bundy): *On Active Service in Peace and War,* (New York, 1948), 454–455.

19. McCormack Memorandum, Origin and Functions, 7.

20. Letter to author by Carter W. Clarke.

21. Ibid. Clarke wrote the author that he spent his entire career connected to intelligence except for periods when he attended the various service schools.

22. McCormack Memorandum, Origin and Functions, 7.

23. From an 8 May 1942 directive to Clarke described in a memorandum from Clarke to Strong, 11 July 1942, subject: Signal Intelligence Activities, ACSI #40, NSAH (classified).

24. Memorandum from Colonel Thomas Betts to Lieutenant Colonel David G. Erskine, Counterintelligence Group, MIS, 22 July 1942, ACSI #40, NSAH. See also Winkler-Bidwell papers in ACSI #6, NSAH. (classified) The latter consists of questions posed by Mr. Winkler, an ACSI and later DIA employee, to Colonel Bidwell on Army COMINT history. The latter's responses were too highly classified to include in his own MID history.

25. *History of the Special Branch*, no author given, 1945, ACSI #2, NSAH, 9–13.

26. Memorandum from Strong to chief of staff, 25 June 1942, subject: Signal Intelligence Service activities, ACSI #49, NSAH.

27. While the NSAH carbon of the Strong memorandum does not show the drafter, it may be stated as a certainty that it was written by Carter W. Clarke.

28. From a conversation between Colonel Clarke and Colonel Minckler as reported in memorandum from Clarke to Major General Clayton Bissell, ACS, G-2, 1 December 1944 (classified), ACSI #49, NSAH. I have not seen contemporary documents containing the actual stated objections to Strong's proposal.

29. The peculiar nature of special branch is apparent from contemporary correspondence and MIS organization charts. The branch does not always appear in the latter. Clarke reported to the ACS, G–2 and not to the chief of MIS.

30. *SSA History*, vol. 1, 81–86.

31. Letter from the Adjutant General (TAG) to the CSO, 18 April 1942 (relaying MIS instructions), ACSI #49, (classified).

32. Signal Security Division, *Annual Report* FY 1943. (Hereafter cited as SSD FY 1943).

33. Ibid.

34. George F. Howe, manuscript history of Army tactical COMINT in the European and Mediterranean theaters, NSAH, Chapter 1, 5–6, (hereafter cited as Howe Mss.) (classified).

35. TAG letters of 31 March 1942, Intercept Directives, ACSI #49, NSAH (classified).

36. See a document headed "Radio Intelligence Companies Location, 3-20-42" and "Directives of Army and Navy Monitoring Stations," ACSI #49, NSAH. This is an important source document listing Army COMINT assets early in the war.

37. *SSA History*, vol. 1, 86–87.

38. The following contemporary nomenclature will be used: SIS: 1930-1942; SSD: 1942-1943; SSS: 1943; SSA: mid-1943-1945.

39. Message from MacArthur to TAG, 1 April 1942, ACSI #49 (classified).

40. Message from Marshall to MacArthur, Clarke drafter, 3 April 1942, ACSI #49 (classified).

41. Letter to the author by Professor Sinkov.

42. Ibid.

43. Message from TAG to commanding general, American forces in the Far East, 30 March 1942, Carter W. Clarke, drafter, ACSI #49 (classified). This message does not discuss cryptanalysis or any other details of processing.

44. See *History of CBB*, Part 1, tab A, 1945 (no author) for an administrative overview.

45. Howe Mss, Part 1, 10-13.

46. Ibid.

47. Interview of Mr. Alfred Jones by the author. Notes in NSAH.

48. Howe Mss, chapter 2, 22 ff and chapter 6 (unpaged).

49. Ibid., chapter 6.

50. N*avigating the Rapids*.

51. Memorandum from Safford to DNC (retyped copy), 23 January 1942, folder marked "Op-20-G Organization," NSAH.

52. McCollum Oral History, 463-464.

53. In later years Safford would state that he was forced out by a conspiracy of senior officers who wanted him to be a scapegoat for Pearl Harbor. See the unpublished Safford manuscripts (copy), obtained from the Division of Naval History, on file at NSAH. Safford prepared the manuscript in the '50s and '60s. It is a maze of material worthy of close, if highly cautious, attention.

54. Memorandum from Joseph R. Redman to all section heads, 12 February 1942, "Op-20-G Organization."

55. Oral history of the late John R. Redman (1969), transcript in possession of the U.S. Naval Institute, Dr. Jack Mason, custodian. (Hereafter cited as *Redman Oral History*).

56. Admiral Noyes seems to have been a difficult person. An alternate version of his relief as DNC is suggested by Mr. Elliott Glunt, NSA employee. Glunt was a LTJG at Op-19 (Navy Department Communications or "Radio Central") in 1942 and recalled for the author a heated argument that Noyes had with certain senior officers. Noyes claimed the right to read all Navy Department messages as he was the DNC. He was replaced soon after this argument. Noyes subsequently commanded a task force in the fighting off Guadalcanal. His unhappy performance there led to his relief.

57. For a discussion of the role of CNO and COMINCH, see Rear Admiral Julius A. Furer, USN (Ret) *Administration of the Navy Department in World War II*, (Washington, DC, 1959). This book is an exhaustive treatment of Navy organization from 1939-1945.

58. Letter to the author by ONI historian Captain Wayman Packard, USN (Ret), April 1976.

59. Admiral Horne's papers are on file at the Library of Congress (Courtesy of the Naval Historical Foundation, owner of the papers). Regrettably, they contain nothing of interest concerning his wartime activities.

60. Memorandum from John Redman to Admiral Wilson.

61. See vol. 1, *Allied Communication Intelligence and the Battle of the Atlantic,* 1945, NSAH, 80 ff., for information on U-boat circuits and early intercept; Ibid., 21–22, for ENIGMA breakthrough.

62. For JN-25 see folder "FY History," NSAH, especially manuscript draft history of GY-1. For merchant codes, see a draft in same folder regarding GY-3.

63. These clandestine operations, into the summer of 1942, are discussed by Commander Kramer in Kramer memorandum – 8 June 1942. For the SIS noninvolvement, see Rowlett interviews. Mr. Rowlett recalled how before the war General Mauborgne admonished the Navy not to undertake any covert operations against the Japanese embassy in Washington for fear of compromising the PURPLE machine breakthrough. ONI covert operations must partially be deduced, as Kramer is understandably circumspect. The Japanese merchant shipping code was certainly obtained in this fashion; their attaché code doubtless was too. Other systems secretly copied may have been: Vichy French, Portuguese, Spanish, and Latin American. There is further discussion of this subject in the aforementioned *History of the Signal Security Agency in World War II* – see vol. 2 (*General Cryptanalysis*) for a chapter on this topic by Mr. Rowlett.

64. "FY History" folder, draft manuscript of GC history, 16, NSAH.

65. This is a confusing subject. Suffice it to say that Op-20-G did control certain CONUS teletype links from the beginning of the war, but overseas radio was through Radio Central, which handled all the Navy Department traffic to and from Washington. However, Radio Central did not have the special cipher systems used to encrypt/decrypt Op-20-G traffic. These systems, using the external indicators COPEK, CETYH, and GYROF, were held only by the COMINT centers. The ECM was used for encryption of COMB and TUNA collective messages.

66. "FY History," 12–14.

67. McCollum Oral History, 480–81. McCollum recalled that Captain Howard Kingman, the assistant DNI "was just crushed when this decision was made to take it entirely out of ONI hands because here we'd worked on this thing together for all these years." Kingman, like Kramer and McCollum, was one of the Navy's veteran intelligence officers. He had headed Op-20-G for a time during the '30s and had been the district intelligence officer for the Third Naval District, New York City. For further light on these changes of June 1942, see memorandum from Joseph Redman to Admiral Horne, 20 June 1942, Op-20-G Organization Folder; Redman opined that naval COMINT must be solely under the DNC. Admiral Horne clearly accepted this.

68. Memorandum from COMINCH (signed by Admiral R. S. Edwards, deputy chief of staff) to VCNO, subject: Radio Decryption Traffic, 6 August 1942, folder marked "Op-20-GI." This memorandum is rather muddled, and much of it is a restatement of existing COMB addressee arrangements.

69. Memorandum from Admiral King to CIC, Atlantic Fleet, CIC, Pacific Fleet, subject: Control of Dissemination and Use of Radio Intelligence, 20 June 1942, in folder marked "RI Dissemination," NSAH.

70. Captain Safford had by then been relegated to the position of a section chief, subordinate to the newly created position of assistant DNC for communications security (who was only a commander!).

71. Memorandum from Wenger to DNC, 14 February 1942, in "FBI-Coast General File," NSAH, hereafter cited as "General File."

72. The Kramer memorandum – 8 June 1942. This oft-cited document is the basic source for Captain Hastings's activities during 1942. It is the source for the origin of the Kramer-inspired coordination conference described in this section.

73. Ibid.

74. The USCG unit was known as Op-20-GU later in the war. For most of the post-merger, it was headed by Commander Leonard T. Jones, a USCG regular with long experience in COMINT. Elizabeth Friedman and other USCG analysts continued to work as a unit, though now under 20G auspices. Mrs. Friedman suggested to the author a personnel strength in Op-20-GU of "not more than twenty." This of course did not include the USCG intercept operators (also merged into 20-G).

75. Letter from Admiral Wilkinson to Mr. Berle, 28 March 1982, "General File."

76. Memorandum from John Redman to DNI and DNC, 3 April 1942, "General File."

77. Ibid.; also memorandum from General Strong to Mr. Berle, 3 April 1942, "General File."

78. Redman memorandum.

79. Memorandum from J. B. W. Waller, ONI to Lieutenant Commander Kramer and Commander Redman, 10 April 1942, "General File." The precise connection between the 2 April Berle Conference and this IIC meeting is not absolutely certain. Mr. Berle had suggested forwarding the problem to the "Intelligence Committee," which perhaps meant the JIC, then being revitalized. The IIC was under Mr. Berle's own informal chairmanship, and this may be what he meant. The FCC was not a party to the IIC or JIC.

80. Memorandum from De La Fleur to Colonel Moore, 7 April 1942, "General File."

81. Interview of George Sterling by the author; also extensive material in boxes 5, 6, and 7 of RG 173.

82. *Report of the Subcommittee of the Interdepartmental Intelligence Conference Appointed to Explore the Cryptanalytical Work of the War Department, Navy Department, and Federal Bureau of Investigation*, 23 April 1942, "General File."

83. The *clandestine problem* was partly investigative. But the committee was supposedly studying all COMINT, a subject rather broader than counterintelligence investigations. But as the IIC was a counterintelligence body, the members may have felt they had to fit their conclusions and recommendations into that framework.

84. *Report of Conference Appointed to Study Processing and Dissemination of Radio Intelligence*, 25 May 1942, "General File." The decline of ONI as a policymaker is evident. Although Commander Kramer was in attendance as the ONI representative, he was assigned full time to Op-20-G and must be considered as a part of the latter organization.

85. Ibid.

86. The Kramer memorandum – 8 June 1942. The operation in New York involved Lieutenant Commander Charles Radcliff Haffenden, chief of investigations for ONI in the Third Naval District. Haffenden was continuing the long-standing ONI/Op-20-G technique of covertly gaining access to foreign cryptographic materials. Unfortunately – in the eyes of Washington – he allowed the FBI and British to become involved. Haffenden would later testify before the Kefauver Committee on the circumstances of his recruiting Charles "Lucky" Luciano as an ONI informant. (See U.S. Congress, Senate, *Hearings Before the Special Committee to Investigate Organized Crime in Interstate Commerce, Part 7*, New York-New Jersey, March 1950). 1187–1198.

87. Ibid.

88. Memorandum from Redman to Horne, 12 June 1942, "General File." This memorandum is signed by Redman, but, as it is marked "tentative," it is not certain if it was delivered. It undoubtedly was used in a verbal presentation to Horne, however.

89. This is a remarkable admission and one restated by the Navy on subsequent occasions. At least for Op-20-G, the committee was a less than sincere undertaking. Seen another way, Redman's remark does not make sense. The Navy had after all initiated the Berle meeting, to which the FBI was logically invited.

90. Redman, if grudgingly, recognized the FBI, COI, and FCC as intercept organizations. Actually the FBI did very little of its own intercept, depending rather on the FCC's RID for radio intercept and the censorship office for mail and cable material. The COI/OSS did undertake some radio intercept operations during the war, always in the face of Army and Navy objections.

91. Extract of minutes of 17 June 1942 IIC meeting, signed by Lieutenant Colonel David G. Erskine, MID, "General File."

92. Memorandum from JIC (signed by Admiral Wilkinson) to JCS, 18 June 1942, subject: Limitation of Cryptanalytical Activities, "General File."

93. Memorandum from John R. Redman to Admiral Horne, via DNC, 25 June 1942, subject: Cryptanalytical and Decryption Operations on Diplomatic Traffic, "General File."

94. Memorandum from Wenger to Op-20-G, 1 June 1943, subject: Future Cooperation Between Army and Navy, "General File."

95. Rowlett interviews.

96. "Report of Conference Appointed to Study Allocation of Cryptanalysis," 30 June 1942, "General File."

97. Memorandum for the President, signed by General Marshall and Admiral Horne (for Admiral King), 6 July 1942, "General File."

98. Memorandum for director of budget, 8 July 1942, "General File."

99. Miscellaneous papers in box 5, RG 173; also Sterling interview.

100. Memorandums of 21 and 22 October 1942, which are enclosures to Joint Staff Planners Report, 15 June 1943, ACSI #50, NSAH.

101. Joint Staff Planners Report; OPD Disposition Form addressed to G-2, 19 January 1943, ACSI #50.

102. See Vernon Davis for a good account of the development of the OSS mission and its relationship to the Joint Chiefs. I have made no effort to see the OSS records on file at CIA because this is peripheral to my subject.

103. "Report of the first meeting of the Standing Committee for Coordination of Cryptanalytic Work," dated 9 September 1942, "General File," signed by Colonel Alfred McCormack, MIS; E. P. Coffey, FBI; Commander Joseph Wenger, Op-20-G. Also in attendance were Colonel Bullock and Mr. Friedman of SIS; Commander Jones and Commander Kramer, Navy. It is to be noted that Colonel McCormack, MIS, acted as chief spokesman for the Army rather than the SIS representative. This corrected, it may be supposed, an oversight in the 30 June report.

104. "Report of Meeting of Cryptanalysis Coordinating Subcommittee of the Joint Intelligence Committee," report dated 15 September 1942, "General File." In attendance were Commander Wenger, Colonels McCormack and Bullock, Mr. Friedman, and W. G. B. Blackburn for the FBI.

105. There is of course much more to the story of Army-Navy-FBI relations during this period. These matters cannot be treated in detail because they were side issues. It should be noted in passing that during December 1942 and January 1943 the MIS, ONI, and FBI agreed that the Army would operate a DF network in Latin America to locate clandestine radio stations. This network was to be run by American Intelligence Service, a branch of the MIS formed in 1942. The network was really run by the FCC (RID), and the Army role is problematical. Op-20-G was ultimately drawn into this arrangement, and the State Department made

arrangements with the host governments. (There are various items on this in "General File" and in the ACSI collections.)

106. See an Op-20 survey of FCC activities conducted as a highest priority project in July 1942, in folder marked "FCC and RI 1939–45," NSAH; also Sterling interviews; RG 173 at the National Archives; and letter from Admiral Nimitz to Secretary, Joint U.S. Staff Planners, 16 November 1942 in Nimitz Papers (copies), NSAH. According to Mr. Sterling, the malicious force behind the Navy's effort against RID was Joseph Redman, who, like his brother John, was a longtime acquaintance of Mr. Sterling.

107. RG 173 has hundreds of items pertaining to requests from the Army especially; also FBI, State Department, BEW, ONI, Op-20-G, other Navy, etc. In an entry in his diary on 28 April 1942, Assistant Secretary of State A. A. Berle praised the FCC for "smashing the Rio spy ring," a dangerous German intelligence and subversion operation. This was one of the most dramatic RID successes.

108. Birch, *Naval SIGINT*, vol. 1, 71–73 (classified).

109. Reference to a message on this subject appears in a summary entry in ACSI #45, NSAH.

110. *Naval SIGINT*, vol. 5(a), 177.

111. Ibid. This same theme had been, and would continue to be, advanced to Op-20-G by BCCS.

112. Kullback's *Report*, dated August 1942, ACSI #45; also a British background paper, not dated, headed "General Marshall's Letter to Field Marshall of 23/12/42" in ACSI #44 (classified).

113. Above-cited British background paper. According to this source, Colonel Bicher (SIS-ETOUSA) and General Stoner, chief of the Signal Corps' Army Communications Service, also were shown the ENIGMA exploitation process at about this time.

114. Message from Travis to War Department, 13 May 1942, ACSI #45 (classified).

115. Memorandum for General Marshall, 9 July 1942, ACSI #45 (classified).

116. Memorandum from Strong to Marshall, 9 July 1942, ACSI #45 (classified).

117. Memorandum from Marshall to President Roosevelt, 11 July 1942, ACSI #45 (classified).

118. See Birch, *Naval SIGINT*, vol. 5(a), 176 ff, and vol. 5(b), 547–555, for a detailed discussion of the Sandwith mission from the British point of view and a reprint of the report of the British-Canadian-U.S. discussions, 6–17 April 1942 (classified). I was unable to get USN records on this matter. Records do exist at the NSG records center, Crane, Indiana.

119. "Notes on U.S. Naval Intelligence Organization," signed by Captain Humphrey R. Sandwith, 15 June 1942, "Op-20-G Organization" folder.

120. Birch, *Naval SIGINT*, vol. 5(a), 179–180 (classified).

121. Ibid., 179–184 (classified).

122. This is further described in the next section.

123. Mr. Birch's objections to the agreement are presented in great detail in his *Naval SIGINT*, vol. 5(a), 181–184 (classified). Subsequent agreements are characterized by detailed attention to means of COMINT communications between the Allies. See *GC History* for a discussion of the various means of Anglo-American communications, 14–15 and 20ff.

124. "Report on Canadian Naval Y Organization," prepared by Captain Sandwith, 19 March 1942; also paper titled "Canadian HF and DF Stations, etc.," 30 December 1942. Both in Wenger File, NSAH.

125. Memorandum from S. W. Norman to Mr. Jett, 16 April 1942, box 5, RG 173 (Declassified).

126. Memorandum from George Sterling to Mr. Jett, 20 July 1943, box 6, RG 173 (folder marked "Chief Engineer–1944" (Declassified).

127. Ibid.

128. Ibid.

129. Ibid. And see also memorandum from C. A. Ellert, acting chief of RID to Mr. Jett, 4 August 1943, box 6, RG 173, for a discussion of the dissolution of the committee.

130. See RG 173, boxes 61 and 62 for hundreds of memorandums exchanged between BSC-RID 1942–45. Much of the intercept and technical data are in boxes 63 and boxes 34–57 of this record group. The official British history of World War II COMINT, *GC&CS History*, the Secret Service SIGINT series, vol. 1, contains an exceptionally cynical commentary on the RID on pp. 55–57. The suggestion there is that RID was unworthy of trust because it was a "political" organization. The documentary evidence, however, suggests that the BSC-RID association was mutually useful and friendly.

131. The author hastens to observe that the complexity and confusion of these relationships did not prevent the accomplishment of the mission. In spite of everything, German intelligence traffic was generally intercepted and read; clandestine stations and agents were exploited or suppressed. Here the Allies were fortunate in the enemies' own disarray. Another observation is in order. While the German intelligence/clandestine traffic was a relatively small matter in the COMINT war, the Allied concerns of the time were valid. German activity in Latin America, West Africa, and Iberia was alarming.

132. Fabian interviews by Captain Wayman Packard.

133. Ibid.

134. McCollum Oral History; also Fabian interviews. Also see Clay Blair, *Silent Victory*, (New York), 1975, which is an account of the USN submarine war in the Pacific. This book has incredible detail on a range of topics including COMINT.

135. Memorandum from Joseph Redman to Admiral Horne, 20 June 1942, Op-20-G Organization Folder, for glowing praise of Fabian.

136. McCollum Oral History, 357 ff.; also unsigned memorandum for Admiral Horne, November 1942, subject: Personal Letter of Admiral Nimitz, November 5, 1942, and other Nimitz correspondence, all in the *Nimitz Papers* folder, NSAH. The memorandum for Admiral Horne recapitulates the matter from March–November 1942.

137. McCollum Oral History, 357 ff.

139. *SSO History*, vol. 4, 850, tab A, manuscript item, no author. (See the Sources section of this study for a discussion and explanation of the SSO histories, which are really a collection of individual typescript memorandums.)

139. Ibid.

140. Letter from Nimitz to Admiral King, 16 November 1942, *Nimitz Papers* folder, NSAH. The story of Rochefort's relief and ill treatment is described in much detail in Clay Blair's *Silent Victory*.

141. Memorandum from Joseph Redman to Admiral Horne, 20 June 1942, subject: Radio Intelligence Organization, Op-20-G Organization folder.

142. King to Nimitz, 28 October 1942; Nimitz to King, 16 November 1942; Horne to Nimitz, 1 December 1942, all in *Nimitz Papers*.

143. Wenger file, "Historical Review," 13–16, 24, NSAH.

Chapter 3
Army-Navy Policy and Organizational Development during 1943

THE COMBAT INTELLIGENCE DIVISION AND OP-20-G

Though it had now been settled that naval COMINT was under the control of the DNC, the cart had been put before the horse. The decline of ONI still left the division of intelligence responsibility at the top as far as the evaluation and use of COMINT and other forms of intelligence were concerned. OP-20-G, the intelligence producing subdivision of 20-G, provided its product to F-11 (Fleet Intelligence) and F-35 (Operational Information) of the COMINCH staff and OP-16FE (the Far East section of ONI). Each of these units had a role in the evaluation, dissemination, and use of COMINT albeit ONI was not involved in the Battle of the Atlantic (insofar as COMINT was concerned.)[1]

On 29 April 1943 a management report regarding naval intelligence was forwarded to Admiral King.[2] There were four recommendations. One dealt with domestic counterintelligence, but the other three are of special interest:

1. Create a "Combat Intelligence Branch" on the staff of COMINCH, "unifying therewith the product of communications intelligence...."

2. Combine most of the foreign intelligence functions of ONI and MIS relating to preparation of strategic surveys and monographs with the research and analysis branch of OSS.

3. Create a new JIC directly responsible to the JCS.

Only the first came to pass, although, as may have become apparent, the other recommendations were most perceptive and wise. But the time was not yet right for true interservice intelligence coordination.

The study of these proposals was apparently undertaken by Admiral Horne and his staff. On 12 June he recommended to Admiral King a variation of the management study suggestions. On the 26th Admiral King announced his decision for what was to be the final wartime configuration of naval intelligence.[3] A Combat Intelligence Division (F-2) was to be established on the COMINCH staff. This new organization would be charged with evaluation of COMINT for the Navy. To that end OP-16FE (ONI) was no longer to receive COMINT. Thus all COMINT at the Navy Department/COMINCH level would go to one place: the Combat Intelligence Division.

Rear Admiral Roscoe E. Schuermann became assistant chief of staff for combat intelligence effective 1 July 1943, when F-2 was formally created. In September 1943 Admiral Schuermann also became the DNI, though ONI and combat intelligence retained separate staffs. The general line of demarcation between ONI and F-2 was that the latter was responsible for operational or tactical intelligence with full use of COMINT, while the former dealt with counterintelligence and strategic studies with limited access to COMINT.

The Combat Intelligence Division was divided into two main sections: F-21 (Atlantic) and F-22 (Pacific). The principal duty of F-21 was intelligence for the U-boat war. To control antisubmarine and convoy operations of the USN, Admiral King had created the Tenth Fleet (FX) during the busy summer of 1943. The Tenth Fleet was a desk-bound organization that coordinated the movements of convoys and the operations of the ships and planes hunting German submarines. F-21 served as the "operations room of the Tenth Fleet, both convoy routing and U-boat plotting information being correlated on common charts."

The duties of F-22 were different because of the different nature of the enemy's naval forces. Japan's submarine forces were in no way comparable to Germany's, but Japan had (unlike Germany) a full range of surface forces. The general responsibilities of F-22 were to prepare daily intelligence summaries for COMINCH and other key personnel, prepare weekly compilations of Japanese fleet, aircraft, and merchant shipping distribution, and maintain a current situation plot of the Pacific theater.[6]

At this point it may be useful to briefly summarize the information OP-20GI prepared for F-21:[7]

1. German naval traffic (translated in OP-20GI-A)

    U-boat Atlantic

    U-boat non-Atlantic

    Blockade runners

    Naval attaché

2. Japanese naval attaché

3. German clandestine traffic

4. Vichy French, Spanish, Portuguese naval traffic

5. Diplomatic (from the Army)

This went to F-21 in several ways: a copy of every translated German message, interpretive memorandums, daily summaries of U-boat ULTRA and non-U-boat ULTRA, and special studies.

Just prior to these broad changes in naval intelligence, Admiral Horne had made a final definition of the role of OP-20-G vis-à-vis the centers in Hawaii and Australia. This was done in a letter to the commandant of the Fourteenth Naval District (Pearl Harbor) and the commander, Seventh Fleet.[8] While there was little here that was new or was not at least tacitly understood, this letter may be considered the definitive Navy Department statement on lines of authority and division of the worldwide COMINT effort. The basic statement was this:

> The Washington communication intelligence center (OP-20-G), under authority of the vice chief of naval operations, exercises control over the centers at Pearl Harbor and Melbourne as necessary to coordinate all efforts for maximum efficiency of the organization. Each of the latter two centers normally operates in accordance with general policies and specific assignments outlined by the Washington center and disseminates all information obtained to designated fleet commanders, to the other two centers and to other authorities as directed by the vice chief of naval operations.

The principle of "certain latitude" by the fleet commanders in controlling operations of the centers was reaffirmed, but where the fleet commanders temporarily diverted the centers for special purposes, OP-20-G was to be advised. Existing allocations of cryptanalytic tasks were restated or clarified.

1. Washington was to work new enemy systems and discover initial breaks. The other centers were to assist as practicable.

2. Washington was also to solve systems requiring special equipment and a large amount of statistical data. "This will apply to the bulk additive recovery in system JN-25. ..."

3. All centers were to work incomplete systems, operational codes, and search for cribs.

4. Washington was to work on minor and obsolete systems.

5. All centers were to decrypt current traffic as their primary function.

The VCNO (DNC) reserved for himself control of personnel strength, transfers, and promotions. Personnel strength, current and upper limits, were set as follows:

Washington   3,000 by early summer 1943; 5,000 upper limit

Melbourne   204 at present; 300 upper limit

Hawaii   900 by late summer 1943; 1,149 upper limit

Intercept and DF stations within the CONUS remained under OP-20-G, control being exercised through 20-GX, the radio DF and intercept section and 20-GF, the DF control section (responsible for the Atlantic).[9]

By summer 1943 OP-20-G had become an elaborate organization. Its primary intercept stations in the U.S. were Bainbridge (Station S) on the West Coast and Chatham,

Massachusetts. Chatham had replaced Cheltenham, Maryland, as the primary station for interception of U-boat traffic by early 1943. A particularly important development in the expansion of OP-20-G was the initiation of an exclusively COMINT radio net. As was described in chapter 2, OP-20-G controlled some CONUS teletype links and communicated with the overseas centers via regular Navy Department radio facilities using private cipher systems. OP-20-G, formerly limited to encryption-decryption of dispatches and messenger activities, took over the intercept traffic teletypes in June 1943.[10] In August the "RI Fox" schedule came into being. This was exclusively for radio traffic addressed to FRUPAC and FRUMEL by Negat (the Washington center, i.e., 20-G). It was transmitted from Station I, Imperial Beach. In October this system was refined with the installation of a new teletype circuit, LL7050, exclusively used for transmitting traffic from Negat to Station I for "RI Fox" radio transmissions to the Pacific centers. Within a month the whole system was further upgraded by the availability to OP-20-G of Army radioteletype from the Presidio of San Francisco to Hawaii.

Every expansion of 20-G communications increased the opportunity for technical control and coordination of the Pacific centers.

THE ARMY COMINT BREAKTHROUGH IN 1943

What might be called an explosion in Army COMINT occurred during the spring of 1943. There were so many significant developments in these few months that for ease of explanation and study they are divided among several parts in this chapter and form the whole of chapter 4.

W. Preston Corderman, chief SSS
(1955 photo as major general)

The Army's COMINT accomplishments into 1943 were by no means insignificant. However, there had been no breaks into enemy mainline military systems after more than a year of war. On 1 February 1943, Colonel W. Preston Corderman replaced Colonel Frank Bullock as chief of the Signal Security Service (SSS), formerly known as the SIS. Bullock had been relieved at his own request because he felt that he should return to general signal corps duties (in fact, he would head the SIS in the China-Burma-India [CBI] Theater).

He had been considered an excellent partner by MIS as he and Colonel Clarke of Special Branch had worked closely in expanding Army COMINT facilities. At the request of MIS, Secretary of War Stimson approached Byron Price, director of censorship, and asked for the release of Colonel Corderman, then one of Price's assistants. Price agreed to this.[11] Corderman was an exceptionally good choice because he had served prewar tours in SIS as a student, instructor, and practitioner of cryptanalysis, and he was a section chief in the old intelligence division prior to Pearl Harbor.

Colonels Clarke and Corderman promptly undertook the study of one of the major policy problems of Army COMINT – the relationship of SSS to the field commands as to production of COMINT and dissemination of the finished product. There were two main issues here. First there were the SRI companies and the overseas COMINT headquarters (such as SIS ETOUSA and CBB) under the theater or field commands. Then there was the matter of dissemination of high-level COMINT to the theaters and commands by the War Department (MIS Special Branch).

On 12 February 1943, Colonel Clarke sent a study of these problems to General Strong, the ACS, G-2. His conclusion was that all highly skilled cryptanalytic personnel then in Australia, the U.K., and North Africa should be called back to SSS headquarters at Arlington Hall Station (AHS).[12] Clarke believed that a War Department General Staff directive was needed to implement his suggestions. Several weeks later Colonel Clarke forwarded a revised study to General Strong. This study had been prepared by Colonel Corderman.[13] It was the strongest possible pitch for a completely centralized, worldwide Army cryptologic service. These were the main recommendations:

1. Operational control of all Army COMINT personnel, installations, and units, including SRI companies was to be under the War Department (chief signal officer/SSS).

2. A special COMINT communications system was to be created and controlled by SSS.

3. There was to be wider dissemination of COMINT to theater commanders by the MIS.

The activities of the overseas centers in Australia, North Africa, and the U.K. were criticized on the grounds that they were counterproductive. "It is absurd to expect that a local commander in one relatively small theater should be able to solve material with which the SSS, with a very large staff and worldwide facilities for intercept coverage, is struggling." And further predictions were added, to the effect that CBB could never solve Japanese army high command systems any more than the COMINT units in North Africa could read German air force or army high-level traffic. There was frustration at SSS because these overseas COMINT headquarters were not sending progress reports to AHS, and their activities were almost unknown. Thus even coordination was impossible.

Behind all this was the nagging example of the Navy, where, as Colonel Corderman recognized, the DNC had effective control of all naval COMINT. Nor should we overlook the fact that the Navy, perhaps partly as a result of its centralized system, was reading Japanese and German high-level naval traffic.

The assets of Army COMINT in early 1943, both SSS controlled and theater controlled, were these:[14]

SRI Companies

There were approximately thirty-five companies in training or in operation overseas or CONUS. The greatest number were in training status or on alert for overseas.

COMINT "Headquarters" Groups Overseas

These were a mixed bag consisting of parties rushed to the field from SIS or organized in the theater. The most important were the 837th Signal Service Detachment (the U.S. component of CBB) with fifty-six officers and enlisted personnel, the SIS ETOUSA, and the detachments in North Africa.

SSS Fixed Stations

Headquarters and processing center at AHS. The detachments of the Second Signal Service Battalion were as follows:

MS-1   Vint Hill Farm Station, Virginia

MS-2   Two Rock Ranch, California

MS-3   Fort Sam Houston, Texas

MS-4   Fort Shafter, Territory of Hawaii (soon renumbered MS-5)

MS-5   Fairbanks, Alaska (soon renumbered MS-7)

MS-6   New Delhi, India (not operational)

MS-7

This was a complex arrangement to fully integrate, especially during this transitional period when SRI companies were en route or newly assigned to theaters. For whatever reason, no directive to centralize was forthcoming from the War Department General Staff.

A major new source of traffic came available to SSS during the summer of 1943 with the opening of MS-4 (Hawaii became known as MS-5 again) in Asmara, Ethiopia. This was operated by a detachment of the Second Signal Service Battalion and provided AHS with a priceless source for Berlin-Tokyo traffic. It was one of the most productive COMINT sources of World War II.

On 7 April 1943 the Army achieved its first break into enemy high-level military systems. This was the solution of the Japanese army water transport code (Indicator System 2468). On 2 June 1943 AHS published its first formal translation of a water transport code message. The break seems to have been made simultaneously at AHS, CBB, and the British center in India at the Wireless Experimental Center (WEC).[15]

Thereafter other Japanese military systems were broken and exploited. Even more dramatic results were obtained from the capture of a Japanese army administrative code publication at Shio, New Guinea, by Australian forces in January 1944.[16] Naturally this break led to further expansion of SSS and the MIS Special Branch. And the development of a COMINT communications system was hastened. The most important sources of this now exploitable traffic became Two Rock Ranch (MS-2) and CBB.

A month prior to the 2468 breakthrough, the MIS had given the SSS a revised set of priorities for intercept and processing. This superseded the priority directive of 18 April 1942 and was far more elaborate.[17] The priorities were divided into groups A through G, in order of importance, and the unreadable systems were ranked by numbers as "special research projects." Group A consisted of the following:

Japanese army ("#1 special research project")

European and African theater weather traffic

Diplomatic traffic (including military attaché) between

- Japan–Russia (Japanese traffic)
- Japan–Germany (Japanese, Italian, and German traffic)
- Japan–Italy (Japanese, Italian, and German)
- Japan–Vatican City (Japanese and Italian)

German military traffic, the top priority in 1942, was placed in Group B as "#3 special research project." However, as will be described in chapter 4, this was a very hot issue indeed. The placement of German traffic in Group B was an important policy change as it recognized the wisdom of placing heaviest U.S. emphasis on Japan. This was in line with the USN-British COMINT understanding regarding the Pacific theater.

Within the MIS Special Branch itself, where Army COMINT policy was formulated, there had been a slow growth of personnel, and these were spread exceedingly thin. The SSS product was published daily in the *Bulletin* and delivered to Special Branch (four times per day) for analysis and dissemination. For this, Special Branch had only thirty-nine officers and civilians, of whom just twenty-seven were available for analysis and preparation of the finished intelligence that appeared in the "MAGIC Summary" and special studies.[18] It is representative of the revolution in Army COMINT, caused by the entry into Japanese army codes in 1943 (and the access to ENIGMA described in the next chapter), to note that Special Branch had 382 people by June 1944.[19]

The demands on personnel were even greater at AHS. The civilian force there had grown to 2,300 by April 1943, and there were 766 military personnel. In spite of this tremendous growth in only a year and a half, only a fraction of the available traffic could be fully processed. This was not only because Japanese army codes were unreadable but also because the readable traffic could not be completely handled.[20] The force at AHS would more than double during the next year to take advantage of the emerging sources. To that end the MIS, through the adjutant general, addressed the commanding general of the Army Service Forces on 11 August 1943 directing that the SSS be provided additional personnel, equipment, and facilities as soon as possible, ". . . with a view to exploiting to the maximum recent successes in obtaining intelligence from certain enemy radio traffic. . . ." And also that ". . . the maximum possible quantity of this intercepted and analyzed material be completely processed and that the transmission of the derived intelligence to the Special Branch, Military Intelligence Service be expedited."[21]

Arlington Hall Station employee at a decipherment machine

It was again becoming apparent that the subordination of the (newly renamed) Signal Security Agency (SSA) to the chief signal officer and the Army Service Forces was a problem. This had been recognized by General Strong in 1942 when he attempted to have the SIS placed under MIS. The issue was now raised by Colonel Otto Nelson, assistant to the deputy chief of staff. On 18 October 1943 he wrote General Strong citing the personnel allotment problems of the SSA. He noted that the SSA obtained its personnel through the OCSigO and the Army Services Forces, while it existed mainly to serve not these organizations, but rather the Special Branch, MIS.[22] Recommendations were sought.

General Strong replied on 23 October. He suggested that the SSA be removed from the Signal Corps and made an independent agency.[23] As the SSA was "our most important source of secret intelligence," it ought not to be "under the command of those who have no concern with the intelligence produced." For administrative purposes, General Strong suggested the SSS could be under the Military District of Washington, but *direct operational control* would be from the chief of staff acting through the ACS, G–2 (i.e., MIS).

This was a reasonable proposal and would ultimately be adopted by the Army after two more rounds of administrative struggle. But for now the Nelson-Strong exchanges came to nothing and the SSA remained under the OCSigO and ASF. It is, however, undeniable that more personnel and equipment for SSA were quickly forthcoming.

By the end of 1943, the field components of SSA, represented by the Second Signal Service Battalion, had again been realigned. The detachment at Fort Sam Houston, one of the oldest in the Army, was disestablished. The centrally controlled sites were now:

MS-1 Vint Hill

MS-2 Two Rock Ranch

MS-4 Asmara, Eritrea

MS-5 Territory of Hawaii

MS-7 Fairbanks, Alaska

MS-8 New Delhi (only partially operational)

CENTRAL BUREAU BRISBANE

In this section the policy and organizational developments in Central Bureau Brisbane, the COMINT organization of the SWPA theater, will be traced from 1943 to the end of the war. (The early story has been described in chapter 2.) Effective 27 January 1943, the CBB was placed under the direct control of GHQ, SWPA. Its mission was specified as follows under GHQ Instruction #27:[24]

1. Supervision, coordination, and operational control of the COMINT activities of the theater's ground and air forces

2. Cryptanalysis, translation, and dissemination of traffic

3. Traffic analysis and DF.

Simultaneously a study committee was created to make recommendations to GHQ on the requirements of CBB. The committee recommended, and GHQ approved, general expansion, procurement of special equipment, and the formation of seven Australian army field sections and eight RAAF wireless units. The latter were the intercept units. As the availability of U.S. Army SRI companies (or similar USAAF units) was still uncertain, all intercept was to be done by Australian forces. Perhaps we can see in microcosm General MacArthur's oft-cited complaint that the SWPA was treated as a second-class theater of operations by tracing the slow availability of U.S. Army SRI companies.[25]

A platoon of the 121st SRI Company reached Australia on 19 April 1942. It was redesignated First Operating Platoon, 126th SRI, soon thereafter. It did not begin intercept operations until November 1942, and the bulk of the company (the 126th) did not reach the SWPA until March 1943. The other companies that General MacArthur was to receive reached the SWPA as follows:

- 112th SRI arrived in Guadalcanal on 29 January 1944
- 125th SRI arrived in Hollandia on 16 July 1944
- 111th SRI arrived in Hollandia on September 1944

Nor were these companies immediately operational upon arrival in the theater because more training or equipment might be needed. All the SRI companies were operating under CBB control by the beginning of 1945.

Up to the COMINT breakthrough of April 1943, CBB tasks were roughly divided as follows:[26]

1. The Australian army was doing most of the intercept, some translation.

2. The RAAF was doing a share of the intercept, studying enemy air activity, and providing bearings.

3. The U.S. contingent was doing a "fair share" of the solution and translation and all the statistical studies. The 126th SRI was beginning to provide intercept.

After the break into the Japanese water transport code, the arrangement became more complicated, as Washington and London became involved to a greater degree. There now were two major aspects: division of the cryptanalytic effort between the centers and provision of traffic by CBB to SSA Washington and to London. It was not always a happy situation for CBB. On 17 August 1943 CBB radioed SSA that the load was too great to continue sending all four-figure traffic to Washington by radio. Traffic in certain systems, including the famous 2468, would continue to be radioed, but others were to be microfilmed and flown to Washington.[27] A month later there was a strong message to SSA from Abraham Sinkov at CBB citing the problems being encountered in receiving messages that SSA was routing via British channels and that the SSA suggestion on a division of cryptanalytic labor was "received here [i.e., CBB] with poor grace," because Washington had taken the most productive aspects for itself. But the harshest complaint by CBB was that "your continued duplication for much of this effort [is] deplored here."[28]

Thus the heart of the problem. CBB, as a processing center not under SSA or MIS or any other War Department office, was beginning to exploit high-level Japanese army traffic, which was also the highest priority target of SSA. There were by the end of 1943 five organizations working this cryptanalytic problem, in by no means coordinated fashion: SSA, CBB, GC&CS, WEC, and to a very modest degree, the U.S. Army's SIS-CBI in New Delhi. The matter would be resolved in favor of SSA after conferences in London in 1943 and Washington in early 1944.

Prior to considering the undertakings reached in conference, comment is needed on the complex method of traffic and technical information exchange used by SSA in communication with CBB. At the suggestion of the British (July 1943), this was done by way of Washington to BSC New York and thence to GC&CS.[29] The SSA messages were to employ special prefixes to show how GC&CS was to retransmit to the field. These prefixes were

- FRESCO – for GC&CS and WEC, New Delhi, with GC&CS to pass to CBB
- SERENA – for GC&CS, WEC, and CBB
- MERMAN – for GC&CS and CBB

For this purpose the British TYPEX cryptographic machine with special settings was to be put in use by CBB, WEC, AHS, and GC&CS. CBB would route material via GC&CS rather than send it directly to Washington.

On 19 July certain Japanese army systems (JA 3366, 6633, and 3636) were assigned exclusively to the WEC in India for cryptanalytic attack.[30] Not until March 1944, however, was there final agreement between the parties or control of anti-Japanese COMINT. From 13 to 24 March the second conference on Japanese army communications was held in Washington. The most important agreements were that SSA would be the coordinator for cryptanalysis on high-level systems and for allocation of traffic analysis studies. Likewise, "requests for coverage and assignment of specific intercept missions will be coordinated by SSA...."[31] Arrangements were made for extensive additions to the existing communications system between the various centers. Specific assignments were made concerning some of the Japanese army systems.

These developments were not paralleled in CBB-U.S. Navy (FRUMEL) relations. There simply was no significant cooperation between these organizations until almost the end of the war. Commander Fabian, head of FRUMEL until December 1943, later opined that CBB had nothing to offer FRUMEL as it was a less-advanced organization having, in his opinion, entirely different interests and objectives. As Fabian put it, "FRUMEL was concerned solely with information on Japanese naval circuits. The Central Bureau was not."[32] It was not quite that simple. In fact, the lack of cooperation was such that Captain Hastings, the GC&CS representative in Washington, called a conference in March 1943 with Commander Wenger, Colonels Carter Clarke and Al McCormack, and Major Harold McD Brown to air the views of Major A. W. Sandford, the Australian army's senior officer at CBB, who was then passing through Washington en route to London.[33] As Major

Sandford explained it, CBB had freely made its product available to FRUMEL until the last month. But as FRUMEL consistently declined to reciprocate and "had openly refused to have any dealings" with CBB, the contact terminated. Major Sandford believed that Commander Fabian had withheld valuable information from CBB (such as a captured callsign book) of a type that was not solely of interest to the Navy.

As Commander Wenger saw the situation, based on correspondence from Commander Fabian, there was another side to the story.[34] Fabian had written in mid-1942 that the CBB had grandiose plans but few trained personnel. In January 1943 Fabian had reported to OP-20-G that while CBB had always been anxious to join with FRUMEL, this was pointless because the Army had nothing to offer, and worse, employed such poor security practices as to be a "menace."

This disagreeable controversy may be attributable to other factors too. It seems likely that there were serious personality problems involving the relationship of certain British and Australian personnel with FRUMEL. Hopefully this had been solved when, by terms of the Holden Agreement of November 1942, FRUMEL was placed solely under the USN. But one of the British officers of FRUMEL, who was to return to London, went to work with CBB instead, thus aggravating the situation.

Another matter of difficulty was that both CBB and FRUMEL provided COMINT to General MacArthur, but did so independently. The matter of competition cannot be discounted. But as General MacArthur later told one of the War Department special security officers, he did not care where he got COMINT, just so long as he got it.

More than a year later, in June 1944, the matter of CBB was again discussed between Clarke and Wenger under the auspices of the newly formed Army-Navy COMINT Coordinating Committee (ANCICC).[35] Clarke told Wenger that the status of CBB as it related to the War Department had still not been clarified.

So, CBB and FRUMEL continued on their separate paths, the former specializing in Japanese naval air and army air and ground communications and the latter on fleet circuits. The thread of CBB's relationships will be taken up again in chapter 8 in the context of the development of the War Department Special Security Officer (SSO) system.

By the end of the war, CBB and its field intercept units had reached a personnel strength of 4,339 men and women operating in Australia, the Philippines, New Guinea, Borneo, Morotai, and Okinawa. Represented were the U.S. Army, RAAF, Australian army, Canadian army, and a few representatives of the British and New Zealand services.[36] Most, though not all, of CBB's processing center had moved forward to Manila before the end of the war and CBB processing elements had accompanied MacArthur's headquarters in each advance, to Hollandia in August 1944, Leyte at the end of 1944, and Manila in March 1945.

By late 1944 CBB headquarters had reached its final organizational structure. Since 1942 it had been headed by General Akin with day-to-day operations remaining under his three deputy directors: (1945 ranks) Colonel Abraham Sinkov, USA; Lieutenant Colonel A. W. Sandford, Australian army; Wing Commander H. Roy Booth, RAAF. Commander Booth was the executive officer as well as one of the deputy directors. The branches, at the time of the final organization, were as follows (this by way of further showing the multinational and interservice character of CBB):[37]

Designator	Description	Chief(s)
A	Administration	Captain W. G. B. Cassidy, AIF Flight Lieutenant P. F. Ward, RAAF Major G. A. Tanner, USA
B	Solution	Captain T. E. Nave, RN Lieutenant Colonel H. L. Clark, USA Flight Lieutenant J. Walsh, RAAF
C	Communications	Major A. G. Henry, AIF Squadron Leader W. J. Clarke, RAAF Major B. E. Small, USA
D	Photography	Lieutenant K. E. Campbell, USA Petty Officer H. L. Stevens, RAAF
E	Traffic Analysis	Major S. R. I. Clark, AIF
G	Machine	Major Z. Halpin, USA
H	Translation	Lieutenant Colonel Hugh S. Erskine, USA
I	General intelligence and liaison	Captain B. Lehane, AIF

In a critique of CBB operations written soon after the war, the deputy directors made a number of interesting observations on administration and policy.[38] They suggested that CBB and G-2 ought to have been combined (presumably under G-2 and control). Their reasoning was not unlike that repeated in Washington throughout the war by Carter Clarke, George Strong, et al. On the other hand, the deputy directors saw the CBB concept of total coordination of both the field effort and the processing as the reason for CBB's success. They left no doubt where they stood on the question of who should control the SRI companies (or similar Australian units) – unless the company could perform all functions, including cryptanalysis and translation, control should meet with the center rather than the field commander. In that regard there was one peculiar situation that developed late in the war. The Army Air Force radio squadrons mobile (RSM) were an unwelcome and uncooperative element introduced into the SWPA. As theoretically self-sufficient COMINT units, extremely well-equipped, they did not willingly join the CBB team. (The RSMs will be briefly discussed in later chapters.)

This section will close with a few comments on CBB's dissemination of COMINT. As CBB was a creature of the theater commander, General MacArthur, there was never any question that the COMINT product would be promptly and directly given to his G-2. When the SSO system was introduced in late 1943 and greatly expanded in late 1944, the War Department gained certain control over COMINT dissemination, especially of ULTRA material, the high-level decrypts. Until mid-1944 the policymaking users of CBB COMINT were in one place – first Melbourne and then Brisbane. The material was distributed daily by CBB couriers to the intelligence staffs of GHQ SWPA, Far East Air Force [FEAF], RAAF, and Australian army.[39] More extensive dissemination of CBB COMINT came about during 1944 and 1945.[40] The daily UBJ report (high-grade decrypts) was disseminated as follows during this later period:

- SWPA – G-2, USN, General Akin, Australian MI, Allied air forces
- Overseas – War Department and the Allied Cryptologic Centers

By then the matter of COMINT dissemination was governed by regulations common to the Army and Navy in all theaters, and to the British.

PROPOSALS FOR CLOSER ARMY-NAVY COOPERATION

During 1942 tentative proposals were made by the OCSigO to upgrade the position of the Signal Corps by placing the chief signal officer on the General Staff.[41] General Olmstead, the CSO, was only too aware that his authority did not seem to match his heavy responsibilities and that, unlike DNC Captain Joseph Redman, he was not really in charge of Army communications.

There were several developments that grew out of this reexamination of Signal Corps authority. One was a study of the merger of certain Army and Navy communications functions to prevent overlap and duplication. A section of the resulting report, which was issued on 19 February 1943, dealt with COMINT. The ad hoc committee came to the conclusion that "The intelligence and security activities of the Army and Navy provide one of the finest examples of complete coordination and cooperation. There is no evidence of any duplication of effort."[42]

This conclusion, coming as it did from a junior ad hoc group, by no means represented the final thinking of the time. A few weeks later, Captain Stone of OP-20-G alerted the DNC to "determined efforts" being made by the Army to merge Army-Navy COMINT.[43]

Stone cited as evidence the Army's recent offer to assist in anti U-boat COMINT which had been accompanied by a request to OP-20-G for U-boat traffic. Further, the CBB in Australia was seeking to merge with FRUMEL, and of greatest significance were statements by General Strong ". . . in which he affirmed positively his belief that there should be a single cryptanalytic bureau in Washington for the Army and Navy." Stone concluded that the Navy would lose in any merger but that OP-20-G assistance to the Army's COMINT program was a good idea.

The matter was of sufficient concern to the Navy for Admiral Horne to forward Stone's observations to Admiral King. Horne commented that he agreed with Captain Stone and that the integrity of Navy COMINT must be preserved under direct Navy control.[44] Admiral King commented, "This is a clear case where the Navy can render services to the Army that the latter could *not* duplicate."

The Army had still other proposals for mergers. During March the deputy chief of staff and the chief of the air staff suggested to the Navy that two super agencies be created – an Army-Navy Far Eastern Intelligence Service under Navy Department control and an Army-Navy Atlantic and Middle Eastern Intelligence Service under the War Department. On 1 April the DNI advised Admiral Horne that these ideas were not acceptable to the Navy.[45]

On 10 May 1943 General McNarney, DCS, appointed a board to study Army communications.[46] One of the members of the board was Colonel Carter Clarke. The board was created to consider suggestions by General Olmstead that the CSO should have more authority and to generally consider the state of Army communications, as there seems to have been growing dissatisfaction at high levels. The board concluded that Army communications were "inadequate, unsatisfactory and confused." In its report issued on 21 June, the board recommended that a communications and electronics division be created and placed on the General Staff and that it have wide powers to direct Army signal matters. This was disapproved at high levels. A few days after the board concluded its work, General Olmstead was dismissed as CSO and forced to retire. He was replaced by Harry C. Ingles.

The board seems not to have studied Army-Navy COMINT consolidation. Testimony was taken from Joseph Redman, probably to examine the Navy's communication management. There was testimony on COMINT from General Strong, General Stoner, and others. Strong testified to the poor equipage and inefficient deployment of the SRI companies, which, he said, should be placed under War Department control. General Stoner voiced the usual Signal Corps position that intercept and processing should remain in the Signal Corps.

During the period that the board was meeting, General Strong approached Admiral Train, the DNI, with a new plan for Army-Navy COMINT cooperation. He submitted to Admiral Train the draft of an agreement, for their joint signature, that would establish a joint Army-Navy COMINT summary to be written (presumably daily) by MID.[47] This summary would be distributed within the Army and Navy only. Material to be disseminated outside the services would continue to be done by the service that produced the intelligence.

Admiral Train submitted the Strong draft to Joseph Redman. Redman's response was negative.[48] He observed that General Strong's draft was vague in use of terms but, most importantly, "This agreement would practically result in the establishment of the Unified Radio Intelligence Organization that General Strong has been promoting, which the Navy opposes." Also it would take dissemination away from the COMINT producing agency. So, the proposal was rejected. General Strong may not have been proposing anything more than a "super MAGIC Summary," an expanded version of the existing MIS Special Branch product. Nonetheless, if General Strong was a promoter of a joint COMINT agency, this could certainly have been a first step in that direction.

On 1 June Commander Wenger, possibly prompted by the Strong proposal, prepared a study paper for Captain Stone concerning future Army-Navy COMINT cooperation.[49] He reviewed the circumstances that had led to the Army undertaking all diplomatic COMINT a year before. Commander Wenger believed this should now be reviewed and had informally discussed this with Colonel Doud of SSS. Doud had told him that the Army still looked on diplomatic traffic as their "bread and butter." The matter seems not to have been pressed at the time.

Commander Wenger returned to the matter of Army-Navy cooperation a few months later when he prepared a comprehensive review of this subject for Admiral King (this paper probably did not get beyond the DNC).[50] Wenger recommended that the Army and Navy create a joint board modeled on the British "Y" board/committee. This board would consist of three officers from each service with an experienced (in intelligence) general or flag officer as chairman. The board would assure better means of COMINT exchange between the services and prompt, safe dissemination of product. The board would be directly under the JCS and report to the JCS ". . . for all matters of policy in connection with the planning and coordination of joint or combined communication intelligence operations, including dissemination of intelligence and security measures pertaining." Wenger added that he did not favor actual merger of Army and Navy COMINT. Captain Stone forwarded Wenger's paper to the DNC. The recommended board was not created, but there seems to have been an increased effort by each service to upgrade the exchange of COMINT.

The SSA surveyed the status of traffic exchange in October 1943 and reported to MIS that, while exchange was significant, the only joint effort (that is, planned rather than incidental) was the Japanese weather problem.[51] The Army was routinely forwarding Japanese weather and naval attaché traffic and German naval attaché traffic to OP-20-G. The SSA was intercepting the naval attaché material incidental to its diplomatic coverage.

The Navy provided SSA with diplomatic traffic, Japanese army traffic on naval circuits, and Japanese weather.

This type of exchange was in keeping with the 1942 agreements. We should also recall that certain decrypted and translated material was exchanged, i.e., the Navy received the SSA Bulletin and the MIS Special Branch MAGIC or diplomatic summary.

In December Colonel Clarke wrote (the recently promoted) Admiral Joseph Redman to clarify channels of exchange.[52] He urged Admiral Redman to send all Navy COMINT that was to be disseminated within the Army to the Special Branch. Certain items of COMINT were being sent directly to General Staff offices rather than to the Special Branch. Of course *raw traffic* was properly exchanged between the COMINT agencies rather than via MIS.

The time had come to formalize the Army-Navy COMINT relationships. This will be described in chapter 7. Before describing that, this study will describe in some detail the important climax of U.S.-British COMINT relations.

Notes

1. Memorandum from OP-20-G to section heads, 21 May 1943, subject: Dissemination of Information in the Navy Department, OP-20-G Organization Folder (classified). This document details the 20-GI dissemination system. Also, letter to the author by Captain Packard (based on the latter's historical research).

2. Report of Mr. Rawleigh Warner to Admiral King, 29 April 1943, subject: Intelligence Function, *Catalogue*, 2.c.(12) (classified).

3. Memorandum from King to Horne, 26 June 1943, "General File," NSAHC (classified).

4. For much of the information in this section, the author is indebted to Captain Packard. Captain Packard studied numerous sources not seen by the author. Also see Furer, *Administration of the Navy Department in World War I*, 156–157, for an excellent discussion of the establishment of F-2.

5. Letter from Captain Packard.

6. Furer, 158.

7. Volume 1, *Allied Communication Intelligence and the Battle of the Atlantic*, 4–5 (classified).

8. Letter, VCNO serial 0833920, 19 April 1943, *Catalog*, 2.6.(1).

9. OP-20-G Subdivision Order No. 55, 16 April 1943, subject: Cognizance and Functions of Sections Under OP-20-G, OP-20-G Organization File.

10. *GC History*, 25, 43–49. The teletype facilities then in operation were:

    LL7067 – simplex line for Bainbridge

    LL7433 – simplex line from Bainbridge and Imperial Beach

    LL7037 – simplex line from Chatham, Massachusetts

    WA52 – TWX on which traffic was received from Chatham; Jupiter, Florida, Winter Harbor, Maine, Imperial Beach, and Bainbridge.

11. General Clarke, in a letter to the author, described the departure of Colonel Bullock and his replacement by Colonel Corderman. Corderman would head the cryptologic service until after World War II. He was the first commander of ASA.

12. Memorandum from Clarke to Strong, 12 Feb 1943, ACSI #49. Hereafter the term AHS will be used interchangeably with SSS or SSA to mean the Army's cryptologic headquarters. This is in keeping with the style of the period 1943–45.

13. "Control of Signal Security Units in Theaters of Operation," 25 February 1943, ACSI #49. This is a significant document and presents a thorough policy statement from the AHS point of view, though with limited mention of the role of MIS.

14. Ibid.; *Radio Intercept Survey* forwarded to Colonel Clarke by Colonel Corderman, 12 April 1943. There were various changes during this period in the monitoring stations. The long-time station at Corozal, Canal Zone, the former MS-4, was closed as was Fort Hunt (former MS-7). MS numbers changed from time to time. The system of giving MS numbers to sources of traffic outside of SSS (such as the SRI, foreign government, other U.S. services) continued.

15. Memorandum from Colonel Harold Doud to Colonel Corderman, 9 April 1943, subject: Solution of Indicator System 2468 Japanese Army Code, ACSI #49; also, *History of SSA*, vol. 4 (Language Branch), 23 ff. Details of how the break was made and the timing of who did what are beyond the scope of this study (and the author's understanding of cryptanalysis).

16. *History of SSA*, vol. 4, 32 ff. Solution of the Japanese army codes presented incredible difficulties for the Allies. Fortunately, Japanese army communications were largely Morse, so the problems of intercept were less severe than might have been the case had more sophisticated equipment been available.

17. Memorandum from General Strong, ACS, G-2, to the chief signal officer, 8 March 1943, subject: Priorities for Operations of the Signal Security Service, ACSI #49 (classified).

18. McCormack memorandum, *Origin and Functions*, 44–45. McCormack lists a number of important Special Branch analyses prior to April 1943. Among them, (a) correct prediction in July 1942 that Japan would not attack the USSR; (b) information on the Spanish attitude following the North African invasion; (c) Latin American matters to guide U.S. policy there; and (d) Japanese economic plans in the Far East.

19. *History of Special Branch*, 60 (classified).

20. *Origin and Functions*, 20–21 (classified).

21. Memorandum from General Strong (Carter W. Clarke, drafter) to AGO, 11 Aug. 1943, directing preparation of memorandum to CG, ASF. The latter sent to ASF on 13 Aug. 1943, ACSI #49 (classified).

22. Memorandum from O. L. Nelson to ACS, G-2, 18 Oct. 1943, subject: Signal Intelligence Activities in Washington, D.C., ACSI #49 (classified).

23. Memorandum from Strong to deputy chief of staff, 23 Oct. 1943, subject: Signal Intelligence Activities in Washington, D.C. ACSI #49 (classified).

24. *History of CBB*, tab A, 3–4.

25. Ibid., Tab J. The politics of this situation ought not to be belabored because the Australian units may have been able to provide sufficient coverage up to the time of the invasion of the Philippines. The history of the 125th SRI is especially interesting. It had operated against Japanese army communications since 8 December 1941 from West Coast sites, especially Fort Lewis, Washington. It may be considered a predecessor to MS-2, Two Rock Ranch, as an important source of Japanese army traffic.

26. Letter from A. Sinkov to S. Kullback, January 1943, attached to CBB Progress Report #4, January 1943, NSAH.

27. Message number Q4104, CBB to War Department (for SSA). Folder 311.5, CXG-114, BII, NSAH.

28. Message number Q1429, CBB to War Department (sent as Akin to CSO/Sinkov to Kullback), 21 September 1943, in ibid.

29. Message from Commander Travis to Colonel O'Connor (GC&CS representative in Washington), 3 July 1943 in ibid.

30. SSA Routing and Work Sheet, 26 July 1943, initialled by Lieutenant Colonel Earle F. Cook and Lieutenant Colonel Harold McD. Brown, in ibid.

31. GC&CS History, *The Organization and Evolution of British Army SIGINT*, vol. 3, 56 ff.

32. Fabian interviews by Captain Wayman Packard.

33. Memorandum from Commander Wenger to chief, OP-20-G, subject: Collaboration between RI Unit and "Central Bureau," Brisbane, 20 March 1943, *Catalog* 3.g. Details of this conference as well as background information on FRUMEL-CBB are contained in this seven-page memorandum, which is a detailed exposition of the controversies in Australia.

34. Ibid.

35. *Outline of Collaboration*, a background paper prepared by Commander Wenger, 18 August 1944, *Catalog* 2.c.(12), 54.

36. See the various appendices to tab A, *History of CBB*, (Part I), NSAHC.

37. *History of CBB*, tab A, appendix B. Lieutenant Colonel Erskine of the translation branch had gone to Australia in April 1942 with Colonel Sinkov and was thus an original member of CBB.

38. *Critique* in *History of CBB*, Part I. This paper was signed by Booth, Sinkov, and Sandford (classified).

39. *SSO History*, vol. 3, tab A: Memorandum prepared by Major John R. Thompson, deputy special security representative (classified).

40. *CBB History*, tab A.

41. *The Test*, 546.

42. *A Survey Looking to the Merger of Army and Navy Communications Services, Initially to Involve Removal of Duplication and Overlaps etc.*, 19 Feb. 1943, *Catalog* 2.c.(7). This document has a good overview of SSS and OP-20-G organization. The survey was not mainly directed toward COMINT; however, COMINT was just one of many signals areas under consideration.

43. Memorandum from Stone to DNC, 9 March 1943, quoted in Wenger's *Outline of Collaboration* (see note 35 above). We may assume that Wenger drafted the Stone memorandum (classified).

44. Note from Horne to King, 10 March 1943, in ibid (classified).

45. This is described in Wenger's *Outline of Collaboration*. The Army's DCS at that time was General McNarney. He was never satisfied during the war that Army intelligence was properly organized for most efficient service.

46. All the information on the proceedings of the Board and the relief of General Olmstead is from *The Test*, 544–563 and *The Outcome*, 614–615.

47. Memorandum, with attached draft agreement, Strong to Train (classified) 26 May 1943, *Catalog* 2.c.(8).

48. Endorsement, Joseph Redman to Train, 2 June 1943 (classified) in ibid.

49. Memorandum from Wenger to OP-20-G, 1 June 1943, "Liaison" folder NSAH (classified).

50. This memorandum, dated 23 August 1943, is quoted in Wenger's later paper, *Outline of Collaboration*, etc. (classified).

51. Memorandum from Lieutenant Colonel H. McD. Brown, SSA to Colonel S. P. Collins, 16 October 1943, ACSI #49 (classified).

52. Memorandum from Clarke to Joseph R. Redman, 2 December 1943, quoted in Wenger's *Outline of Collaboration* (classified).

Chapter 4
The Army-British COMINT Agreements of 1943:
The ENIGMA Crisis

THE CRISIS IN BRITISH-U.S. RELATIONS

Beginning in late 1942, British-U.S. Army COMINT relations underwent a most difficult period not eased until a general agreement was reached in May 1943. This may be considered the "ENIGMA crisis," for it involved determined War Department efforts to get full access to ENIGMA material, both means of production and finished product. In the end, the British monopoly of ENIGMA ceased, and a full partnership began.

In January 1943 the routine and long-established British-U.S. Army relationship regarding diplomatic traffic was reaffirmed and clarified in a conference at Arlington Hall. The formal meeting, which lasted less than two hours, was attended by representatives of all interested organizations:[1]

U.K.-Canada	U.S.
Colonel W. W. Murray (Senior Representative)	Colonel Bullock (Chief SSS)
Colonel John Tiltman (GC&CS)	Lieutenant Colonel H. Doud (SSS)
Major Drake (DMI Office, Canada)	Major Telford Taylor (MIS Special Branch)
Captain Kenneth Maidment (BSC)	Major H. McD. Brown (SSS)
Mr. De F. Bayly (BSC)	Captain Rowlett (SSS)
and others	Mr. Friedman (SSS)
	Ensign Daniels (OP-20-G)

The purpose of the meeting was to insure the proper exchange of diplomatic traffic. Major Brown of SSS acted as moderator. He proposed that each country submit a schedule of coverages (circuits) and material desired. Based on these requirements, a working committee composed of Major Brown and Captain Maidment of BSC would make the arrangements. There was a discussion of existing channels of communication between the parties and agreement that exchange through Captain Maidment had proved a successful technique.

Quite separate from this uncontroversial area of cooperation was a problem that had begun a month earlier. On 2 December 1942, Field Marshall Sir John Dill, the British chiefs of staff representative in Washington, had written a note to General Marshall saying that Dr. Alan Turing, then in the U.S. on a scientific mission, had been denied access to a scrambler device being tested by the Bell Laboratories. Sir John asked General Marshall if he could lift this ban.[2]

This led to several days of study and consideration at the War Department, mostly within MID. Carter Clarke suggested to General Strong that the British were acting in a suspicious manner because the approach to the War Department had been made by Captain Hastings, the GC&CS representative, through Colonel D. M. Crawford of the Signal Corps rather than through MID. Crawford had told Captain Hastings that the scrambler could not be shown to Dr. Turing.[3] On 4 December General Strong suggested to General Marshall that a forceful note be sent to the British protesting these "back door" methods.[4] This was not done. However, General Marshall seems to have met with Dill, because on 8 December the chief of staff told his deputy, General McNarney, that Dill had said that Dr. Turing had full access in the U.K. to all secret developments. Therefore, Marshall asked McNarney, "would there continue to be objection to his [Turing] being allowed to see what is going on?"[5]

Dr. Alan Turing, cryptanalyst and mathematician

McNarney's reply is not known, but perhaps General Strong and Colonel Clarke intervened. For on 9 December Marshall wrote to Dill and told him that access to the scrambler was restricted, but that this was not unlike the British policy toward the U.S. Army for, continued Marshall, ". . . there is not interchange of information regarding these ultra-secret developments."[6] Marshall expressed his regrets that Dr. Turing had been embarrassed and suggested that a new request for access to the project could be made through MID.

General Dill, taking General Marshall's letter to mean that the matter would be solved in Dr. Turing's favor, expressed his gratitude to Marshall.[7] Dill said that he had been "horrified" to learn from Marshall that secret information was being withheld. He assured Marshall that he had taken appropriate action and that now "we hide nothing."

Actually the Turing matter had not been resolved and would rapidly become a forum for reviewing the total U.S. Army-British COMINT relationship.

Following Marshall's memorandum to Dill on 9 December, the latter seems to have instructed Captain Hastings to communicate with Commander Travis at GC&CS on the points raised by General Marshall. On 12 and 14 December Hastings met with Carter Clarke and showed him a series of messages from Travis. The theme of these messages was that Hastings and Colonel John Tiltman must convince the U.S. that GC&CS was withholding nothing. Clarke also learned that at Dill's direction Captain Hastings was to formally request MID to grant Dr. Turing access to the scrambler project at Bell Labs. Hastings was to secure a clear yes or no answer from MID.[8] Clarke urged General Strong to refuse the requested access. He said that the British were withholding a great deal from the U.S., specifically German army field traffic, German clandestine traffic, material related to "Slavic" nations, and details of the GC&CS "high-speed analyses."[9]

General Marshall apparently agreed with the Clarke-Strong position. On 23 December he again wrote Field Marshal Dill telling him that, according to MID, the British were holding back the aforementioned items.[10] Dill's response three days later is especially interesting.[11] The field marshal may have recognized that there was high-level confusion at the War Department as to how the British controlled COMINT, while the British were equally confused about the U.S. setup. Dill explained that British COMINT was centralized under GC&CS headed by Brigadier Stuart Menzies. The latter's Washington representative was Captain Hastings, and Colonel Tiltman, in Washington for a liaison visit, was also a GC&CS official. Dill also stated that GC&CS was under the Foreign Office.[12] He acknowledged his own misunderstanding in that Dr. Turing had applied for access through the wrong channels, namely, Signal Corps instead of MID. Dill did not withdraw his request (through Hastings) on behalf of Dr. Turing.

On 1 January 1943, General Strong advised Marshall that he had talked with Colonel Tiltman regarding the U.S. complaints.[13] The SSS would directly resolve the issues with Colonel Tiltman. But General Strong still believed that the British should be barred from the scrambler project. He was supported in this stand by Admiral King, the DNC, and by the Signal Corps. Therefore he suggested that General Marshall either ignore the Dill-Hastings-Turing request or explain to Dill that his (Marshall's) technical staff had advised him to continue to restrict access to the scrambler.

General Marshall did not take any action for several days. But there was heated communication between the British intelligence representatives in Washington and their chiefs on how to satisfy the U.S. and press Dr. Turing's case.[14] On 1 January Commander Travis wired Tiltman: "Can you not plead with Arlington or G-2 to assist in the matter of Turing?" Tiltman replied that the Turing case was being handled at the highest level and that a decision would be forthcoming. Tiltman reported that on his own initiative he had told General Strong that the best way to fulfill U.S. Army intelligence needs would be for Strong to have an Army representative accredited to GC&CS for receipt of all COMINT and related evaluations. Strong had accepted this suggestion and planned to send Colonel Al McCormack (Clarke's deputy in Special Branch) on a short mission to the U.K. to study the implementation of Tiltman's proposal.

Colonel Tiltman's suggestion to General Strong would prove, many months hence, to be the method adopted. The short-term response was hostile. On 4 January 1943 Travis wired Tiltman that "director does not (repeat not) approve of your suggestion" and that if McCormack visited the U.K. he could deal with the British DMI. Fortunately, Captain Hastings intervened with a personal message to the CSS (i.e., the director, Brigadier Menzies) on 5 January. He made it clear that the London response to Tiltman's suggestion was impolitic and that General Strong was the U.S. Army "kingpin for all 'Y' policy." Therefore, Colonel McCormack should be welcomed by GC&CS and not diverted to the DMI.[15] That same day Tiltman wired Travis. He noted that Hastings would send a personal message to the CSS. He opined that one problem now apparent to him was that MID was reluctant ". . . to take advice on policy from Arlington experts with whom all our contact has been hitherto."

Once again Colonel Tiltman had shown great perception. For while the MID (actually MIS Special Branch) had gained authority over Army COMINT policy in May 1942, there was not yet adequate knowledge, by MIS, of what the SSS was doing in technical areas. That lack of knowledge extended to certain SSS and SIS-ETOUSA relations with Britain. For example, there is no indication that Carter Clarke or General Strong were fully aware of the results of SSS liaison training visits to GC&CS during 1942 (i.e., Kullback's visit; Johnson's assignment there). Nor had the British understood who was in charge for the U.S. – that the responsible person was General George Strong, not the chief signal officer or his subordinates. This was further confused by the attitude of SSS. Under Lieutenant Colonel Winkler and Colonel Bullock, access to SSS spaces for MIS (and its predecessor) was very limited. Special Branch analysts did not have personal contact with SSS cryptanalysts or translators. This was changed when Colonel Corderman took command.

Colonel Tiltman also revealed to Commander Travis in the 5 January message that War Department experiments with a new type of Bombe had only been revealed to him the day before. Tiltman restated the position advanced to General Strong by him and Captain Hastings, ". . . we withhold nothing but reserve right to discourage duplication where our interests are vitally affected."

The Dill-Marshall exchange now resumed. On 5 January Sir John formally requested Marshall permit Dr. Turing to visit the project at the Bell Labs.[16] General Marshall's reply, made the next day, seriously confused the issues.[17] He once again rejected the request made on behalf of Dr. Turing. He concluded that other than War Department interests were involved and that he could not resolve these in Dr. Turing's favor. General

Marshall then added his comments on General Strong's desire for more access to British COMINT. According to General Marshall, "... he (Strong) agrees with me that turning this information over to us does actually involve increased hazard. Therefore my opinion is that your people should not release to us more detailed data of this kind than they do at present. As I said before General Strong agrees with this."

The stand concerning Dr. Turing was merely a continuation of what had been going on for over a month. It was not helpful, but it was consistent. However, General Marshall's reversal, and the alleged reversal by General Strong regarding access to highest level British COMINT, is impossible to understand. During this period General Marshall's attention was turned elsewhere. Lacking other evidence, I conclude that he misrepresented the views of General Strong because of some misunderstanding.

The next day General Marshall and Field Marshal Dill had a meeting about these issues. Dill then put his response in writing.[18] Like General Marshall's letter, it is not completely in keeping with known events. Rather than find the apparent Marshall-Strong concession an agreeable matter, Dill was angered. Perhaps he thought that the U.S. agreement not to push for more COMINT access was a sarcastic response or, more likely, that it represented a disbelief that all was being shared. Dill wrote, "It seems to me that the proposals in your letter derogate from the principle of full reciprocity. Our position, I understand, has been made quite clear. We are prepared to show your people everything *in England* [Dill's emphasis], but we reserve the right to refuse to allow 'exploitation' in the U.S. of vitally secret traffic where we are chiefly concerned, unless we are satisfied as to the necessity." Dill noted that the USN had been "allowed" to exploit certain traffic [i.e., U-boat ENIGMA] because it was vitally important to the Navy.[19] Dill was equally strident on the Turing matter. He suggested that if Dr. Turing returned to England empty-handed there would be "an unfortunate effect." He noted the great amount of mistrust and the need to restore mutual confidence.

There is another British response that cannot be specifically dated, though it was probably an enclosure to Dill's letter of 7 January. This is a background paper probably prepared by (or for) Commander Travis, GC&CS, and sent to Dill.[20] It is a refutation of the points raised by General Marshall, on advice of Carter Clarke and General Strong, in his 23 December memorandum to Dill. Among the points disputed were these:

1. Various U.S. representatives in the U.K. had seen the "high-speed analyses" [i.e., the Bombe]. The U.S. was working on one too but had not shared this fact with the British until December 1942.

2. Several U.S. Army personnel were at Bletchley Park working on German army field traffic (SIS-ETOUSA personnel).

3. Some German clandestine traffic (within Europe) may have been withheld from the U.S. prior to the North African landings, and some of this traffic may have been slow in reaching General Eisenhower, but "I believe this has been cleared up."

4. And finally, no "Slavic" traffic was being withheld. Activities in this area were made known to the Sinkov group in 1941, and after the German invasion of Russia "the Y Board decided to cease interception of Russian service traffic." [However, the British would begin to work some of the Russian problem again during 1943 – and not share information with the U.S.]

On 9 January 1943, General Marshall left Washington for the Casablanca Conference and did not return until 28 January.[21] The degenerating COMINT and Turing negotiations now fell to General McNarney, the deputy chief of staff. On the 9th Colonel Tiltman received a message from Travis for General Strong's attention.[22] Travis assured Strong that the RSS was giving all ETO traffic (clandestine) to General Eisenhower and that in general terms of COMINT access "Eisenhower is treated on precisely the same terms as any British commander."

Casablanca Conference, January 1943

The same day General McNarney acted decisively. As Field Marshal Dill had also gone to Casablanca, McNarney sent a memorandum to Lieutenant General G. N. Macready, British Staff Mission, Washington.[23] McNarney wrote that he had directed G-2 to grant Dr. Turing access to the Bell Labs for the purpose of examining the scrambler.

Unfortunately, the resolution of the Turing affair did not clear the way for a general agreement between the War Department and the British on the ENIGMA. Relations grew worse during the next three months.

On 8 February 1943 Mr. Friedman formally reported to Colonel Corderman that Arlington Hall's own "E solving machines" would be installed by 1 April and ready for operations soon after.[24] But, warned Friedman, actual exploitation of German army and air force ENIGMA enciphered communications would not be possible without specially trained personnel, a considerable volume of German service traffic, information from the British about their technical means of dealing with ENIGMA, and special channels of communication (and attendant cryptographic gear) for Arlington Hall. Special training was in progress at Arlington Hall, and special communications presumably could be developed. Only the British could provide the German traffic and the vitally important information on special techniques. The only U.S. Army sources of high-grade German traffic were MS-1 (Vint Hill) and the SRI detachments in Iceland and Newfoundland. These sources were inadequate and would remain so primarily because of geographic considerations. Therefore, proposed Mr. Friedman, a message should be sent to GC&CS announcing the near readiness of Arlington Hall's "E solving equipment" and suggesting that ENIGMA exploitation begin there. GC&CS would be requested to furnish the traffic. Friedman recognized the British concern for security and the attendant reluctance to allow ENIGMA exploitation outside the U.K. The British fears could be overcome by these arguments: Arlington Hall could make a real contribution on its own; as there was a large volume of traffic to work, it could be divided for better coverage; the German army and air force might introduce a fourth wheel into their ENIGMA machines; the Japanese might adopt the ENIGMA; and the U.S. needed practical training for future operations.

This memorandum was shown to Colonel Clarke, and it formed a basis for recommendations made in a memorandum drafted by Clarke that General Strong sent to General Marshall on 17 February.[25] General Strong recounted the chief of staff's correspondence with Field Marshal Dill and then advised that the time had come for the U.S. Army to exploit ENIGMA communications much as the U.S. Navy was doing, with British approval and assistance. General Strong attached a detailed proposal that was essentially a restatement of Mr. Friedman's observations and suggestions. He also enclosed the draft of a letter for Field Marshal Dill that was also a version of Mr. Friedman's ideas.

In this memorandum to General Marshall, General Strong did recognize that U.S. forces in the U.K. and North Africa were "doubtless" receiving intelligence analyses based on GC&CS exploitation of ENIGMA. But this was not sufficient for U.S. needs and was not an adequate exchange for the U.S. gift of the PURPLE machine two years before.

German ENIGMA cipher machine exhibited at the National Cryptologic Museum, Fort Meade, Maryland

The memorandum may have reached General Marshall the same day, for late that afternoon he had an appointment with Dill.[26] His response to General Strong was brief – the matter should be resolved through Captain Hastings.[27]

General Strong's requests of the British (made in his 17 February memorandum to General Marshall) were given to Captain Hastings, who forwarded them to the director of GC&CS, that is, Brigadier Menzies, the CSS. On 26 February the latter wired Hastings that the whole question had been placed before the British chiefs of staff.[28]

Brigadier General Hayes Kroner, Strong's deputy, was in London, and the direct responsibility for negotiating with the British Chiefs of Staff fell on him. He was in an unfortunate position, as he came to accept some aspects of the British position, greatly displeasing General Strong and Colonel Clarke. During the first week of March, Kroner sent a message to G-2 that implied that the dispatch of raw traffic from GC&CS to Washington was undesirable on security grounds. On 8 March Strong cabled an uncompromising reply.[29] Kroner was to insist upon traffic from the British. He was to "press this point to the limit of your ability," and he could call upon the SSS liaison officer at Bletchley Park, Captain Roy Johnson, if he needed technical advice.

Kroner's reply on 11 March clearly showed how difficult his position was.[30] He assured General Strong that he had made the very highest contacts short of Prime Minister Churchill and that the U.S. position had been fully presented. The British were adamant that there could be no exploitation outside of the U.K. because of the danger to security. Kroner suggested that the U.S. had no choice other than to participate at Bletchley Park. An appeal could be made to the prime minister, said Kroner, but he recommended that General Strong wait until the British Joint Chiefs had sent their formal estimations to Dill. Perhaps most telling of the points made by General Kroner was his statement that the British "lay great store" in Marshall's memorandum to Dill of 6 January 1943 (supra) wherein Marshall had written his agreement that traffic should not be sent to the U.S. because of danger to security. Kroner added that *he was not even aware of this letter* which, of course, put him in the position of advancing a proposal already rejected by his own chief of staff.[31]

Probably unknown to General Kroner, the British Chiefs of Staff had already dispatched their instruction to Sir John Dill. Their letter, dated 7 March 1943, refers to some of the preceding correspondence and presents, in the form of a joint regulation, definitions and procedures that are to apply to highest level of COMINT.[32] The term special intelligence (SI) was to apply to high-grade axis codes and ciphers that had been broken. SI was derived from the following:

- All German services' ENIGMA machine ciphers and German secret service and attaché ENIGMA ciphers
- German secret teleprinter
- Italian Hagelin and SIGMA submarine code
- PURPLE
- JN-25
- Japanese military attaché code

Exploitation was to be as follows:

1. Items 1–3 were to be in British hands, although German naval ENIGMA keys would continue to be exploited by the British and the U.S. [OP-20-G].

2. PURPLE would continue to be mutually exploited.

3. JN-25 was to be exploited by the U.S. in the SWPA but "conjointly" with the British unit in Australia and the "... command area of the CIC, Eastern Fleet...."

4. Japanese military attaché code would continue to be mutually exploited.

SI would be disseminated to British and U.S. commanders in chief as needed for conducting operations. Both the U.S. and Britain would be bound by the same SI regulations.

The author has not been able to determine the date when the British Joint Chiefs letter reached Dill and in turn the Combined Chiefs of Staff, G-2. It is interesting to note that from 7–14 March General Marshall vacationed in Florida accompanied by Field Marshal Dill.[33] By 17 March, the War Department was undertaking the study of severing all existing traffic exchange arrangements with the British.[34]

It was a bad time for U.S. Army cryptologic efforts. Not only had the British adopted an uncompromising stand on ENIGMA, but the Army had just recognized that the U.S. military attaché code had been compromised and other U.S. systems were now in doubt.[35]

The War Department seems to have briefly considered a new tack. Perhaps the U.S. COMINT units in North Africa could provide German intercept for the SSS, which now had equipment that could be used on ENIGMA traffic. A series of inquiries were sent to Harold G. Hayes, the SIS veteran who was now the senior officer in the U.S. Army COMINT setup in North Africa. Hayes made it clear that ENIGMA-based COMINT was received by AFHQ (Eisenhower) in Algiers on a special radio link from Bletchley Park. This SI was given to G-2 and not to Hayes as "Y service here has nothing to do with it."[36] The 849th SIS and other Army COMINT units were in no position to provide the SSS with any volume of ENIGMA enciphered traffic.

What was needed now were serious counterproposals to the British from the War Department. On 3 April 1943 Colonel Corderman submitted such a detailed alternative to Colonel Carter Clarke.[37] Corderman generally accepted the British definition of those types or sources of the solved high-grade systems to be known as SI. However, he added two more: the Japanese diplomatic system known as J-19 and the German diplomatic keyword system known as FLORADORA. Thereafter he significantly departed from the British Joint Chiefs' declaration of common policy. The key portions are quoted in full:

> Special intelligence and TA intelligence in all theaters will be exploited cooperatively at all exploitation centers with a full, free, and frank interchange of raw material, technical data, solution data, and collateral intelligence.
>
> Research in cryptanalysis and in the development of cryptanalytic, intercept, DF, and TA apparatus shall be on an entirely reciprocal basis, together with all experiments and findings. Specially accredited U.S. representatives will continue to be welcome at all British signal intelligence centers, and from them nothing in the field covered in this paragraph will be withheld [and the U.S. would reciprocate toward the British].

Corderman changed certain British definitions for joint use. As in the British Joint Chiefs' declaration, Corderman emphasized security of dissemination and operational use of SI.

Corderman's alternative plan was studied at MIS Special Branch by Lieutenant Colonel Telford Taylor. Taylor reported his findings to Carter Clarke on 5 April.[38] Colonel Taylor was favorable toward the Corderman plan but suggested that practical considerations would require certain modifications by way of compromise. Nor did he limit his observations to the Corderman document, but rather he reviewed the entire controversy. He concluded that the severance of U.S.-British COMINT relations would not be tolerated by either the U.S. or British Chiefs of Staff. Therefore, MIS ought to discard that as a serious option. Nonetheless, this was a two-edged sword. Captain Hastings, the GC&CS representative, had implied to the U.S. that the British themselves would sever the existing COMINT relationship if the British Joint Chiefs' proposal was not accepted. Hastings had combined with this threat a continuing disparagement of PURPLE's importance and had generally downgraded the performance of U.S. Army COMINT. Taylor suggested that this could be turned around and that MIS could show the British and U.S. Chiefs of Staff that it was Captain Hastings and company who were promoting a break in relations.

As Taylor and Corderman saw it, the British proposal was unacceptable mainly because it excluded U.S. Army participation in cryptanalysis/decryption of German ENIGMA and TUNNEY (secret teleprinter communications) and in dissemination of resulting SI. The U.S. could not agree to such exclusion and "what we really want *at this time* is to gain a foothold in 'ENIGMA' and develop technical competence and gradually develop a supplementary operation so as to improve joint coverage. What we ultimately want is independence. . . ." Taylor's specific recommendations to accomplish this are a reworking of Corderman's effort. This, combined with some change made by Carter Clarke formed the basis for U.S. Army-British COMINT cooperation for the remainder of the war.[39] The exploitation of ENIGMA and TUNNEY would remain largely a British responsibility, while PURPLE, Japanese military attaché (JMA), and J-19 would be primarily the responsibility of the U.S. Army. But there would be mutual exchange of raw material, technical data, and solution data in *all* the foregoing systems. The U.S. COMINT center(s) " . . . will be able to furnish supplemental coverage at all times and provide security against interruptions in British operations." Secondly, there would be full exchange of SI, that is, final COMINT product, between the U.S. Army and the British via specially appointed officers. This last point recognized the use of the British special liaison unit (SLU) system and was the origin of the U.S. SSO system that continues to this day.

Using this reasonable counterproposal, General Strong placed the matter before General Marshall in a memorandum of 12 April.[40] General Strong also used this opportunity to remind the chief of staff of the fragmented nature of the Army's COMINT organization, which compared poorly with the British system.

General Marshall's response, if any, is not known. But General Strong must have received some high-level encouragement, because on 19 April he met with Brigadier Redman, secretary of the Combined Chiefs of Staff, to whom he presented the U.S. view.

The next day he sent Brigadier Redman a rather nasty memorandum in which he wrote that he alone (Strong) would determine how COMINT would be distributed to U.S. forces (except for AFHQ in Algiers).[41]

By now the MIS-MID feeling toward the British had reached a low point. As Telford Taylor suggested to Colonel Clarke, British intelligence played one U.S. organization against the other and also enjoyed a direct channel to both Prime Minister Churchill and President Roosevelt, something not available to MID.[42]

AN AGREEMENT IS REACHED

The great controversy had actually bottomed out, and reasonable steps were now taken to reach an accommodation. A U.S. mission went to Bletchley Park in late April 1943, and Commander Travis came to Washington in May.[43]

The U.S. mission consisted of Colonel Alfred McCormack, Clarke's deputy, and Lieutenant Colonel Telford Taylor. They were joined by Mr. Friedman of SSS. While the author has not seen their instructions, it is clear that the purpose of the mission was to learn everything possible about British COMINT operations. In this way Field Marshal Dill's promise to General Marshall that "we withhold nothing" was fulfilled.[44]

Arriving in the U.K. on 25 April, the members of the mission went to work at a furious pace. From then until McCormack and Friedman left the U.K. on 13 June, there was a constant flow of detailed messages sent by them to Colonel Clarke and General Strong describing GC&CS organization and technique, the general structure of British intelligence, techniques of dissemination, and operational use of COMINT. Mr. Friedman later supplemented these with a technical report on ENIGMA operations.[45]

Colonel McCormack had personal conferences with the CSS himself and with Commander Denniston, then deputy director (civil) of GC&CS. While Colonel McCormack was not empowered to make general agreements on behalf of the War Department, he seems to have reached a verbal understanding with Denniston. The latter reaffirmed his oft-stated opinion that the U.S. should concentrate on Japanese military systems. He offered the service of GC&CS to fill any gap in diplomatic COMINT that might result from ". . . a supreme effort on Japanese military by Arlington." Denniston also suggested, and McCormack agreed, that Lieutenant Colonel Taylor remain at GC&CS as liaison officer to the civil (diplomatic) portion.[46]

In the meantime, Commander Travis came to Washington where he met with Colonel Corderman, Colonel Clarke, and General Strong. On 16 May Commander Travis formally notified Colonel Clarke that he and Colonel Corderman had worked out most details of U.S.-British COMINT collaboration.[47] The next day Commander Travis and General Strong signed the "Agreement Between the British Government Code and Cipher School and U.S.

War Department." Commander Travis signed on behalf of the British Chiefs of Staff. For some reason the agreement was not forwarded to General Marshall until 10 June. It was then approved on 15 June by the signature of Colonel Otto T. Nelson, Jr., assistant to the deputy chief of staff and on behalf of the deputy chief of staff.[48] The agreement is recognizable as an elaborated-upon version of the Corderman-Taylor-Clarke proposal of early April.

The agreement contained an attempted definition of certain terms, which, however, underwent later change and need not be elaborated upon here. The major features of the agreement are summarized as follows:

1. The agreement would pertain to COMINT derived from Axis military and air forces only. Nonservice or neutral traffic was excluded. (Abwehr traffic – German intelligence/counterintelligence – was included.)

2. There would be a complete interchange of technical data (including CA) through liaison officers in Washington and London, with arrangements for dissemination of SI to field commanders through special channels in accordance with special regulations.

3. U.S. personnel would be allowed to gain experience in ENIGMA solution in the U.K.

4. The U.S. would undertake Japanese military and air force traffic as its main responsibility. The British were to have German and Italian military and air force traffic as their prime responsibility.

5. All decrypts would be available to each country's liaison officers.

6. The SIS and the British Y services would cooperate in and coordinate intercept operations.

7. Regarding German cipher machines (ENIGMA mainly), there were to be special provisions, among these:

    a. U.S. liaison officers at GC&CS would examine decrypted messages and summaries thereof and select those desired for transmission to the War Department and theater commanders.

    b. A U.S. cryptanalytic party would work on these systems at GC&CS and effect independent solutions but in coordination, so as to avoid duplication.

    c. Research into new methods of cryptanalytic attack would be made in Washington. "Formulas will be supplied by Great Britain for use on machines now at Arlington Hall."

Final high-level British approval preceded the similar U.S. action. On 22 May 1943 Brigadier Redman informed Captain Hastings that Field Marshal Dill had shown the Travis-Strong agreement to the chief of the Imperial General Staff [Field Marshal Sir Alan Brooke]. The latter approved, he directed that all further arrangements be worked out at a technical level "direct with the American authorities concerned." As Brigadier Redman concluded, "The matter is therefore passed to you out of the hands of the chiefs of staff committee."[49]

It now remained to implement this important agreement. This would be done largely through the efforts of Colonel Taylor in London, supported by Colonel Clarke in Washington. A new array of special regulations would come into being, and the SSO system would soon be created.

The practical results of U.S. access to ENIGMA and other high-grade German material, so important operationally, can only be touched on in this study.

THE IMPLEMENTATION OF THE AGREEMENTS

The Travis-Strong agreement required two separate areas of development by the War Department: technical operations by or through the SSS and selection and dissemination of COMINT through the MIS.

The technical portion was in turn divided into operations conducted at Arlington Hall and those in the U.K. Operations at Arlington Hall are well beyond the scope of this study. It should be said, however, that significant cryptanalytic operations were conducted there that materially contributed to the exploitation of German ENIGMA and other high-grade systems. The operations in the U.K. were under the "special cryptanalytic project in SIS ETOUSA," codenamed BEECHNUT.[50]

Lieutenant Colonel Frank B. Rowlett

In early 1943, during the U.S.-U.K. negotiations described above, Lieutenant Colonel Frank B. Rowlett, chief of the General Cryptanalytic Branch at SSA, and Colonel George Bicher of SIS ETOUSA made plans to send a small detachment to the U.K. to conduct intercept operations and cryptanalysis in cooperation with GC&CS. The BEECHNUT project was authorized by General Strong on 9 July 1943. During the remainder of 1943, several groups were sent to the U.K.

Headquarters, Project BEECHNUT, was formed with Major Roy D. Johnson, the SSA liaison officer at GC&CS as officer in charge and Major William Bundy as operations officer. BEECHNUT was in turn subordinate to Colonel Bicher's SIS ETOUSA. BEECHNUT became operational in January 1944 with about 250 officers and enlisted personnel divided into the following elements:

- Special Intercept Unit (6811th Special Security Detachment)
- Machine Section of the Special Cryptanalytic Unit (6812th SSO)
- Special Cryptanalytic Unit (6813th SSO)

BEECHNUT headquarters was colocated with SIS ETOUSA in London. A total of nine Bombes, shipped from the U.S., were in use by BEECHNUT by the summer of 1944. Thereafter the BEECHNUT units, working in cooperation with GC&CS, significantly contributed to the ENIGMA attack in both intercept and solution.

Lieutenant Colonel Telford Taylor had remained in the U.K. to implement the Travis-Strong agreement for MIS. As he had no assistance until the end of August, he limited his activities to studying diplomatic material at Berkeley Street and to learning his way around at Hut 3 (intelligence reporting), GC&CS. He cabled a small amount of material to MIS Special Branch – mainly ISK and ISOS decrypts (German secret service traffic).[51] On 23 August Colonel Taylor was joined by another Special Branch veteran, Major Seth McKee, and they cabled the first CX/MSS item to Washington on 27 August. This was the first German military ENIGMA message that had ever been available to the War Department and may be considered the beginning of cooperation under the Travis-Strong agreement.

All did not go well, however, because the CSS, British DMI, and perhaps even General Strong had second thoughts about the scope of Colonel Taylor's operations. The record of this is murky, but one thing is certain: a new and more specific agreement was made on 25 September 1943 following a conference between Colonel Taylor, the CSS, the British DMI, and Wing Commander Jones, the head of Hut 3.[52] It was agreed that Colonel Taylor could select CX/MSS and other texts, as needed, for transmission to Washington. If the intelligence analysis/commentary accompanying the texts was inadequate for Colonel Taylor's purposes, he could contact the appropriate British ministry (i.e., war, air) for elucidation. The ministries could also on their own initiative provide further comments (beyond those prepared at Hut 3) to Colonel Taylor.[53]

Colonel Taylor received reinforcements in November–December 1943. In January 1944 the Taylor operation became known as 3-U.S., the nomenclature being derived from the fact that it was a U.S. contingent working with Hut 3. The duties of 3-U.S. expanded in keeping with the original agreement and with new War Department security regulations concerning the handling of COMINT. By the end of January 1944, Colonels Taylor and McKee were involved in assigning newly arrived personnel to SSO portions. Major Littlefield, a Special Branch veteran, was working at Berkeley Street on diplomatic traffic; Major Calfee, another Special Branch type, was involved in counterintelligence exploitation of COMINT (the Ryder Street operation); while Major F. W. Hilles was in charge of the MIS group at Bletchley Park. This group included ten or more U.S. "advisors" responsible for disseminating high-level COMINT to U.S. field commanders; an equal number of officers studying at GC&CS in preparation for SSO assignments with the field commands; and three MIS officers with a civilian assistant, disseminating COMINT to the MIS Special Branch in Washington.[54]

On 15 March 1944, General Marshall formally notified General Eisenhower of the role of the SSOs.[55] The receipt and control of ULTRA, which was now the common British-U.S. term for high-level COMINT, at the field commands would be by SLU personnel under the control of the director general of GC&CS [i.e., the CSS, Menzies]. MID personnel would work with the SLUs. Each field command authorized to receive ULTRA would have a MID representative who would receive the ULTRA, evaluate it, and "... present it in usable form to the commanding officer and to each of his senior staff officers as are authorized ULTRA recipients, assist in fusing ULTRA intelligence with intelligence derived from other sources, and give advice in connection with making operational use of ULTRA intelligence in such fashion that the security of the source is not endangered."[56]

The remainder of the 3-U.S. story and the European SSO program can be briefly told here (brevity being dictated by the nature of this study rather than merits of the story).

The MID/MIS representatives who went into France in 1944 with the field commands, though serving as SSOs, were more commonly known as SSRs (Special Security Representatives) or simply ULTRA representations or ULTRA officers. These U.S. ULTRA officers received the material from the servicing SLU detachment on varying schedules or according to the urgency of the material. The SLU detachments were composed mainly of British personnel, but there were some U.S. officers trained under the SSO system (by MIS, 3-U.S., and GC&CS) in these detachments. Overall SLU control was by the CSS acting through SLU#8 at Supreme Headquarters Army Expeditionary Force (SHAEF) under the command of British Lieutenant Colonel Gore-Brown.[57] There seems to have been no typical ULTRA officer operation on the continent in 1944–45 because of varied conditions and the personal styles of these officers (and the commanders and G-2s they served). There were ULTRA officers with at least the following commands: SHAEF (for air operations); Eighth and Ninth Air Force; Ninth Tactical Air Command and other tactical air commands; First Allied Airborne; Twelfth Army Group; First, Third, Ninth and Fifteenth Armies; Sixth Army Group; Seventh Army, and ETOUSA.[58]

Two examples of practical operations are included here, but the reader is again cautioned that generalization cannot be made.

Major Ansel E. M. Talbert, USAAF, the ULTRA officer at Eighth Air Force, received ULTRA from the SLU detachment located at Eighth Air Force headquarters. This detachment was entirely composed of British officers and enlisted men and informally functioned as an adjunct of the office of the director of intelligence, Eighth Air Force. The SLU deciphered the messages from GC&CS, typed them, and delivered them to Major

Talbert several times per day. Talbert then appended his own evaluations, distributed the material to a small number of authorized recipients at Eighth Air Force, and kept appropriate files.

At Twelfth Army Group, the activities of the ULTRA officers, Lieutenant Colonel Charles R. Murmane and Lieutenant Colonel Samuel M. Orr, were somewhat more involved. They likewise received typed copies of the GC&CS ULTRA from the servicing SLU detachment. After registering the material, they posted the current situation map if warranted, updated the German order of battle file, made entries in their topical index, and sent messages to the subordinate armies (First and Third) via the SLU link if there was reason to believe that the ULTRA officers at these armies needed additional background material not provided through their own SLU contacts. Twice daily, Colonels Orr and Murmane gave an ULTRA briefing to General Omar Bradley and key members of his staff.[59]

By the end of the war, the 3-U.S. operation consisted of forty-three U.S. officers in the field with SLUs or as ULTRA officers at the commands and fifteen officers at Hut 3 Bletchley Park or in London.[60]

The latter group continued to select material for transmission to the War Department and to the field commands. An appreciation of how complete the U.K.-U.S. Army COMINT cooperation had become may be gained by a description of some of the material made available to 3-U.S. by GC&CS. All German military and secret service traffic was available to the U.S. representatives, and it was a matter of selecting material for transmission. The War Department (MIS) was interested mostly in receiving ULTRA bearing on German order of battle, long-range plans and policy, and manpower matters. Tactical items were also furnished as well as police and secret service traffic. The U.S. also received the so-called "C" series, which were special items furnished to the British DMI and his counterparts. The "C" Series, later called MCC series, were sent "eyes only" for General Marshall, the ACS, G-2, and Carter W. Clarke. After G-2 was reorganized in June–July 1944, Colonel McCormack, acting in the newly created position of director of intelligence, also was a recipient. Especially instructive of the closeness of cooperation was the sharing of the Bay and Stark Series with the War Department and the field commands. This included all manner of diplomatic, commercial, and attaché material, mostly produced at Berkeley Street and published in various logs. Even the RES (reserved) series, which was to have been withheld from the U.S., became available following an agreement made between Carter Clarke and Mr. Peter Loxley of the Foreign Office. This included such items as Vatican, Jewish Agency for Palestine and French secret service traffic. Special procedures for U.S. access to RES remained, but cooperation was now complete.

Before this chapter on U.S. Army-British cooperation is closed, certain technical arrangements made by SSA (and not MIS) will be described. On 24 December 1943 the earlier understandings on exchange of diplomatic materials were updated. An agreement was signed by Colonels Corderman and Earle F. Cook for SSA and P. W. Filby, E. B. C. Thornett, and Colonel H. M. O'Connor for GC&CS. O'Connor had replaced the ambitious Captain Hastings soon after the Strong-Travis agreement. Technical understandings involved cable exchange of Japanese diplomatic traffic, exchange by courier or cable of German diplomatic keys, German diplomatic traffic, and translations (both current items and back traffic).[61]

Working arrangements were made at GC&CS by the SSA liaison officers assigned there and by visitors from Washington. In June 1943 Mr. Robert O. Ferner and Captain John W. Seaman of SSA had been assigned to Bletchley Park to study, and Seaman was appointed as a regular liaison officer later that year. He was in turn succeeded by Captain Walter J. Fried and Albert W. Small. Their work, which seems to have been separated from the large BEECHNUT project described above, was to represent SSA's B-III branch at Bletchley Park. They cabled or pouched nonroutine technical items concerning cryptanalytic research, information on new systems, and special reports to Arlington Hall. Routine exchanges of keys, tables, and the like were made by cable between the operating elements at Arlington Hall and Bletchley Park.[62]

As British-U.S. Army arrangements were involved, it may well be to once again introduce the subject of OSS nonaccess to COMINT. As late as January 1945, the OSS was "carefully excluded from all ULTRA," except the so-called PAIR traffic – Abwehr and S.D. (SS Security Service) traffic.[63] OSS made efforts in the U.K. and Europe to remedy this situation by the creation of a counterintelligence war room in London where, OSS officers hoped, "some operational ULTRA would be made available." A war room was created, but OSS did not get ULTRA by that route because of arrangements made by Telford Taylor with GC&CS and Section V of MI-6.[64]

Notes

1. *Minutes of Meeting of British, Canadian, and U.S. Army Representatives for Arranging Exchange of Intercepted Diplomatic Traffic*, 15 January 1943, ACSI #44, NSAHC (classified).

2. Memorandum from Dill to Marshall, 2 December 1942, ACSI #2(a), NSAHC. Dr. Turing, a mathematician, was one of the great cryptanalysts of the time. He is generally credited with making the GC&CS break into ENIGMA (classified).

3. Memorandum from Clarke to Strong, 4 December 1942, ACSI #2(a) (classified).

4. Memorandum from Strong to Marshall (Carter Clarke, drafter), 5 December 1942, ACSI #2(a). Apparently Clarke et al. considered the British request "backdoor" because it was directed to the Signal Corps instead of MID.

5. Note from Marshall to General McNarney, DCS, 8 December, in ibid.

6. Memorandum from Marshall to Dill, 9 December 1942, in ibid. (classified).

7. Memorandum from Dill to Marshall 15 December 1942, in ibid.

8. Memorandum from Clarke to Strong, 21 December 1942, in ibid. (classified).

9. Ibid.

10. Memorandum from Marshall to Dill, 23 December 1942, in ibid.

11. Memorandum from Dill to Marshall, 26 December 1942, in ibid.

12. During the war GC&CS was under the British Joint Chiefs, who acted through Menzies, the CSS, and the Joint Intelligence Committee.

13. Memorandum from Strong to Marshall, 1 January 1943, ACSI #2(a) (classified).

14. Copies of these messages or extracts thereof are filed in ACSI #2(a) (classified).

15. Hastings added in this message to CSS that he had finally convinced General Strong that Menzies was not the DMI. Obviously neither side had yet gained a clear picture of the other's intelligence structure.

16. Letter from Dill to Marshall, 5 January 1943, ACSI #2(a) (classified).

17. Memorandum from Marshall to Dill, 6 January 1943, in ibid. (classified).

18. Letter from Dill to Marshall, 7 January 1943, ACSI #44 (classified).

19. Sir John's use of the word "allow" is not entirely appropriate. The U.S. Navy, at the time of the Holden Agreement, advised Britain that it would proceed on its own ENIGMA attack because the GC&CS had "lost" the U-boat system for many months and nothing was being read on a current basis. The British then agreed in principle that OP-20-G could proceed and that there would be mutual support.

20. Paper headed "General Marshall's letter to Field Marshal 23/12/42," ACSI #44. This paper was cited in chapter 1 as it is a source for prewar British-U.S. Army COMINT relations.

21. Chief of Staff appointment books for 1943, Marshall Library.

22. Message, in ACSI #2(a).

23. Memorandum from Lieutenant General Joseph T. McNarney to Lieutenant General Macready, 9 January 1943, ACSI #2(a).

24. Memorandum from William F. Friedman to Colonel Corderman, 8 February 1943, ACSI #2(a) (classified). This is a superior exposition of the problem and offers a wise solution. This memorandum was a basis for many later expositions and proposals by MIS and SSA.

25. Memorandum with two tabs from Strong to Marshall, 17 February 1943, ACSI #44.

26. Chief of Staff appointment books for 1943. Shows appointment with Dill at 1515, 17 February.

27. Memorandum for General Strong signed by Colonel Robert N. Young, secretary of the General Staff (dictated by General Marshall), 22 February 1943, ACSI #44.

28. Memorandum from Hastings to Strong, 26 February 1943, which replies to Strong's memorandum of 23 February, (not seen) (classified).

29. Message from Strong (drafted by Carter Clarke) to Kroner, 8 March 1943, ACSI #2(a). This message discusses the previous message from Kroner (not seen by author) (classified).

30. Message from Kroner for Strong (Eyes Only), 11 March 1943 in Ibid. (classified).

31. General Marshall seems not to have had much interest in intelligence matters. There is no lack of evidence to support this. Carter Clarke, in a letter to the author, explained that General Marshall considered intelligence a necessary evil that he preferred to avoid. Experienced MID veterans General Louis J. Fortier and Colonel Paul Robinett have described General Marshall's shortcomings in this area. (See Colonel Robinett's diary for 1940–41 and General Fortier's letters to Marshall by biographer Forrest Pogue on file at the Marshall Library.) However, General Marshall had had many bad experiences with military intelligence leadership, from Dennis Nolan in World War I down through Sherman Miles and the Pearl Harbor mess.

32. *Letter to Sir John Dill by the British Joint Chiefs of Staff*, 7 March 1943, ACSI #44.

33. Chief of Staff appointment books, 1943 Marshall Library. General Lomerwell of the ASF also joined the Marshalls and Dills.

34. Memorandum from Major Harold McD. Brown to Colonel Corderman, 17 March 1943, subject: Traffic Exchange with BSC. This lengthy memorandum is an excellent source for SSS-BSC traffic exchange arrangements, U.S. sources of traffic, agreements, etc. Its purpose as a study of the practical effects of the Army severing the relationships with the British is apparent only upon seeing it in context of the British Joint Chiefs' letter to Dill. As of March 1943, the SSS and the UK (via BSC) were exchanging Japanese army and a broad range of diplomatic traffic only. (No German air or army traffic was involved.)

35. Memorandum from General Strong acting for the Joint Security Control to chief of staff, 3 March 1943. Friedman Papers, NSAHC.

36. Message #1143 from Hayes, signed by Eisenhower, to WAR, 3 April 1943, ACSI #2(a). The actual study of possible ENIGMA intercept by the North African-based SRI companies is contained in other documents in ACSI #2(a).

37. "Agreement Concerning Cooperation in all Matters Relating to Special and Traffic Analysis Intelligence," 3 April 1943, signed by W. Preston Corderman, ACSI #44.

38. Memorandum from Telford Taylor to Clarke, 5 April 1943, subject: Cooperation between United States Signal Intelligence Service and British Y Service, ACSI #44 (classified).

39. The Taylor memorandum bears various handwritten changes made by Carter Clarke (classified).

40. Memorandum from Strong to Marshall, 12 April 1943, ACSI #44 (classified).

41. Memorandum from Strong to Brigadier Redman, 20 April 1943, ACSI #2(a). This memorandum references the 19 April meeting. The memorandum is so harsh that it is possible that it was never actually sent – the copy reviewed by the author does not definitely show that it was dispatched. It was probably drafted by Carter Clarke.

42. Memorandum from Telford Taylor to Carter Clarke, 16 April 1943, subject: Bletchley Park vs. Arlington Hall, ACSI #2(a).

43. I have not been able to locate documents that show the immediate sequence of events that led to McCormack and Friedman going to Bletchley Park. I suspect that there was a British invitation through Hastings. The reader will recall that several months earlier General Strong had proposed sending McCormack to Bletchley Park.

44. See section 1 of this chapter.

45. Many of the McCormack-Friedman-Taylor messages (and other documents) to Carter Clarke are found in ACSI #34, NSAHC. Mr. Friedman's "Report on E Operations of the GC&CS at Bletchley Park" is also in NSAHC (ribbon copy). These are extremely valuable collections of source material. The McCormack mission undoubtedly merits further study.

46. "Memorandum Describing American Liaison at Berkeley Street," 12 October 1945, prepared by Major Louis T. Stone Jr. and included in the *SSO History*, appendix III, part II, NSAHC. Denniston memorandum describing Denniston's views, 21 May 1943, is with Major Stone's paper. Berkeley Street was the common name for the civil side of GC&CS much as Bletchley Park was the name for the services side (classified).

47. Letter from Travis to Clarke, 16 May 1943 (on letterhead of British Joint Staff Mission, Washington), ACSI #44 (classified).

48. The basic agreement, the cover memorandum from Strong (drafted by Clarke) to the chief of staff and the approval signatures thereon are in ACSI #46. (These are the only papers bound in NSAHC's copies of ACSI #46.)

49. This letter, Brigadier H. Redman to Captain Hastings, is reproduced on page 21 of *Army and Air Force Sigint*, vol. 3 (Organization and Evolution of British Army Sigint), GC&CS history (classified).

50. All the information in this section concerning Project BEECHNUT is taken from a paper entitled "History of Special Project Beechnut, SIS ETOUSA," also referred to as the Rowlett Report, NSAHC. This paper was probably prepared in 1945 (classified).

51. "An Account of the Origins and Development of 3-U.S.," a manuscript in vol. 2 *SSO History*, 204–05 (hand-paged), prepared by Colonel F. W. Hilles.

52. Ibid. Colonel Hilles suggests that General Strong virtually cancelled certain provisions of the Travis-Strong agreement, to the detriment of the U.S. I cannot trace this alleged development and have therefore proceeded to the Wing Commander Jones-Telford Taylor agreement of 25 September. The latter is quoted by Hilles. It was in the form of a letter from Jones to the CSS, DMI, and (I think) RAF intelligence representative.

53. It should be noted that at the time of the McCormack Mission, CX/MSS material was reaching commanders of U.S. forces but in the theater only. This material went to AFHQ Algiers, First U.S. Army and the USAAF headquarters in the North African theater. But the distribution was in British (SLU) channels. As has been emphasized, none of this information went to the War Department. (See the Friedman Report on E Operations, 74.)

54. From a study paper prepared by Colonel Hilles in vol. 2 of *SSO History*, 193 ff, (hand-paged).

55. Letter from Marshall to Eisenhower, 15 March 1944, ACSI #42, NSAHC. This letter was drafted by MIS Special Branch (classified).

56. The term MID officers, rather than MIS officers, is used throughout the Marshall letter. This minor point bedevils a person trying to understand Army intelligence organization. The best solution is at all times to consider the terms MID and MIS synonymous. General Strong did not like the MIS concept initiated in the general War Department reorganization of March 1942. He thought of the entire force under his control as MID. (See various discussions of this in Bidwell's History.)

57. Manuscript entitled "The Use of ULTRA Intelligence by U.S. Army Commands in the European Theater of Operations" prepared by Major B. R. Shute in 1945, filed in appendix 2, vol. 2, *SSO History*.

58. Appendix 2, vol. 2, *SSO History* (based on the index of manuscripts, memorandum etc. prepared in 1945–46 by SSO/ULTRA officer veterans).

59. The Talbert and Murmane – Orr operations are in manuscript form in appendix 2, vol. 2, *SSO History*.

60. "An Account of the Origins and History of 3-U.S.," manuscript in *SSO History* vol. 2. See 214 ff, (hand-paged).

61. Paper described as "SSA-GC&CS (Civil) Agreement", 24 December 1943, in a folder of documents labeled, Volume 1 3855A, NSAHC.

62. McCraken Study, ACSI#45.

63. "History of Special Counterintelligence War Room," a memorandum prepared by Colonel Calfee, 27 August 1945 in appendix 4, vol. 2, *SSO History*.

64. Ibid.

Chapter 5
British-U.S. Navy COMINT Agreements of 1943-44

From the U.S. point of view, this is a far less complicated subject than that of the preceding chapter. For that reason the account is very brief.

There were three main reasons why the U.S. Navy's cooperation with the British was smoother and more orderly than that experienced by the Army. First the naval COMINT organization was such that policy matters could be exhaustively addressed by OP-20-G or OP-20. This was especially so after the downgrading of ONI in the summer of 1942. Second, effective cooperation predated the war, especially in the Far East, and a very thorough and far-reaching agreement was made in late 1942 – the Holden Agreement. In fact, it would not be far from the mark to say that the Holden Agreement was, for the purposes of U.S. naval COMINT policy, if not for all practical applications, all that was ever needed to define the relationship with the British. Finally, OP-20-G and its subordinate centers were well able on their own to meet most COMINT needs of the U.S. Navy. The Pacific theater was a U.S. show, and the Battle of the Atlantic became so too. As we have seen, OP-20-G was independently and successfully attacking the ENIGMA enciphered communications of the German U-boat networks during 1942, and there was even more extraordinary success in the Pacific against Japanese naval systems.

During July 1943 there were important conferences in London concerning the British OP-20-G relationship. At the beginning of the month, Rear Admiral Joseph Redman and Commander Wenger visited GC&CS on the invitation of Commander Travis. Wenger met with Mr. Birch of the naval section of GC&CS and Commander Laird of the Royal Navy's Eastern Fleet to work out more details of Pacific COMINT.[1]

The result of these conferences was an understanding reached on 25 July and known to OP-20-G as the Extension Agreement, based as it was on the Holden Agreement of 1942, which remained the basic policy document.[2]

Among the basic provisions of the Extension Agreement were these:[3]

1. Urgently needed raw material would be interchanged between GC&CS and OP-20-G by cable or radio as far as possible.

2. In the field of cryptanalysis, GC&CS would "pay special attention" to machine ciphers, other ciphers ". . . for which British experience and facilities are particularly suited," and certain research matters.

On 1 August further understandings were reached concerning the exchange of recoveries and special intelligence. The latter is especially interesting as there was now to be direct passage of locally produced COMINT from FRUMEL to Columbo and Columbo to FRUMEL.[4]

The overall relationship was enhanced by improved communications between OP-20-G and GC&CS. By November 1943 routine communications (the bulk of the traffic) between the two primary centers was handled via a Western Union landline teletype that linked BSC in New York with 20-GC (20-G's COMINT communications office).[5] BSC communicated with GC&CS by cable or radio. This arrangement relieved the burden on existing facilities, one of which had been a system whereby naval traffic went through BSC but over a landline from Arlington Hall to New York City.[6]

In fact, the BRUSA Agreement of 14 January 1944 may be seen from the U.S. side as more of a COMINT communications agreement than a major policy agreement (of the Travis-Strong type). From the British standpoint, it was otherwise and perhaps the entire matter of British-USN COMINT relations of 1943–44 is more a British policy story than an American one.

The BRUSA Agreement was reached in Washington following negotiations at OP-20-G by Mr. F. H. Hinsley, a young intelligence officer of the naval section of GC&CS, assisted by Colonel O'Connor, Captain Hastings' replacement in Washington. The agreement was in the form of a memorandum to Mr. Hinsley signed by Admiral Joseph Redman. The British had called for the establishment of a "comprehensive U.S.-British circuit, to be called the 'BRUSA' circuit, to be established as early as practicable between Washington, Pearl Harbor, Melbourne, Columbo, and GC&CS, incorporating U S. naval and British circuits at present used for the dissemination of RI material." This circuit would carry technical information, "decryption intelligence," and "traffic intelligence." Traffic would be enciphered on U.S. machines. Changes or modifications to the BRUSA circuit would be made only after agreement between Washington and GC&CS.[7]

This was generally agreeable to the U.S. except that the Columbo-Melbourne circuit was now held to be of doubtful value if FRUMEL was subject to redeployment. And there was a rather general "escape" clause inserted by the U.S., which is quoted in its entirety:

> The extent to which radio intelligence information and recoveries can be exchanged between the 'BRUSA' station will continue to be dependent upon communication and other facilities available and on the need for such exchange.

The BRUSA circuit did not go into effect until 27 June.[8] It was not really to be a new system so much as an expanded version of the existing COMB and TUNA (20-G) collections combined with existing Washington-London and London-Columbo links.[9] On 12 July, 20-G directed USN stations ". . . to put all decryption and traffic intelligence on BRUSA circuits regardless of area involved."[10] This lasted only a few weeks when it became apparent to OP-20-G that the facilities were being overloaded. There followed some months of discussion, and ultimately a new Pacific theater agreement was reached in Washington on 23 October 1944.[11] This agreement, signed by Commander Travis and

Rear Admiral Redman, recognized certain changes that had taken place since the Holden Agreement, but it in no way altered the primacy of the USN in the Pacific. As stated in the preamble, the purpose of the agreement was ". . . to minimize the use of rapid communication facilities and to promote proper coordination by the most efficient employment of personnel, particularly in the solution and exploitation of those Japanese cryptographic systems that require the combined effort of relatively large numbers of persons. . . ." The general agreements were these:

1. The exploitation centers would be OP-20-G, FRUPAC, and Columbo (FRUMEL was being replaced by RAGFOR – Radio Analysis Group, Forward – the COMINT center on Guam).

2. OP-20-G would coordinate the Allied effort and allocate tasks. ". . . Bletchley Park, of course, would be free to make suggestions, requests, or complaints at any time."

3. GC&CS would undertake any tasks assigned by OP-20-G and give these assignments "full priority."

A few specific cryptanalytic assignments (such as JN-25, L-53, and the NAN cipher) were made to GC&CS. It was agreed that a minimum of current traffic would be supplied to GC&CS by electrical means, unless it was a solved system being actively worked by GC&CS. There was no alteration in existing understandings about exchange of intelligence – this would continue to go back and forth. The impact, then, was to reduce the load on the BRUSA circuit for passage of new traffic to GC&CS.

Notes

1. *Naval Sigint*, vol. 5(a); GC&CS History, 240 ff.

2. Details of the Extension Agreement are in ibid., 250, and a background paper prepared by Commander Wenger on 1 July 1944 entitled "Outline of the Collaboration in Japanese Cryptanalysis Between the U.S. Navy and the British" (especially 8–19).

3. *Outline*, 8.

4. *Naval Sigint*, facing 250.

5. *GC History*, 20 ff.

6. Ibid.

7. *Naval Sigint*, vol. 5(b), 316 ff. and reprint of the Agreement on 559–61.

8. These British proposals and others form the first part of the Redman memorandum to Mr. Hinsley.

9. *GC History*, 46–49, for a discussion of BRUSA communications from the 20-G point of view.

10. *Naval Sigint* 5(b), 332.

11. "An Agreement Between GC&CS and Negat on Japanese Cryptanalytic Tasks," 23 October 1944, in *Catalog* 3.h.

Chapter 6
Continued Jurisdictional Problems regarding Clandestine Communications

THE RADIO INTELLIGENCE DIVISION

In spite of having been frozen out of COMINT policy matters in 1942 by the Army, Navy, and FBI, the Radio Intelligence Division (RID) of the FCC continued its extensive intercept and DF operations against clandestine communications. The significance of the RID effort was emphasized by its prominent place in the informal intercept committee that met weekly from August 1942 to August 1943. (See section 5 of chapter 2.) Nonetheless, efforts to dismantle the RID or to incorporate its personnel and equipment into the armed forces continued.

In September 1942 Secretary of the Navy Knox had initiated a high-level inquiry into RID activity when he posed certain questions about "security of military communications activities" to the Joint Chiefs.[1] A JCS study was begun and went on until early 1943. The JCS inquiry was an involved one dealing with the communications security of various agencies as well as the RID's place in COMINT. We need note here only one of the opinions solicited by the JCS. On 16 November 1942 Admiral Nimitz gave his views following the recent staff visit to Hawaii by members of the study group. He stated that all aspects of COMINT, including intercept operations and DF, should be under the Army and Navy, and further, that a "civilian agency could [not] intelligently and efficiently perform any part of these functions without benefit of continuous full and complete military information which, in the interests of security and the war effort, cannot be entrusted to it."[2] On the other hand, the Army, which had depended so heavily on the RID, was not as anxious to do away with the organization.[3]

The JCS comments and recommendations went to Secretary Knox on 1 February 1943 in the form of a letter signed by Admiral Leahy.[4] The COMINT activities of the Army and Navy were broadly described as were those of the FCC. In the JCS view, the FCC was intercepting enemy military, naval, and diplomatic traffic and locating clandestine radio stations. The FCC was also allegedly monitoring U.S. military communications for COMSEC purposes and providing bearing aids for lost planes. In the opinion of the JCS, the FCC's COMINT activities were expanding and were thus ". . . a substantial drain upon available material and personnel." Further, it appears as if these activities were becoming less useful ". . . as the art progresses." This lessening of effectiveness could not be reversed because the military services could not safely disseminate special information to the FCC.

Admiral Leahy concluded that FCC personnel and equipment should be transferred to the Army, and that this could be accomplished by executive order.

Secretary Knox favorably reported the JCS position to President Roosevelt on 8 February 1943 and attached the proposed executive order. The president did not formally respond until 7 September at which time he advised Secretary Knox that the RID would not be disestablished or transferred to the Army.[5] Rather, wrote the president, the FCC was performing too valuable a service for such civilian agencies as the FBI, State Department, Censorship, Bureau of Economic Warfare, Weather Bureau, and Coordinator of Interamerican Affairs. The president suggested that jurisdictional matters should be worked out by the Board of War Communications. Actually, the latter body, chaired by Mr. Fly of the FCC, had never had anything to do with COMINT (and would not in the future).

The matter did not rest there, however. Later in 1943 a congressional committee looking into the FCC's supervision of the broadcasting industry created some disarray by delving into RID activities.[6] A more thorough, and equally hostile, scrutiny of RID activities took place in congressional budget hearings in January 1944. Both in public and closed sessions, Mr. Fly and George Sterling explained the wide range of RID (and FBI) operations.[7] They claimed that there was no overlap of operations insofar as enemy military communications were concerned, as the RID intercepted enemy military communications only on the request of the services. Extensive documentation was presented on and off the record. The result of all this was that RID did suffer some budgetary cuts and had to contract certain of its overseas operations.

This may not have been unjust because the RID, by early 1944, had ended a number of the auxiliary projects it had begun early in the war under the Army, which especially was so desperately short of COMINT assets in Hawaii, Alaska, and on the West Coast. In March the RID notified OP-20-G that the latter would no longer receive copies of clandestine intercepts because operations were being curtailed.[8] However, the RID continued to serve its other customers, notably the FBI and the British, through the end of the war. At its peak in 1944, the RID intercept and DF facilities included twelve primary monitoring stations, fifty-nine secondary stations, and eight mobile units.

Before closing this account of the RID, several more of its operations will be listed to again emphasize the diverse work of this organization and the many requests made of it by the services.

1. Throughout 1943 and into 1944, the RID station at San Leandro, California, engaged in extensive radio communications with U.S. Army guerrillas in the Philippines. This was done at the urgent request of the War Department.

2. In Alaska the monitoring personnel met requirements levied by RID and the SSA in Washington and the G-2, Alaskan Defense Command, Colonel L. V. Castner. The

Alaskan group also worked deception operations against Japanese naval units and trained the 102nd SRI Company personnel on their arrival in Alaska.

3. It covered Soviet Far East weather and clandestine traffic for the SSA.

4. It recorded scrambled German voice traffic for SSA.

5. It periodically, and on specific request, intercepted German, Japanese, and Italian submarine communications for OP-20-G.

How are we to square the accomplishments of the RID with the abuse from and ingratitude of the organizations it so loyally served? There were institutional reasons which were of paramount importance to the services: the RID was a civilian organization outside of any military chain of command and at the same time was (so it was alleged) tinged with partisan politics. The latter charge in fact relates only to FCC chairman Fly, who was not in any case involved in day-to-day RID work. The large budget of RID, with the resultant availability of modern equipment, must have galled the services. And, especially for the understrength Army COMINT organization, the RID's wealth of experienced and well-trained communications personnel probably seemed a tremendous embarrassment. Last and not least, there were the personality clashes involving those same worthy, if irascible, men who were in many a policy fray: Admiral Joseph R. Redman and John Edgar Hoover.[10]

THE NAVY-FBI CONTROVERSY AND THE ATTENDANT DISPUTES REGARDING THE BRITISH

A theme that has run through this study is that the U.S. COMINT services established separate and often secret-from-each-other arrangements with British intelligence. These arrangements in turn led to a great deal of interservice bickering. As suggested in the first chapter, all of this must be seen against the background of the intense passions aroused because of the expanding role of the OSS, which often had very special (if not in COMINT) understandings with the British. This section will further examine these relationships, insofar as they involved the clandestine COMINT picture.

The U.S. Coast Guard COMINT unit, a part of OP-20-G since 1942, had been designated OP-20-GU by the beginning of 1944. In fact, by a subdivision order of 14 April there was both a separate staff department known as G-70, office of the Head of Clandestine Department, as well as GU, the operating element. The entire operation remained under Commander Leonard T. Jones, USCG. The responsibilities of this organization had not changed, and it still operated as a semi-independent organization responsible for all phases of clandestine work: interception, cryptanalysis, translation, and liaison with counterpart British offices. The dissemination of its product, however, was the responsibility of OP-20-GI. OP-20-GU remained a rather small organization in

Washington.[12] The intercept came from the USCG operators at, primarily, South Hampton, Long Island, and New Smyrna, Florida, as well as Winter Harbor, Maine; overseas monitoring sites were in the Dominican Republic, Brazil, Peru, and Chile.[13]

OP-20-G had continued its tradition of success against clandestine systems. In fact, its independent solution of the "Green" ENIGMA in January 1943 caused great consternation in British circles coming as it did in the midst of the tense Army-British COMINT negotiations growing out of the Dr. Turing affair (see chapter 4).[14] On 11 February 1943 a most secret and immediate message was cabled from the CSS to Captain Hastings asking him to look into reports from Captain Maidment, BSC, that the Coast Guard was deciphering messages on a Cologne-South America circuit and giving results to the FBI. The CSS pointed out that these messages were enciphered in ENIGMA (to which Captain Maidment did not have access) and that any action taken on this intercept, or any leaks, could jeopardize the entire ENIGMA situation. While it was believed (said the CSS) that, because of poor German cryptographic discipline, the messages could be broken without knowing the ENIGMA wiring, the USCG had in fact obtained the wiring information from Major Kullback of SSS (this last information reported to CSS by Colonel Tiltman). The message concluded "matter is most serious, keep me informed of developments."

Hastings replied to "CSS Only" on 13 February and assured London that the significance of the U.S. breakthrough was recognized by Commander Wenger and MIS and that the results had *not* been passed to the FBI.

Clearly, in the eyes of the British as well as the U.S. services, there were limits to what could go to the FBI. For a time at least, the FBI may have received disguised summaries derived from ENIGMA enciphered traffic, but they never received verbatim translations.[16]

In May 1943, OP-20-G tentatively decided to stop disseminating clandestine COMINT to the FBI.[17] This move was approved by the DNC. This action was recommended by Commander Wenger because the Navy received nothing from the FBI and because there were the important restrictions, noted above, for FBI receipt of ENIGMA material. And, recalled Wenger, the 1942 agreement had concerned only the Western Hemisphere. Even that had been done only to "obtain some measure of control over the cryptanalytic efforts of the FBI." In Wenger's opinion, the recent MIS-ONI-FBI agreement about the former agency's responsibility for operating a DF network in Latin America nullified the clandestine terms of the 1942 agreement.

Nor was the FBI's situation helped by the knowledge, at least in ONI, that there were "side agreements" made in 1943 between the FBI representative in London and the British whereby the FBI would receive certain COMINT in the U.K. Allegedly General Strong, the ACS, G-2, had not objected to this, although it was not referred to or approved by his own Special Branch, much less ONI or OP-20-G.[18] That the FBI was receiving COMINT from the British in London seems to have been known to SSA.[19]

Matters were further clouded by the so-called Colonel Ferguson incident of October 1943. The real meaning of this affair is uncertain, and we have only the ONI account.[20] On 7 October Tom Welb, an FBI liaison officer, brought to ONI counterintelligence five enciphered intercepts that he said had been received from the FBI representative in London, who in turn had obtained them from a Colonel Ferguson, allegedly an officer of ONI (in London). Apparently the FBI wanted the Navy to decipher these messages. Also the FBI may have used this as a pretext for chiding the Navy about not having given these intercepts, which were Western Hemisphere clandestine, directly to the FBI in Washington. The upshot of all this was the discovery by ONI that Ferguson was a British MI-6 officer dealing with the FBI in London, and that the messages in question had been intercepted by OP-20-GU and provided to the British. This incident was seen by ONI and OP-20-G as an example of the devious methods of the FBI and the British and was cited as such in various Navy COMINT policy reviews in 1944.

But possibly the FBI had made its point, for on 20 October 1943 the Navy revised its recent, tentative policy of nondissemination to the bureau. Under the new formula, agreed upon by Carter Clarke for the Army and Admiral Schuermann (DNI) and Captain Stone for the Navy, the 1942 agreement would be observed.[21] The FBI was entitled to Western Hemisphere clandestine COMINT. The Army and Navy would now forward clandestine material to the FBI in summary memorandums without revealing the source or quoting intercepts verbatim. Both MIS and ONI agreed to tell each other what had been disseminated to the FBI.

The problem was not resolved by this measure. On 8 December 1943 Director Hoover sent a grim memorandum to the DNI.[22] He bluntly said that the Navy was not cooperating with the FBI, and that the latter, therefore, was unable to fulfill its counterespionage responsibilities in the Western Hemisphere, especially in Mexico and Argentina. The FBI had been furnishing the Navy messages, obtained in various ways, "for decoding," but "no decodes" were received from the Navy. Hoover recognized that the Navy furnished summaries of intelligence that appeared to be from message traffic, but the "information furnished is fragmentary, the source which is essential to our investigation withheld, and it is by no means a full picture, which is so necessary." Equally intolerable, wrote Mr. Hoover, was that certain information was not made available to the FBI in London because it was allegedly available to the FBI, via ONI, in Washington. Thus the FBI was being blocked from information in various ways. Director Hoover then summarized his case: the FBI could be effective in counterespionage only if it were aware of the identity of foreign agents and had access to their channels of communication. Paraphrases or summaries of clandestine messages were not adequate.

The director closed with a threat. If the Navy refused to cooperate, the FBI would begin seizing foreign agents in Latin America and closing clandestine radio stations – this in spite of the preferred technique of "controlling" enemy espionage nets by having secret access to their communications.

The response from Admiral Schuermann was not conciliatory.[23] The DNI disclaimed any lack of cooperation by the Navy and assured Director Hoover that the FBI would continue to receive material from clandestine traffic when pertinent. But the Navy would not furnish verbatim translations. Admiral Schuermann said that the Navy had no information anyway on clandestine stations in Mexico, while COMINT-based or clandestine traffic to and from Argentina was "fragmentary." The DNI requested advance notice should the FBI decide to close clandestine stations, but he deplored this action as it would surely require the cooperation of Argentine authorities, which was tantamount to notifying the Germans. He warned Director Hoover that should Argentine authorities be told that clandestine messages were being solved, then Germany would receive information of "great value," especially as there were "details in this connection which I am not at liberty to divulge." The latter reference, of course, was to the use by German agents of the ENIGMA and the total Allied exploitation of that system.

Hoover did not carry out his threat to close down all clandestine stations and seize agents, though stations were closed and arrests made from time to time, depending on local conditions in the particular country. At the end of the war a number of German stations that had been located were still operating (and being monitored).

In January 1944 the U.S. solicitor general issued a ruling to redefine the authority of British Security Coordination in the U.S.[24] In keeping with changed conditions, the covert operations of BSC were now severely restricted. The BSC liaison function remained, but the use of informants in the U.S. and the independent conduct of investigation was forbidden. The principle of considering the FBI as BSC's primary point of contact was emphasized, and BSC was required to transmit to the FBI "all information pertaining to, or which in any way affects the Western Hemisphere. . . ." The solicitor general recognized that there were conditions of a purely military nature wherein BSC-USN/USA liaison was appropriate. This ruling probably had no real effect on COMINT relationships, and it may be doubted if the FBI reaped any new benefits in the COMINT field.

The story of FBI-Navy noncooperation goes on through 1944 and into 1945. No solution was ever reached, and only a few more major events will be described.

In April 1944, ONI again stopped disseminating COMINT to the FBI, this time because of the perceived need to tighten security before the Allied invasion of France.[25] This decision was reinforced by the FBI's alleged revelation to the press of its codebreaking capabilities vis-à-vis foreign agents, and its inability to keep COMINT out of court in espionage prosecutions.[26]

In May, Colonel Clarke, Admiral Schuermann, and Lieutenant Colonel Cowgill of MI-6 formulated the "3-N Agreement," another step in tightening preinvasion security.[27] It was agreed that COMINT derived from Latin American German clandestine traffic would not be disseminated ". . . by telegram or pouch in complete or disguised form to any person in South America for information or investigation." Further, any "transcript" of such

COMINT given to the British by the Army or Navy or to the Army and Navy by the British would be annotated with the caveat that it was for the personal use of the recipient only and that no further dissemination was authorized. Any exceptions to 3-N required the mutual agreement of the CSS, the ACS, G-2, and the DNI. While there is no reference to the FBI in this agreement, its terms precluded that agency from receiving the material and certainly from being able to use it in Latin American operations. Similarly State Department personnel, ONI MIS, and British officers in Latin America would not have received this material to assist in counterintelligence or political maneuvers.

Commander Wenger tackled the FBI-Navy problem in mid-May 1944 and prepared a lengthy appreciation of the situation for Carter Clarke.[28] Wenger recommended that the COMINT services reach a new general agreement or obtain a presidential order. The new agreement, or executive order, would limit Western Hemisphere clandestine COMINT production to the Navy. All dissemination of the product to the FBI would be through the Army's MIS. If, however, the Navy had to directly disseminate COMINT to the FBI, it would be under strictest Navy security regulations, and the FBI would have to make certain promises about its security practices.

Nothing came of this because Colonel Clarke opined that the matter of COMINT allocation should not be reopened. Rather, the Army and Navy should "sit tight" and welcome any move by J. Edgar Hoover to appeal to the president.[29]

The situation was such that by August 1944 Commander L. T. Jones, head of OP-20-GU, would write that his organization had had no direct contact with the FBI or COMINT (or at least cryptanalytic) matters for "almost a year and a half."[30] At the same time, Jones described for Commander Wenger the 20-GU capability for taking over the entire clandestine field. Jones was aware that the FBI had sources not available to GU – intercepted courier dispatches, certain cable communications, and mail, as well as what the FBI derived from the German stations in the U.S. that operated, as double agent activities, under FBI control. Jones felt that these sources could be made available to GU (except for the FBI double agent operations) if necessary.

Actually there was no way for the Navy to take control of the clandestine field without the assent of the FBI and FCC or an executive order. Instead, OP-20-GU contented itself with rearranging its intercept facilities and attempting to get greater coverage of German intelligence communications within Europe.

In the midst of these ongoing controversies, the FBI's own COMINT organization, the Cryptanalytic Section of the Technical Laboratory, continued to function. At its peak in 1944, there were thirty-eight FBI agents, clerks, and special employees at bureau headquarters working German clandestine traffic under the direction of Special Agent I. Woodrow Newpher. The main sources for their traffic were the RID and BSC. Their cryptanalytic activities were generally successful; at least this is the evaluation later made by Mr. Newpher.[33] There is no indication, however, that the FBI broke or exploited

ENIGMA enciphered communications of German agents. The full story of FBI COMINT activities remains to be told. FBI cryptanalysis existed in a vacuum because there was no technical exchange with OP-20-G or the SSA. Even the British do not seem to have provided the bureau with significant technical assistance in cryptanalysis.[34]

There was still another thorny area of clandestine COMINT policy during 1943–44, this involving the Army and Navy. By late 1943 the SSA began processing Abwehr (German Intelligence Service) traffic on instructions of MIS. This seemed to the Navy to violate the basic 1942 agreement. The Army response was that Abwehr traffic was not meant to be included in the 1942 agreement.[35] The Army position was incorrect in that most clandestine traffic from Latin America was, and always had been, Abwehr. The larger issue of general Abwehr traffic in other areas, particularly Europe and Africa, was another matter. This traffic was often other than "clandestine" as there were Abwehr links between Germany and German-occupied territory. The Army viewpoint was that this type of communication was military in nature and therefore not to be processed by, or disseminated to, the Navy. Had the basic 1942 agreement used the term "intelligence" or "secret service" traffic instead of "clandestine" traffic, the ground rules might have been clear from the beginning.

Not until later 1944 did the Army and Navy come to an understanding on this class of Abwehr traffic and freely exchange the material.[36] The Navy was probably not deprived of any information vital to its operations, but this dispute does expose the odd nature of the U.S. COMINT structure and the rather primitive nature of the basic 1942 agreement. Some of the anomalies were not lost on the chief policymakers. During his visit to GC&CS in the spring of 1943 (see chapter 4), Colonel Alfred McCormack learned that while the British had offered continental (European) intelligence traffic to the USCG unit, the latter had shown little interest, preferring to concentrate on the Western Hemisphere.[37] Quite probably the MIS instructions to SSA to resume work on German clandestine and other intelligence systems were made because of Colonel McCormack's findings. The Coast Guard was simply not taking advantage of the wealth of information available from British sources. Regardless of the arrangements subsequently worked out by OP-20-GU and the Army in Washington, from the summer of 1943, once the Army gained full access to the German intelligence communications being exploited by the British, the Army's requirements were met. This was accomplished through Telford Taylor's 3-U.S.

The conclusion must be that OP-20-GU never fully realized the potential available through the 1942 agreements. Aside from any question of the narrowness of 20-GU's outlook, the technical problems cannot be ignored. The Coast Guard did not have the intercept capability to cover certain continental circuits while the British did. What is curious, though, is that the RID, operating from monitoring sites in the Western Hemisphere was able, like the British, to cover a great deal of Abwehr (and SD) traffic within Europe and Africa.[38]

Notes

1. U.S. Congress, *Hearings before the Subcommittee of the Committee on Appropriations, House of Representatives, 78th Congress, Second Session on the Independent Office Appropriation Bill for 1945*, Government Printing Office. The FCC portion of these hearings appears on pages 1149–287, testimony taken on 19 January 1944. Among those appearing for the FCC were Chairman James L. Fly; E. K. Jett, chief engineer; George E. Sterling, RID. Information on the Knox letter is on pp. 1253–64.

2. Letter from Nimitz to Secretary, Joint U.S. Staff Planners, 16 November 1942, subject: Responsibility for Conduct and Security of Military Communications Activities, Nimitz Papers, NSAHC.

3. See *The Test*, 445–46, which contains the suggestion that the CSO concurred in President Roosevelt's subsequent decision to preserve the RID. See also *Hearings* for various items introduced during the course of FCC testimony.

4. Letter from Admiral Leahy to Secretary Knox, 1 February 1943, quoted in *Hearings*, 1253 ff.

5. Roosevelt to Knox correspondence, in ibid.

6. This was the Cox Committee. Congressman Cox owned a broadcasting company and did not like Chairman James Fly. Cox went to some length to discredit Fly and the FCC and unnecessarily exposed certain RID activities. (Sterling interview; *Hearings*; miscellaneous material in RG 173).

7. See ibid., 1253–64, and various files in RG 173, National Archives.

8. Cited in memorandum from Commander L. T. Jones, OP-20-GU to OP-20-G, 7 September 1944, subject; Clandestine Radio Intelligence, General File, NSAHC. This is a detailed account of the clandestine COMINT problem, as seen by the Coast Guard Unit. Hereafter cited as Commander Jones memorandum.

9. See especially Boxes 5 and 27, RG 173; also *Hearings*; Sterling interviews.

10. George Sterling summarized it this way in the author's interviews: Admiral Redman was a longtime personal friend of Sterling. But the admiral missed no opportunity to downgrade RID, especially to Congress. In Sterling's opinion, Admiral Redman felt that the RID, in an unauthorized COMSEC capacity, was monitoring U.S. Navy communications. For Mr. Hoover it was a personal matter. He intensely disliked Chairman Fly because of an obscure quarrel about the fingerprinting of radio operators on U.S. merchant marine vessels. Hoover and the FBI gave RID no support at the congressional hearings.

11. OP-20-G Subdivision Order No. 69, 14 April 1944, signed by Captain Philip R. Kenney, Chief of OP-20-G, Organization File, NSAHC.

12. Mrs. Friedman told the author that there were rarely more than twenty people directly working on CA and translation.

13. Memorandum from Commander Jones to OP-20-G-1, 25 August 1944, subject: Clandestine Communications, General File.

14. See *History of Coast Guard Unit 387*, 231 ff., for a complete discussion of Green ENIGMA and other ENIGMA solutions by the USCG. Sources for the British concern are discussed in the next source note.

15. A copy of this message and the reply message are in General File. The message numbers are CXG 358 and CXG 898.

16. Commander Jones memorandum.

17. Memorandum from Wenger to OP-20-G (Captain Stone), 28 May 1943, General File. This memorandum contains a favorable endorsement by Stone as well as the notation of DNC approval.

18. Memorandum from Captain Wallace S. Wharton, OP-16-B-7 to DNI, 19 December 1944, subject: Control of Dissemination of Intelligence Derived from Radio Interception to Civilian Agencies of the United States, General File (classified). This document, hereafter cited as Wharton memorandum, is an involved account of Navy-FBI-British intelligence relations. "Buck" Wharton was a reserve officer with political connections in the Pacific Northwest. He headed ONI counterintelligence (B-7) through most of the war. This memorandum must be read with some caution because ONI was no longer involved in Navy COMINT policy and had access to COMINT only in counterintelligence matters. The author's efforts to trace the FBI-British "side agreement" of 1943 through FBI records was unsuccessful.

19. Rowlett interview. Mr. Rowlett advised that the FBI representative in London was Mr. Simperton. A Mr. Thurston was also an FBI representative there.

20. Memorandum from Captain Wallace Wharton to DNI, 12 October 1943, General File.

21. Memorandum from Captain Stone to DNI *via* DNC, 20 October 1943, General File. See also Wharton memorandum (classified).

22. Memorandum from Hoover to Admiral Schuermann, 8 December 1943, General File (classified).

23. Memorandum from Schuermann to Hoover, 10 December 1943, General File (classified).

24. Letter from Hugh B. Cox, assistant solicitor general to BSC, 22 January 1944. See also the Wharton memorandum.

25. Wharton memorandum.

26. Ibid.

27. Agreement dated 1 May 1944, in General File. See also Wharton memorandum.

28. Paper entitled *Outline of Controversy Between the Navy and the FBI*, 17 May 1944, General File (classified).

29. Memorandum from Clarke to Wenger, 20 May 1944, General File (classified).

30. Memorandum from L. T. Jones to OP-20-G10, 25 August 1944, General File.

31. Memorandum from Kinney to various subdivision heads, 31 August 1944, General File.

32. Commander Jones memorandum.

33. Author's interview of Mr. Newpher, 1975.

34. Vol. 1, *Secret Service Sigint*, GC&CS History, 55–56 (classified).

35. Memorandum from L. T. Jones to OP-20-G, 18 November 1943, General File (classified).

36. Wharton memorandum; see also Commander Jones memorandum for a good discussion of the meaning of the terms involved.

37. See various items in ACSI #34, especially the report headed *Coast Guard Liaison with British on Clandestine Traffic*.

38. Sterling interview and Sterling article, "The U.S. Hunt for Axis Agent Radios."

Chapter 7
The Army and Navy Move toward Full Cooperation, 1944–45

THE ARMY AND NAVY FORMALIZE COOPERATION

A recurring and major theme of this study has been the development of Army-Navy COMINT cooperation. The culmination of these trends, the creation of the Army-Navy COMINT Coordinating Committee (ANCICC) and the Army-Navy Communications Intelligence Board (ANCIB), will be described in this chapter. Although the Army's continuing attempts to put its own COMINT structure in order are important in considering interservice cooperation, these will be treated separately in the next chapter.

While General Strong had long favored more cooperation or even consolidation of the Army and Navy COMINT services, the actual agreement that was the first step in that direction was based on a Navy concept. The credit probably goes to Commander Wenger who, though opposed to outright merger of the COMINT services, had during 1943 prepared sound proposals for better coordination and high-level planning.

By the end of 1943, the Army had access to information of undoubted operational value to the Navy. This was from the now-exploitable Japanese army codes. From the standpoint of MIS Special Branch, the Navy had never properly reciprocated for the steady volume of material that came from the Army in the form of Special Branch MAGIC Summaries, SSA's Japanese diplomatic translations, material obtained by MIS from the British. Colonel Clarke decided that Japanese army material would not be made available to the Navy unless a reciprocal agreement was reached.[1]

This led to an exchange of views between MIS and OP-20-G, the former represented by an ad hoc committee composed of Clarke, Colonel Al McCormack, and Major Perdue. They sought a "simple traffic exchange" type of agreement (actually an exchange of translations rather than raw traffic).[2] The Navy countered with the suggestion that liaison officers should be exchanged and that these officers would have free access to the other service's COMINT files. The Navy proposal became the basis for the agreement that was in the form of a document signed by Admiral King on 4 February 1944 and forwarded to General Marshall. The latter signed on 12 February 1944, making it effective.[3]

This agreement, hereafter referred to as the King-Marshall Agreement, was to apply only to anti-Japanese COMINT matters and only among the various headquarters agencies in Washington. This was a practical first step given the U.S. primacy in the Pacific both in the narrower world of COMINT and in the wider arena of high-level strategy. Such an agreement did not have to consider the British position. The basic terms of the King-Marshall Agreement were these:[4]

1. Army liaison officers would deal with the Pacific section (F-22) of the Navy's Combat Intelligence Division and have access to OP-20-G files concerning anti-Japanese COMINT.

2. The Navy liaison officers would have similar access to MIS Special Branch and SSA.

3. These liaison officers would take whatever information they needed, but the service producing the COMINT would continue to control handling, dissemination, and use.

4. There would be common rules governing the security of ULTRA (i.e., highest-level COMINT).

Colonel Clarke, who had not favored the exchange of liaison officers in the first place, was, not surprisingly, unhappy with the early applications of the King-Marshall Agreement.[5] He gave the Navy liaison officer full access, without restrictions, to Special Branch material, and copies could be made of any material. Major Snow, the Special Branch liaison officer to the Navy, was unable to copy all material, as the Navy reserved the right to determine what the Army could have. Clarke suggested to the ACS, G-2, that the Army perhaps should reconsider the agreement.

But as this agreement had been signed by the chiefs of staff, it was not to be discarded at the first sign of trouble. Rather the oft-suggested, by each service, idea of a COMINT coordinating body was resurrected. One may be confident that the idea came from Commander Wenger, though the author has found no record.

On 18 April 1944, the ANCICC came into being. Its first meeting was attended by Colonel Clarke of MIS, SSA chief Colonel Corderman, Commander Wenger and his chief Captain Kinney, from the Navy, and Captain Smith-Hutton of F-22. They agreed that their purpose would be to coordinate future plans in the Pacific, coordinate relationship and agreements with the Allies, and consider postwar plans.[6] The following month an ANCICC charter was drawn up defining its purpose as ". . . to improve the general collaboration of the Army and Navy communication intelligence organizations by coordinating plans and agreements affecting joint operating arrangements in support of properly approved policies, preparing recommendations for desirable changes in policies, and settling such controversial matters as can be resolved without reference to higher authority."[7]

Nowhere was there criticism of the King-Marshall Agreement or a suggestion that it had not become a basic COMINT agreement. The MIS continued its regular assignment of liaison officers to the Navy, and the latter did likewise. At least by June 1944, the SSA had a technical liaison officer, Captain John N. Seaman, at OP-20-G.[8] The SSA/OP-20-G liaison was vigorously pursued, and a wealth of sensitive technical data was freely exchanged.[9]

Meanwhile, a separate technical agreement had been made on 7 April 1944 between the SSA and OP-20-G for collaboration on Japanese weather systems.[10] Each service would freely exchange intercepts as well as cryptanalytic data. The Navy would be responsible for primary work on the main Japanese weather system, JN-37. This agreement, which just predated the first ANCICC meeting, seems to have been made without reference to MIS or the Combat Intelligence Division.

THE WORKINGS OF ANCICC AND THE CREATION OF ANCIB

The members of ANCICC promptly plunged into a number of jurisdictional problems of mutual concern. At the first meeting on 18 April, the members had decided to withhold clandestine COMINT from the FBI.[11] This decision, as was shown in the preceding chapter, was put into effect by ONI. The committee also resolved to again discourage OSS attempts to enter the COMINT field and to take no action on the relationship of FRUMEL and CBB until the responsibilities of the latter were made clear.

While a meeting-by-meeting account of ANCICC's work in 1944 will not be given here, some of the highlights will be shown in the following paragraphs. These illustrate the remarkable degree of cooperative effort that had come into being.[12]

Although the King-Marshall Agreement had called for free exchange of all material of interest via liaison officers, this seems to have been slow in coming about (at least according to Colonel Clarke – see section 1). However, at the 10 May 1944 meeting ANCICC specified that all Japanese military attaché and all Japanese naval attaché (JNA) COMINT would be exchanged between the services. At this same meeting, the committee went so far as to undertake preliminary planning for a complete Army-Navy COMINT merger. Commander Wenger and Colonel Earle F. Cook of SSA were appointed as a subcommittee to consider this. The specific details of this early merger planning do not appear in the ANCICC minutes, but it is likely that the intent was to consider postwar organization rather than anything in the near future.

Legal aspects of COMINT, of no great concern since Pearl Harbor, were also considered by ANCICC. At issue were the existing U.S. communications laws (specifically the 1934 law that had, among other things, created the FCC) that seemed to prohibit many COMINT activities.[13] A legal matter that had been of continuing concern was how to protect COMINT from unauthorized disclosure. The ANCICC recognized that specific legislation was needed and draft legislation, initiated in the committee, ultimately reached the chiefs of staff. This, however, is a postwar story.

Immediate wartime needs were of course discussed. Colonel Clarke, at Navy urging, agreed to dispatch Special Branch officers to serve as SSOs at JICPOA, (actually CIC) Pearl Harbor. The activity and employment of U.S. Army Air Force Radio Squadrons Mobile and the all-service integration and coordination of radio fingerprinting (RFP), intercept, and DF were studied and discussed. These discussions resulted in specific cooperative operations in the Pacific.

In November, ANCICC, in regular operation for six months, moved toward still greater formalization of its activity and an expansion of responsibility. Extensive subcommittees involving officers of MIS, SSA, OP-20-G, and Combat Intelligence Division were formed.[14] The authority of ANCICC was now "... to determine the major policies and to take such action as may be necessary to coordinate methods, procedures, operations, and equipment – in all matters involving communication intelligence," and "ANCICC has the authority to implement its decisions except on matters of major policy, which will require the approval of higher authority." The regular members of ANCICC would now be:[15]

Position	Incumbent on 10 November 1944
Commanding Officer, SSA	Colonel W. P. Corderman
Deputy Chief, MIS	Brigadier General Carter W. Clarke
Assistant Director Naval Communications, OP-20-G	Captain J. N. Wenger
OIC, Naval Communications Annex	Captain Phillip R. Kinney
Assistant, Combat Intelligence Division	Captain W. R. Smedberg III

The subcommittees included Intercept and DF, TA, COMINT Communications, Collateral Information, Cryptanalysis, Intercept Coordination, Research, and Intelligence/Security.[16]

Whether or not by design, the ANCICC did not make any new general agreement to replace the allocation and dissemination agreements of the summer of 1942. To do so would probably have required the participation of the FBI, a most unlikely circumstance. This is of more than passing interest, because as late as December 1944, OP-20-G and SSA, through individual representatives rather than through the ANCICC, debated the meaning and authority of the 1942 agreement as it applied to "trade codes." Throughout much of the war, the SSA had worked Japanese commercial, that is, economic messages, although the 1942 agreement allotted Japanese "trade codes" to OP-20-G.[17]

At the end of 1944, the Navy took the initiative once again and suggested that ANCICC, which had originated with discussions at the COMINT and intelligence services level only, should become even more formal and permanent and have the approval of Admiral King and General Marshall. The exact sequence of events that led to the creation of what would be known as ANCIB is not clear, but it cannot be too wrong to see Captain Wenger and Captain W. R. Smedberg (who found interservice infighting intolerable) as inspiring the move.

A draft proposal establishing the new organization was prepared for Admiral King's signature on 22 December 1944 but was not sent to him, probably because more discussion with the Army was needed. Another version was signed by Admiral King on 14 February 1945 and sent to General Marshall.[18] The Navy proposal noted that ANCICC had operated successfully for almost a year but as "an unofficial committee." As the results had been good, a permanent, formal committee was needed because "war experience has demonstrated the logic of centralizing control and coordination of this most valuable but very easily lost source of intelligence in an [Army-Navy] committee. . . ." The proposed body, to be known as ANCIB, would be outside the framework of the JCS, the Joint Intelligence Committee, or the Joint Communications Board. ANCIB would be responsible directly to the chief of staff and the COMINCH/CNO. ANCIB would consist of two officers from each service, and Admiral King intended to name the DNC and the assistant chief of staff for combat intelligence (who was also the DNI) as his representatives.

The King proposal went to the MIS for recommendations. The response from Brigadier General Carter Clarke, sent to the deputy chief of staff, was extremely negative and seems to have been a low point in the formulation of COMINT policy. But it must be said that General Clarke was probably weary from the struggles he had just completed regarding operational control of the SSA (to be discussed in the next chapter). Clarke's first response, a draft dated 24 February and intended for the DCS, does not seem to have been signed by the ACS, G-2, General Bissell. The next effort was far more detailed and was signed by General Bissell on 2 March 1945.[19] In this memorandum, Clarke and Bissell agreed that the proposed ANCIB was a worthy idea, comparable to the British Signal Intelligence Board. However, U.S. COMINT was not as centralized as that of the British, and there were these factors to consider:

1. Navy COMINT was centralized under the DNC. Army COMINT was fragmented with SRIs and RMSs under theater control; semi-independent theater SIS groups; and the SSA, which was partly under MIS control. The SSA, though the main processing center and having its own intercept stations, still depended on units not under its control for the bulk of its traffic.[20]

2. The King proposal was good for the long range.

3. ". . . The Army can hardly participate in an interservice project of this sort as long as its own signal intelligence activities remain as decentralized as they now are."

The recommendation was for a noncommittal response to Admiral King and an Army staff study before making a final reply.

This was most displeasing to General Thomas T. Handy, the deputy chief of staff. In two bristling memorandums to General Bissell on 7 March, he suggested that the latter's objection to the King proposal were not valid.[21] He suggested (in the second memorandum) that Bissell's negative comments were ". . . due to what you conceive to be faulty organization within the Army – a view that is not accepted by other responsible agencies. Such reasoning does not appear to be sound." A draft acceptance was therefore directed.

On 9 March 1945 General Marshall sent a brief memorandum to Admiral King accepting the establishment of ANCIB. He also enclosed an agreement that he had signed, which required Admiral King's signature. Admiral King signed the ANCIB agreement on 10 March.[22]

The ANCIB was established effective immediately with the following membership:

Army	**Navy**
Major General Bissell ACS, G-2	Rear Admiral Joseph Redman, DNC
Colonel W. Preston Corderman, Commander, SSA	

Because of the different organizational structures of the Army and Navy and by virtue of Admiral King's initial suggestion regarding the membership of ANCIB, neither General Clarke nor Captain Wenger was on the board, while Colonel Corderman, actually subordinate to Clarke, was. But the ANCIB agreement called for the creation of a "new" ANCICC that was to be the working committee of the ANCIB. Predictably the members of the "new" ANCICC were as before: Clarke and Corderman for the Army; Wenger, Kinney, and Smedberg for the Navy.

The ANCIB charter as stated in the agreement was as follows:

2. With respect to all matters pertaining to collection, research, production, compilation, dissemination, and security of communication intelligence, the Board will:
   a. Coordinate the plans and operations of the communication intelligence organizations of the Army and Navy.
   b. Formulate joint agreements as to procedures pertinent thereto.
   c. Negotiate and coordinate with other intelligence organizations.
3. The Board will function outside the framework of the Joint Chiefs of Staff and report directly to the chief of staff, U.S. Army, the commander in chief U.S. Fleet, and the chief of naval operations.

The creation of ANCIB was a logical development, if some three years late. In fact, ANCIB belongs to the postwar period rather than to World War II, as it was the U.S. framework for interservice COMINT cooperation that preceded the formation of the Armed Forces Security Agency (AFSA) in 1949. Although attempts to draw exact parallels are probably useless, it is worth saying that ANCIB brought the U.S. COMINT services into an organizational and policy position reached by the British ten years before.

Notes

1. Memorandum from Carter W. Clarke to Major General Clayton Bissell, ACS, G-2, 4 March 1944, subject: Army-Navy Agreement Regarding ULTRA, ACSI #42. This is a lengthy document filled with complaints about the lack of cooperation since the beginning of the war.

2. Ibid.

3. *Joint Army-Navy Agreement for the Exchange of Communication Intelligence* in *Catalog*, 2.c.(9).

4. Ibid.

5. Clarke to Bissell, 4 March 1944, see footnote 1.

6. *Outline of Collaboration* (prepared by Wenger), 33 ff.

7. Ibid.

8. Routing and Work Sheet with entry for 1 June 1944 in SSA file folder marked *Reports (Liaison with Navy)*, NSAH.

9. See *Reports (Liaison with Navy)* folder. There are forty-eight reports on file prepared by Captain Seaman and his successors, Captain Walter J. Fried and C. P. Collins. Most are addressed to Colonel Rowlett and deal with such matters as the Navy Bombe, German clandestine traffic, attaché and diplomatic traffic, GC&CS, and U.S. machine processing. There is a great volume of detail on specific cryptanalytic processes in these reports.

10. *Joint Army-Navy Conference Concerning Japanese Weather Information*, 7 April 1944, signed by Colonel W. Preston Corderman and Commander J. N. Wenger, *Catalog*, 2.c.(10).

11. *Outline of Collaboration*, 33 ff. The proceedings of many of the 1944 meetings of ANCICC are reproduced in this study by Commander Wenger.

12. All the examples are from Wenger's *Outline of Collaboration*.

13. In the prewar period, there is no doubt that the U.S. intelligence services understood that at least diplomatic COMINT operations were illegal under the 1934 law. However, COMINT activities had been authorized by President Roosevelt, the secretaries of the services, the CNO, and chief of staff. According to the thinking of the time, that was sufficient legal justification. Once war began, the president's war powers caused any legal question to evaporate.

14. All information on the November expansion of ANCICC is from *Army-Navy Communication Intelligence Coordinating Committee General Information – No. 1, Note by Secretaries*, 10 November 1944, signed by J. V. Connorton, Lieutenant, USN, and Rhea M. Smith, Captain, USA, in *Catalog* 4.b.

15. Ibid. Wenger had replaced Captain Kinney as head of OP-20-G and as an ADNC on 6 November. This will be discussed in the next chapter.

16. The subcommittee roster contained in the 10 November document is an interesting "Who's Who" of the COMINT community late in the war. Joseph J. Rochefort had returned to favor in the COMINT business and was appointed to the Intelligence/Security Subcommittee.

17. *Report of Meeting between Army and Navy on Allocation of Commercial Traffic*, 13 December 1944, signed by Lieutenant B. K. Buffham, SSA, in *Catalog*, 2.c.(13). In February 1945 a similar discussion arose between Army and Navy representatives over definition of diplomatic COMINT. See *SSA History*, vol. 1, 100–103, and Rowlett interviews, tape #3.

18. Memorandum to chief of staff, subject: Army-Navy Communications Intelligence Board – Establishment of, 14 February 1945, in *Catalog*, 4.d.

19. The unsent draft and the 2 March 1945 version are in ACSI #4, both drafted by Carter W. Clarke for the signature of General Bissell.

20. I am not sure if this was correct unless traffic from the British is counted. CBB was the largest source of U.S. Army traffic after the SSA's own traffic.

21. These two memorandums from Handy to Bissell, both 7 March 1945, are in ACSI #4.

22. Memorandum from Marshall to King, 9 March 1945, and Agreement (no date), both in *Catalog* 4.e. The date of 10 March for the ANCIB agreement is in the Winkler-Bidwell material in ACSI #6. The ANCIB Agreement was in the form of a memorandum to the DNC, DNI, ACS, G-2, and commanding general, SSA.

Chapter 8
Internal Army and Navy Organizational Developments, 1944–45

SSOS IN THE PACIFIC

Having seen in the preceding chapter how the Army and Navy, beginning in early 1944, found a regular means for cooperation and exchange, we return to the organizational and policy developments within each service. The ordering of this topic has been difficult as it precedes some of the developments just described in chapter 7, but, on the other hand, it continues beyond the creation of ANCIB (March 1945) to the end of the war. Unhappily, there is a certain timelessness to some of the events that follow, for there has been a repetition to the present day.

The watershed of any history of Army COMINT during World War II, be it one of policy and organization or of operations, is March–May 1943, when the first breaks into the Japanese army codes were made and when the Army gained full access to the British exploitation of ENIGMA. Among the administrative results was the creation of the Special Security Officer (SSO) system to securely distribute and control ULTRA information and a series of War Department regulations that sought to safeguard ULTRA in accordance with British and U.S. Navy standards. A serial description of the Army COMINT regulations is too tedious a matter. Suffice it to say at this point that the first ULTRA (or ULTRA Dexter) regulations were promulgated in September and October 1943, and that the role of the SSOs was specifically, if narrowly, stated in the latter regulation:

> Special Security Officers assigned to the staff of a command shall have sole charge of bringing ULTRA Dexter intelligence to the attention of the commander and shall advise the commander on all problems of security in connection with the receipt, transmission, handling, and use of ULTRA Dexter intelligence. Recommendations made by such officers concerning security shall be followed.

The European Theater version of the SSO system, under the direction of Colonel Telford Taylor, has already been described in detail. Beginning in the fall of 1943, SSOs were sent from MIS to the other theaters: Major James Ashly to SWPA, Captain John F. B. Runnals to CBI, and Major Edwin E. Huddleston Jr. to Pacific Ocean areas (Hawaii). In order to familiarize the commands with the SSO system, Colonel Clarke visited the Pacific-Asian theater prior to the dispatch of the aforementioned officers. He met personally with General MacArthur and overcame the general's objections to having a

War Department-controlled officer in his command.² The matter of War Department control of the SSOs remained a sensitive issue in the SWPA.

By spring 1944 the MIS undertook the selection and training of additional officers for SSO positions in the Pacific. This was because major offensives were to commence against Japan, and there would be a greater need to disseminate ULTRA below the level of theater commander. In July the War Department ULTRA regulations applicable to the Pacific and Asian theaters were revised to allow dissemination to numbered armies and the equivalent USAAF commands and to corps that might operate independently. This new group of SSOs (about twenty officers) went overseas in September 1944. Ultimately there were War Department SSOs not only at MacArthur's headquarters but also with the Sixth and Eighth Armies in the Philippines, the Far East Air Force (FEAF) and its subordinate elements, the Fifth, Thirteenth, and (much later) Seventh Air Forces. In Hawaii, SSOs were with naval intelligence officers at JICPOA and the advance headquarters in Guam. In the CBI, SSOs were at various headquarters in Ceylon, India, and China. At least two SSOs went into Okinawa during the invasion.³ In theory, all these officers were under Carter W. Clarke, originally when he was chief of Special Branch and later when he was deputy chief of MIS and SSO War Department.

The operations of the SSOs in the Pacific and Asian theaters are too varied for an easy summary and are a part of the operational history of COMINT. Certain administrative and policy arrangements must be described, however.

The expanded SSO system, still under War Department control, was resisted by General MacArthur. In June 1944 he had sent a message to General Marshall decrying the principle of having officers not under his command in his theater. He said that he supported the idea of an SSO system and the new security and dissemination procedures but not Washington control. His conclusion was grandly put: "Many disasters in history can be charged directly to such long distance control of functions that properly belong to a responsible field commander."⁴ General Marshall did not directly respond, but he did order the dispatch of the new ULTRA regulations and the attendant SSO augmentation.

The experience of Major John R. Thompson tends to show how General MacArthur's views were acted upon.⁵ Thompson and four assistant SSOs were sent to SWPA to serve at the Central Bureau. The GHQ SWPA and the FEAF (both served by SSOs) had already moved forward to Hollandia and thence to the Philippines. The Thompson group was to select CBB and MIS ULTRA material for transmission from Brisbane to the forward area. However, General Richard K. Sutherland, General MacArthur's chief of staff, purportedly at the urging of Spencer Akin, squelched this procedure. General Sutherland told Thompson that the War Department ULTRA regulations allowed the SSOs to merely advise on ULTRA security and to decipher/encipher ULTRA product messages. Only SWPA G-2 officers would select and disseminate CBB material. In the end, the SSO team, with the aid of an SWPA G-2 type, did the ULTRA selection, editing, and transmission anyway.

In the China-Burma-India (CBI) theater, the SSO was at first colocated with the theater SIS in New Delhi. His duties included typical SSO operations, as well as liaison and coordination for the War Department with the large British COMINT organization in India (the WEC).[7] CBI SSOs were assisted by the theater G-2 personnel in order of battle work but nonetheless maintained control over ULTRA information and, as elsewhere, held their own private crypto systems. The SSOs in the CBI seem to have been welcomed by the command, and their duties extended to evaluation of COMINT as well as secure dissemination.[7]

Lest the SSO function become too involved in the telling, these points are made to place it in context:

1. The SSOs personally received all ULTRA produced in Washington and disseminated by MIS. In other words, the Signal Security Agency, through intercept received from, mainly, MS-2 at Two Rock Ranch and CBB, produced ULTRA for the Pacific and Asian theaters. This was evaluated and forwarded to the SSOs by MIS Washington.

2. Locally produced ULTRA – as by CBB or SIS New Delhi – was usually, by late 1944, disseminated by the SSOs.

3. The SSOs disseminated Navy-produced ULTRA; Navy ULTRA available to the Army was extensive and of highest value.

If these operations seem rather too extensive for a few dozen SSOs, we should note that lower-level COMINT, called Pearl (solved low-level cryptographic systems) and Thumb (TA and DF), as obtained for CBB by the SRI companies and independently by the USAAF Radio Squadrons Mobile, did not necessarily go through the SSOs. A substantial portion of the COMINT was in the Pearl and Thumb categories, and the term "low-level" ought not to be interpreted as "low significance."

DEVELOPMENTS AT THE WAR DEPARTMENT

General Strong had been ACS, G-2, for almost two years when illness incapacitated him in February 1944. He was replaced by Major General Clayton D. Bissell, a controversial Air Force officer without intelligence experience. Strong had never favored the MIS concept and ran G-2 as though the MID staff and MIS were one and the same. Within days of his departure, a board headed by John J. McCloy undertook a study of the reorganization of G-2. Serving with McCloy on the board were General Bissell, General John Smith, the Army representative to OSS, and General Otto L. Nelson, who had been a prime mover in the March 1942 reorganization of MID. General Nelson, a fixture on the General Staff since the beginning of the war, was almost certainly the force behind this reorganization too.[8] The McCloy Board had the following objectives:[9]

1. a renewed attempt to separate MID and MIS
2. an end to extreme compartmentation
3. emphasis on anti-Japanese and German intelligence
4. maximum exploitation of productive intelligence activities
5. establishment of an intelligence specialist system

The end to extreme compartmentation was surely directed at the Special Branch, which, it may be recalled, was a product of the thinking of Secretary of War Stimson, Mr. McCloy himself, and his former law partner Colonel Al McCormack. The personnel growth of the Special Branch was probably a factor too. By June 1944 the branch had a strength of 382 officers, enlisted, and civilians (a substantial portion in all categories being women), while the rest of MIS in Washington numbered only 356. This seemingly odd situation was actually an honest recognition that COMINT was the most valuable type of intelligence. But it had led to the development of parallel subdivisions: there was a Special Branch unit (B section) analyzing Japanese military matters and preparing the "Japanese Army Supplement" to the daily MAGIC Summary, while at the same time the "other," i.e., non-COMINT portion of MIS also had a Japanese military section.[10] It was often difficult for Special Branch's Japanese and German order of battle analysts to deal with their MIS counterparts who were not authorized access to ULTRA.

Major General Clayton Bissell
assistant chief of staff, G-2

The reorganization and establishment of a new MIS/MID did not take place until July 1944. The former Special Branch disappeared and its COMINT analysts were divided among specialists' desks and research units of the new intelligence division of MIS headed by Colonel Al McCormack, as director of intelligence (or director of information). A new Special Branch was created to supervise COMINT liaison and the SSO program. Carter Clarke became deputy chief of MIS and was soon promoted to brigadier general. Army

COMINT policy remained the personal responsibility of General Clarke, and, as the SSO War Department, he directly controlled the new Special Branch too." Once again MID was separated from MIS as a pure policy and staff agency. Both MIS and the MID staff remained as before under the ACS, G-2.

The McCloy Board had also considered the matter of control of Army COMINT.[12] The board had forwarded its overall recommendations to the deputy chief of staff on 23 March 1944. Included was the apparent advocation of the merger of SSA into the MIS.[13] Unfortunately, this advocacy was hedged in that certain questions requiring staff study were posed.

General Bissell answered these questions in a memorandum to General Marshall on 15 June 1944. His case (perhaps prepared by Carter Clarke) was that unified control of Army COMINT was needed, and that could be accomplished by placing SSA and its monitoring stations under MIS. General Bissell requested authority to take that action at the appropriate time but "not immediately" as MIS was too deeply involved in critical intelligence production and was receiving good support from the Signal Corps. The landings in Normandy had taken place only nine days before, and the general reorganization of MID/MIS was in progress too.

We cannot know what might have happened if General Bissell had asked for immediate control of SSA. What followed were months of interminable wrangling within the War Department. The matter is too repetitive to recount memorandum by memorandum, argument by counterargument. Certain highlights are instructive, and the basic concepts must be described because there has never been a thorough resolution in the intelligence community.

John J. McCloy saw General Bissell's memorandum to the chief of staff. He urged General Marshall to have G-2 immediately take control of SSA.[14] But it was General Nelson, the assistant deputy chief of staff, who responded to General Bissell on 22 June. He asked for specific plans to implement the G-2 assumption of control over SSA and for an analysis of the effect on other Signal Corps activities.[15]

Carter Clarke reviewed the matters faced by Nelson, and a reply to the office of the deputy chief of staff was made on 11 July.[16] The response did not include detailed plans, but rather the proposal that the transfer would take place thirty days after it was approved and that the Army regulation (AR 105-5) giving the CSO COMINT and COMSEC responsibilities would be changed, as would Signal Corps and MIS personnel allotments. Detailed plans for a MIS-SSA integration and reorganization would come *after* the transfer.[17]

The commanding general, Army Service Forces, and the CSO were quick to answer this challenge. General Somervell wrote the chief of staff on 22 July to enter his strong objection to the G-2 proposal. He reassured him that several previous G-2 attempts to take over the SSA had been disapproved and that this latest effort had neither increased efficiency or better organization to recommend it. He recommended that there be no change in the existing setup and that "the subject [should] remain closed for the duration." Included with General Somervell's memorandum to General Marshall was a lengthy exposition of the matter prepared by General Harry Ingles, the CSO.[18] General Ingles raised these objections to the transfer of SSA from the OCSigO to MIS:

1. MIS was not like the Signal Corps, an established branch of the Army, authorized by Congress.

2. MIS would gain control of only the SSA and Second Signal Service, leaving the Signal Corps to still train and man the numerous other Army COMINT elements (i.e., the SRI companies, etc.).

3. MIS could not train the specialists needed for COMINT.

4. The production of COMINT was largely a signals undertaking. Similarly, cryptographic processes were a signal matter.

5. If the SSA, operating under the OCSigO had not fulfilled its mission, the MIS should state its complaints to the CSO. There had been no complaints.

General Ingle's arguments were in turn subjected to predictable rebuttals from Carter Clarke.[19] Of greater interest were the observations of Mr. McCloy, made in a memorandum to General McNarney, the DCS.[20] McCloy wrote that he was in complete disagreement with Generals Somervell and Ingles because the entire COMINT operation belonged "under one roof." But he went beyond the immediate circumstances and looked toward the postwar period. He wrote:

> In my judgment one of the chief pillars of our national security system after the war must be an extensive intercept service. If we are to be a military power or, indeed, if we are to take an active role in world affairs, we cannot afford to leave this field entirely to the British and the Continental powers. *It is one of the best sources of intelligence that there is and I would take it out of any existing service agency immediately in the hope and belief that it would develop into an organization which would stand a better chance of perpetuation in peacetime.*

Mr. McCloy then went on to the personnel problems of military intelligence. He observed that "the curse of our so-called intelligence service to date is the attachment to it of only those officers who have social acceptance and means enough to enable them to pursue a life of relative ease." He concluded that the best example to follow was that of the British who, he believed, had brought together under actual control all the elements that make up communications intelligence.

Assistant Secretary McCloy simply lacked the authority to implement his recommendations. There is no record, unfortunately, to show where Secretary of War Stimson stood. So the arguments and counterarguments returned to military channels.

The MIS position was given to the DCS in greater detail in September in a paper possibly prepared by Colonel McCormack and signed by General Bissell.[21] The entire COMINT process, from intercept through analysis and dissemination, was described as a single intelligence operation that should be in the hands of intelligence officers, not divided between signal and intelligence officers. The successful British system was given as an example of the wisdom of consolidation. The existing system impeded overall Army COMINT, placed the U.S. in a weak position in dealing with the British, and worsened the "... present unavoidable division among the Army, the Navy, and the FBI of responsibility for U.S. signal intelligence activities." A new feature was introduced into the MIS argument. Under the present system, sophisticated forms of radio deception, beyond mere manipulation of traffic volume could not (or would not) be carried out by SSA. The British were able to practice real deception based on their knowledge of what communications the enemy could exploit. With MIS planning and control, the U.S. too could enter this field.

At the end of November 1944, the CSO offered a compromise. The SSA would remain under the OCSigO, but the MIS could communicate directly with that agency and would be given some authority over transfer of key personnel.[22] The matter of direct MIS-SSA contact was not as elementary a matter as it seemed. Most correspondence from MIS had had to pass through the OCSigO en route to SSA. And as late as 1943 the MIS Special Branch analysts had been forbidden by Signal Corps policy from dealing person to person with the translators or editors in SSA. The contact was in writing at the level of chief, Special Branch-Chief SSA. Colonel Corderman had, however, dropped these restrictions long before this offer of compromise by the CSO.[23]

The CSO's compromise was not acceptable to G-2. Likewise an offer by General Ingles to work the matter out through a personal discussion with Carter Clarke was rejected.[24] A few days later General Ingles tried again. He presented the new DCS, General Thomas T. Handy, a document for signature that would give operational control of the SSA to the ACS, G-2, leaving the CSO the "command and administration" of the SSA/Second Signal Service.[25] The new delineation between the authority of the ACS, G-2, and the CSO was set out in some detail, and while certain arrangements were simplified and were in favor of G-2, the dual control remained.

General Handy must have liked the Ingles proposal because, over the objection of General Bissell, he directed the latter to prepare a draft order transferring operational control of the SSA and Second Signal Service to G-2 but leaving these organizations under the CSO for administration, training, and supply.[26] General Handy signed the directive on 10 December 1944 making the new arrangement effective on that date. It was not just a rewrite of General Ingles's draft, but it was far from what G-2 had wanted. The main points were these:[27]

1. "Operational command and control" of the SSA and the Second Signal Service was transferred to the ACS, G-2.

2. Activities charged to the CSO under AR 105-5 would continue to be performed by SSA and the Second Signal Service.

3. COMINT liaison with U.S. and foreign agencies was to be the responsibility of the ACS, G-2.

4. The ACS, G-2, was to have control over personnel transfers where intelligence operation might be affected. G-2 was also authorized to shift personnel between MIS and SSA for reasons of intelligence production.

5. The CSO was to continue to be responsible for the SSA and Second Signal Service other than as specifically excepted by this directive.

Upon assuming operational control of these organizations, General Bissell notified the CSO that he would exercise this control through the MIS.[28] The major commands and the British CSS were notified of these changes on 16 December 1944.[29]

Neither the MIS nor the Signal Corps was completely pleased with the outcome. While MIS had been given adequate authority to regulate the COMINT production of SSA, the CSO and the Army Service Forces remained in the SSA chain of command. From the not insignificant standpoint of careerism, it must have been a trying situation for regular Signal Corps officers assigned to SSA. General Frank Stoner, chief of the Army Communication Service, later summarized the Signal Corps position this way:[30]

> [Only the Signal Corps] could have handled the vast construction of highly specialized plant required for this operation. At no time during its operation by the Signal Corps was any requirement by G-2 unfilled and all initiative for new action and pioneering came from the Signal Corps. The most awkward condition, if any, was caused by having to fight four rear guard actions with G-2 to preserve the general value of the war effort.

Not surprisingly, this is not how the MIS saw it. There were some concrete and almost immediate intelligence gains made now that MIS was in charge. Certain Japanese circuits in Southeast Asia, which were overcovered by SSA, were dropped in favor of hitherto untouched Japanese traffic bearing on the home islands, Korea, China, and Manchuria. In the field of cryptanalysis, MIS insistence that lower-level Japanese systems be attacked reaped considerable benefits. And more selectivity was introduced into SSA translation efforts.[31]

ATTEMPTED ARMY CONSOLIDATION IN THE THEATERS AND THE CREATION OF ASA

The 10 December 1944 directive that gave the ACS, G-2, operational control of SSA and its intercept sites did not result in the centralization of Army COMINT. The tactical intercept units (the SRI companies, RSMs, etc.) remained under theater, Army, or Corps control, and the CBB and SIS New Delhi were likewise under the theaters. But now the

ACS, G-2, and the MIS were in a more favorable position for direct contact with the theaters on COMINT matters. In reality the MIS effort for complete worldwide control of all Army COMINT units and activities never ceased. Generals Clarke and Bissell remained in the forefront of this effort.

Aside from the activities of 3-U.S. and its SSOs and the BEECHNUT Group, Army COMINT in Europe was to remain under the commander there. The bulk of high-level intercept and COMINT production remained a British show. While there is some evidence that the MIS after the 10 December directive sought to centralize Army COMINT in Europe under the War Department, this did not come to pass.[32]

The tactical COMINT organization, though not under central direction, expanded tremendously after the Normandy assault. Curiously, the structure that had been building in the U.K. in preparation for D-Day was supplanted by a provisional one, almost at the last moment in at least one case. A month before D-Day there were eight SRI companies in the U.K.[33] However, these units were perhaps too large and inflexible for the assault and beachhead phase of the Normandy operation. Several months before the invasion, First U.S. Army was authorized, by the theater commander, to form three provisional tactical COMINT companies. The units, known as Signal Service Companies, went into France as follows:[34]

Assault Corps	Signal Service Company in Support
V	3250th
VII	3251st
XIX	3252nd

The experience of the 3252nd Signal Service Company exemplifies the organizational structure and the COMINT doctrine of the last year of the war in Europe.[35]

The 3252nd was organized by First Lieutenant Albert Jones, who commanded the unit through the end of the war. He obtained his cadre from the 124th SRI Company, stationed in the U.K., and filled the unit with personnel from other SRI companies and with men arriving from the U.S. Rapid training and requisition of equipment followed. The unit reached France five days after D-Day with a complement of 7 officers and 121 enlisted men. The unit had intercept operators, cryptanalysts, DF personnel, and translators. Their mission was, and remained, to intercept and fully process German army tactical communications in direct support of Corps' combat operations. The company was directly under the Corps' or Army Signal Office for general administration and signal support. However, intelligence requirements came from G-2, XIX Corps, and the resulting COMINT was furnished directly to Corps G-2 by telephone, messenger, or, very rarely, radio. As the company was able to read the intercepted German field codes, total processing was possible. The company remained "on the line" until the German surrender. At no time did Lieutenant Jones receive any instruction or requirements from the CSO, the MIS, or the

MIS representatives (3-U.S.) in London. He was not aware of the SSO-SLU system or that high-level ciphers were being exploited.[36]

By late summer 1944 there were nine SRI companies in the theater supporting Headquarters, Twelfth Army Group, and the numbered armies. There were also fifteen Signal Service Companies supporting the various corps.[37] Most of these units were under the administrative control of the appropriate Army or Corps Signal Officer, but the real working relationship was with, and the operational direction came from, the G-2. There was also Colonel Bicher's Signals Intelligence Service, European Theater of Operations,

SID ETOUSA, Headquarters, SI Division, 59 Weymouth Street

U.S. Army (SIS ETOUSA), which had controlled the training and disposition of the COMINT companies prior to D-Day. Now, an operating arm of SIS ETOUSA, SID (Signals Intelligence Division) ETOUSA came into the picture. The advance party of SID ETOUSA, known as SID "D," actually controlled the operations of two SRI companies in France – the 114th and 118th. Other SID parties remained in the U.K., one at Bletchley Park SID, and SID "D" had varied responsibilities toward the tactical COMINT units and the commands – technical support, personnel support, and staff guidance.

It was the closest thing in the European campaign to a centralized control of tactical COMINT.[38] Colonel Bicher's staff, unlike the SRIs and Signal Service Companies, was in contact with the 3-U.S. and SSO organization. His organization also remained as the link between the field commands and the Signal Corps/SSA for personnel and equipment requirements.

Tactical COMINT units in Italy remained under the control of the 849th SIS (See chapter 2). As the Mediterranean theater was under British command, ULTRA seems to have come directly to General Mark Clark from the SLU. U.S. Army SSO personnel surveyed the situation there, but there seem to have been very few SSOs permanently assigned to the theater. Tactical COMINT in Italy was characterized by the same provisional and ad hoc arrangements made in France – smaller units made up of SRI company personnel combined with 849th SIS specialists.[39]

But it was to the Pacific and Asia that the War Department turned its centralization efforts. In March 1945, General Bissell, in replying to General Handy's caustic statements on G-2 resistance to the creation of ANCIB (see chapter 7), suggested immediate consolidation within the War Department of all Army COMINT centers and COMINT units.[40] Thus, the SRIs and related units, CBB, and SIS New Delhi would be placed under SSA control. And the latter was already under MIS operational control. General Bissell went even further and suggested that all U.S. COMINT might be put "under a single agency placed in whatever position in the executive branch of the government [that] may appear most suitable."[41] This echoed the earlier proposal of Assistant Secretary McCloy.

The general discussion of Army COMINT centralization was renewed during March–April 1945. No decision was reached although Brigadier General Henry I. Hodes, who had replaced Otto Nelson as assistant deputy chief of staff, observed that General MacArthur would have to be "sold" on any centralization plan.[42]

The impetus for a decision came not from within the War Department but from Lieutenant General Dan Sultan, commanding general of the India-Burma theater. In a message to General Marshall, Sultan proposed that the War Department establish an agency to coordinate all Army "intercept and signal intelligence agencies in the Pacific, China-India-Burma theaters...."[43] General Sultan suggested that this agency should be located in Luzon.

The initial reply to General Sultan was merely one of acknowledgement and assurance that the matter was already under consideration.[44] General Bissell was prompted, however, to review the suggestion that he had made to the DCS in March.[45]

The chief signal officer reentered the policy struggle as his comments on the March-April memoranda and messages had been requested by General Hodes. Not without caustic and perceptive humor, General Ingles noted that the ACS, G-2's proposals seemed to suggest that the Army should adopt the Navy's mode of centralized COMINT.[46] As the Navy's centralization was under the director of naval communications, he wrote G-2 could hardly be recommending the same procedure for the Army. General Ingles repeated his previous position that the Signal Corps should run Army COMINT, especially during the postwar period when funds for this type of activity might not be available to G-2. The existing situation with the Signal Corps running COMINT activity through G-2 operational supervision seemed satisfactory. Ingles also found that the role of the SRI companies was misunderstood (by MIS). Their purpose was to provide immediate tactical intelligence for theater, Army group, and Army commanders, and, thus, these units should not be transferred to SSA. On the other hand, General Ingles was in accord that all high-level COMINT should now be centralized in SSA.

The response from Bissell and Clarke was that the SRIs should indeed be under central control because their operations had been rife with problems and inefficiency.[47]

On 8 May the War Department went directly to the theater commanders with the proposal that all Army COMINT units engaged in the war against Japan should be centralized. This would mean consolidation of SSA, the SRIs, RSMs, and theater signal intelligence services (i.e., CBB and SIS New Delhi).[48] The purpose of this action was to ensure fullest Army-Navy-British coordination, to avoid duplication, and to make best use of scarce skills, especially Japanese linguists. Comments were solicited.

Generals Wedemeyer and Sultan expressed their approval although the latter opined that the personnel involved should remain under the theater commander.[49] General MacArthur, whose operations were far more affected, did not concur.[50] He objected to "absentee control" of COMINT from thousands of miles away and the likely disruption of CBB operations and the excellent CBB-theater headquarters relationship. Most important, he might not get COMINT as fast as needed.

In all this, General Sultan's original proposal for having the centralized COMINT headquarters *in Luzon* seems to have been lost. Undoubtedly that would have appealed to General MacArthur. General Bissell gathered arguments to counter General MacArthur's fears, and in a paper prepared for General Bissell (probably by General Clarke) two rather interesting points were made.[51] First, more Japanese army traffic was being intercepted at MS-2, Two Rock Ranch, California, than anywhere else. This material was processed at Arlington Hall Station and sent to the theaters. Second, though CBB considered alone was a good operation, its activities were "wasteful" since "they are uncoordinated with other much more extensive signal intelligence operations of the U.S. Army and the British."

The 1944 Signal Corps-MIS struggle was now to be repeated, this time involving disputes between various parts of the General Staff as well as MacArthur's headquarters (now known as Army Forces Pacific-AFPAC). Once again it is too tedious to include every detail of the conflicting opinions.

General Bissell, having reviewed the theater comments, two of three being favorable, proposed sending messages to the Pacific-Asia commanders implementing the War Department centralization plan. General John Hull, chief of the Operations Division of War Department General Staff (WDGS), did not concur. Rather, the SRIs and the related units should, he said, remain under theater control while the "cryptanalytic bureaus of the fixed station type" should come under War Department control.[52] General Hull put his position and that of General Handy this way: "We must provide the field commander with the means under his direct control of obtaining signal intelligence as pertains to the area under his influence. This, I am sure, is the principle upon which General Handy bases his objection to your proposal. . . ."

In line with General Hull's position, new messages to the commands were drafted in MIS and forwarded to Operations Division (OPD) for consideration on 14 June.[53] The revised messages were never sent, for reasons shown below, but are sufficiently significant to outline here. The theater commanders were to be told that the SRIs, RSMs, and Signal Service Companies would remain under their command. Fixed stations and personnel and facilities devoted to high-level cryptanalysis and high-level TA would be placed under the command of chief, MIS. The SRIs and related units would accept intercept missions assigned by MIS, when not otherwise occupied. Subject to the authority of ANCIB, the ACS, G-2 would be responsible for coordination of Army COMINT, in the Pacific-Asia area, with the U. S. Navy and Allies. Specific orders would be issued progressively.

All of this would have meant placing CBB and SIS New Delhi under MIS but leaving the intercept units under the commanders. Ambiguities were not lacking. In any event, War Department action was defended.

At this point General Bissell departed for London presumably for conferences on the postwar role of the MIS in Europe. While he was there, General Akin sent a message to the War Department suggesting that General Bissell attend a COMINT conference in the Philippines to work out policy differences. In spite of General Clarke's advisory to the contrary, General Bissell proceeded to MacArthur's headquarters.[54] There he was won over by General MacArthur, and with the latter's concurrence, he radioed a new position to the War Department on 5 July.[55] He reported that General MacArthur considered that the creation of a worldwide, centrally controlled Army COMINT organization was essential but that AFPAC units should not be absorbed in such a system until the "decisive operations" in the Pacific were completed. Until then the AFPAC COMINT units were to retain their existing organizational structure. Bissell reported that MacArthur was agreeable to continuing electrical transmission to AHS of all Japanese traffic intercepted by AFPAC, and that he wanted to receive solution data and results by the fastest means. The AFPAC units would contribute to overall intercept coverage to the maximum extent possible.

Bissell's message was poorly received by Generals Marshall, Handy, and Clarke. General Marshall's reply to General Bissell is quoted in full:[56]

> Your summary of the MacArthur-Bissell conference of July 4 and 5 leave situation in status quo. This is understood here to be reversal of views you had when you left the United States and that you no longer recommend centralization at this time. If such is case do you desire to withdraw your previous recommendations and your proposed plan for centralization?

General Clarke followed this with a personal message to General Bissell urging him to hold to his previous stand and that "your position both personal and official will be much stronger if you adhere to your recommendation and are overruled by higher authority, than it will be if you withdraw your previous recommendation."[57]

General MacArthur's stand and General Bissell's acceptance thereof can hardly be faulted. While MacArthur was not told of the existence of the atomic bomb until shortly before the first one was dropped on Hiroshima (6 August), he had probably concluded at the time of his conference with Bissell that a sudden Japanese surrender was quite possible soon. There was COMINT to that effect.[58] It would therefore have been unreasonable to reorganize AFPAC intelligence in the midst of decisive decisions. But then General MacArthur had always been resistant to War Department interference.

General Bissell, in a follow-up message on 10 July, replying to the criticism from Marshall and Clarke, had some interesting observations.[59] He was prepared to modify his position based on what he had learned in the field. He still favored a centralized, Washington-controlled COMINT organization, but "such a system would produce maximum results only if fully accepted and loyally supported by Army signal intelligence elements in MacArthur's area." As MacArthur had enough to worry about, said Bissell, the War Department ought to assist him in the manner that he (MacArthur) thought most helpful.

Two paragraphs of General Bissell's message provide such a useful, if highly judgmental, historical perspective of COMINT in the SWPA that they are quoted in full:

> Akin has built a signal intelligence empire in Central Bureau which in my opinion, judged by results in other areas and by other agencies, is not very efficient. It must have much support from Washington if it is to produce. We have been and will continue to give it all possible support.
>
> MacArthur has told me that he has been very well satisfied with the intelligence furnished to him for his operations and stated that he has always known the enemy's strength, dispositions, and usually enemy intentions in sufficient time to take appropriate action. MacArthur is not much concerned with where the intelligence comes from as long as he continues to receive promptly all that can be provided from every source.

A month later, on 14 August, Japan agreed to surrender. No time was wasted in MIS, and the next day General Bissell wrote the chief of staff calling his attention once more to the centralization of Army COMINT.[60] He reminded General Marshall that General MacArthur had agreed to centralization when the war ended. General Bissell recommended that the chief of staff immediately approve centralization of Army COMINT and COMSEC activities, and that directives to the field commanders be issued. The approval came from the office of the deputy chief of staff, after OPD concurrence, on 23 August.[61]

During the first weeks of September, implementing directives were prepared by MIS. By Adjutant General's Office (AGO) letter of 6 September 1945, the Army Security Agency (ASA) was established effective 15 September 1945. ASA as a War Department agency was to comprise all COMINT and COMSEC units of the Army including SSA and Second Signal Service; the SRIs, RSMs, Signal Service Companies, and detachments; RI platoons and all other units and activities performing COMINT functions. ASA would be responsible for all Army COMINT and COMSEC.[62] On 19 September the command relationship was described:[63]

> Command of the Army Security Agency will be exercised by the War Department through the chief, Military Intelligence Service, who is specifically charged with the direct supervision of the Army Security Agency.

So the Clarke-Bissell formula of complete and direct MIS control of all Army COMINT and COMSEC came into being. The creation of ASA was no more than a name change because the MIS had intended to exercise its centralized control through an enlarged SSA.

DEVELOPMENTS IN NAVY COMINT ORGANIZATION IN WASHINGTON AND THE PACIFIC

A certain amount of repetition may seem to be present in this section. This is because the Navy's COMINT position in the Pacific was, by late 1944, augmented by full Army cooperation. Thus, Army COMINT and the role of the USAAF COMINT units is reintroduced.

OP-20-G underwent a major reorganization in November 1944 and also received additional duties. Effective 6 November, Joseph N. Wenger, recently promoted to captain, became head of OP-20-G as assistant director (naval communications) for communications intelligence. Captain Kinney, until then head of 20-G, became OIC of the Washington Supplementary Activity and the Naval Communications Annex.[64] This command change gave final and formal recognition to the fact that Captain Wenger had been running 20-G since the replacement of Captain Safford in early 1942.

Captain Joseph N. Wenger, assistant director naval communications, Op-20-G

A useful organizational principle was also recognized – the Washington COMINT center, Negat, hereafter known as Supplementary Radio Activity, Washington. OP-20-G would be one of the Navy's COMINT centers, theoretically on a par with FRUPAC, carrying out tasks assigned by the now separate 20-G. The "new" OP-20-G retained staff and supervisory functions but few operational ones. In spite of the odd renumbering of the Supplementary Radio Activity Washington as OP-20-3, which seemed to place it somewhere under OP-20, the DNC, rather than 20G, Wenger's authority was clear: he would "plan and operate the entire communication intelligence organization."[65] Or as the final division order stated, he had "supervision of the entire U.S. naval communication intelligence organization."[66] OP-20-3 in reality served as more than another center as it carried out many of the worldwide control and coordination functions, as well as the COMINCH/CNO-support COMINT production that OP-20-G had performed. The bulk of the Washington-based 20-G people went into the new OP-20-3, making the change somewhat illusory.

At the same time, by authority of Admiral King, a Pacific strategic intelligence unit was established within OP-20-3. It was to study, compile, and disseminate strategic information, derived from COMINT, pertaining to the war to the Pacific.[67] This unit, known as OP-20-3-G-51, Strategic Information Coordinator, seems to have been created to ensure that sources of strategic information would be available at, or coordinated from, one place. This meant appropriate contact with 3-GI, F-22, OP-16-FE, within the naval intelligence structure, and externally with MIS and the British. Needless to say, the prestige of the naval COMINT organization was further enhanced by this move.[68]

The OP-20-G COMINT communication network continued to expand to meet the Navy's own needs and to support the BRUSA agreement. There were important developments during the spring and summer of 1944. In May it became possible to exchange encrypted raw traffic by radioteletype between the Washington and Pearl Harbor COMINT centers as well as the advanced center at Kwajalein. By the end of the year, Navy COMINT sites at Adak, Bainbridge, Guam, and Melbourne were involved in this radioteletype setup.[69] Also in May the Army made available to 20-G certain communications facilities (primarily radioteletype) between San Francisco, Hawaii, and Australia. At the same time, the Army gave the 20-G a duplex radioteletype circuit on its Washington-London multichannel circuit.[70] Thus 20-G had access to and/or controlled a vast COMINT communications network. This was all added to the important and long existing CONUS landline teletype system that linked 20-G to its primary intercept sites at Chatham, Massachusetts, Bainbridge, Washington, and to BSC, New York.

There were new developments in the field by late 1944. Pearl Harbor (FRUPAC) became the sole major COMINT center in the Pacific. The former center FRUMEL had been downgraded because of changing conditions. FRUPAC continued to serve the commander in chief, Pacific and his subordinate elements in the Pacific via an elaborate intelligence gathering, analysis, and dissemination system (CIC-JICPOA-fleet intelligence officer).

After the capture of Guam in August 1944, plans were made to create a forward joint-service COMINT correlation center on the island. Commander Linwood S. Howeth, a 20-G veteran, was appointed to supervise this operation.[71]

This operation, known as RAGFOR (Radio Analysis Group, Forward) seems to have started up by late 1944. A CICFOR (Combat Intelligence Center, Forward) was in operation on 15 January 1945.[72] Both RAGFOR and CIC were Navy controlled but interservice in manning and overall operation. They were established as forward elements of FRUPAC and CIC-JICPOA, and their role became extremely important when Admiral Nimitz himself moved to Guam in early 1945.

RAGFOR was charged by CINCPAC/CINCPOA with examination of all "local" intercept accomplished at Guam (or subordinate areas) by the two Army SRI companies, the 130th and the 111th (a detachment thereof); the Air Force's Eighth RSM; a Second Signal Service Detachment operating MS-11; and the Navy's own intercept site, Station A. From this intercept, RAGFOR would select certain high-priority items, especially relating to Japanese air operations, and conduct the necessary processing and exploitation of "any enemy low-level cryptographic systems capable of being processed in the field. . . ."[73] The processed material would then be furnished to the local evaluating and disseminating agency and to the Army and Navy COMINT organizations in Washington and Hawaii.[74] The local evaluation-disseminating units were CICFOR and the SSO representatives. The duties of CICFOR went beyond handling the RAGFOR production and included dealing with COMINT from CIC Hawaii, and other Army and Navy sources.[75]

That these activities on Guam were truly cooperative and joint-service is apparent from the identification of the intercept sources serving RAGFOR. Further, CICFOR had both Army and Navy watch officers, teletype operators, and clerks. The importance of this experience was not lost on Commander Richard W. Emory, the CICFOR commanding officer, who wrote at the time of the Japanese surrender:[76]

> War experience has proved it essential that the Army and Navy combine their CIC personnel and information to form a single intelligence organization.... At CIC Pearl since August 1944 and at CICFOR during its brief existence, the Army and Navy have functioned as one....
>
> War experience has proved the absolute necessity of combining all sources of information into a single intelligence product.

Joint service developments were also present in the Philippines though not on so extensive or formal a basis. There an SSO was assigned to the headquarters Seventh Fleet at Tolosa, Leyte, in January 1945. It was the experience of SSOs in the Philippines, especially those supporting FEAF and its subordinates that the ULTRA available from the Navy was "the primary source of intelligence of immediate tactical use."[77] The experience there suggested to one SSO, as it had to Commander Emory, that a single "ULTRA Agency" ought to be established.[78]

Had it been necessary to invade Japan, there were plans to establish a COMINT center on Okinawa under USAAF auspices and in connection with RAGFOR and Central Bureau in Luzon.[79] This would have involved "low-level" COMINT and might or might not have developed into an all-service advanced center. The Navy planned to support the invasion of Japan with the existing COMINT facilities and some twelve intercept and analysis teams afloat on flagships. These were to provide early warning of air attacks.

This final look at Navy COMINT policy and organization, though brief, may help to again emphasize the relatively consistent developments within that service, based on policies established early in the war by highest-level directive and tacit understanding. Naval COMINT remained under the DNC in Washington, without interference from any other organization. At the same time the center in the Pacific served Admiral Nimitz according to his needs. This could not have been otherwise considering the rapid growth of his reputation and his good standing with Washington.

Notes

1. AG 312.1, 14 October 1943, Security of ULTRA Dexter Intelligence. A copy of this regulation, and the other ULTRA regulations, is filed in *SSO History*, vol. 1, behind Tab A.

2. Seven-page manuscript entitled *History of the Operations of Special Security Officers Attached to Field Commands*, undated, no author, at the beginning of *SSO History*, vol. 1. I have not found a detailed account of

Colonel Clarke's trip. While it is certain from this source that he met with General MacArthur, I am less sure of his visits to Hawaii and CBI. In a letter to the author, Clarke mentions being in the CBI in December 1943.

3. Ibid. Various manuscript accounts in vol. 4 of *SSO History*.

4. Message #BG290, no date, For Clarke from O'Connell, Eyes Alone of Marshall from MacArthur, ACSI #33.

5. See various War Department papers of early July 1944, filed in ACSI #33.

6. Manuscript of Major John R. Thompson in Tab A, vol. 3, *SSO History*.

7. Manuscript entitled *Report of Special Security Operations in the China-Burma-India Theater,* etc., no date, no author, vol. 5, *SSO History*.

8. Letter to the author by Carter W. Clarke; Nelson's own book *National Security and the General Staff,* 526 ff.; Bidwell, *History of the Military Intelligence Division,* Part Five, 12–13, 15, 26, 215 ff.

9. Nelson, 526 ff.

10. *History of Special Branch,* 52, 60–63.

11. Part 3(?) of *History of Special Branch,* a document that deals with the period 1944–45. The author of this document is unknown, NSAH.

12. Because of the top secret nature of this work of the McCloy Board, there is no discussion of it in Nelson's *National Security and the General Staff.*

13. I have not seen the McCloy Board report. But see Memorandum from Bissell to chief of staff, 15 June 1944, subject: Reorganization of the Military Intelligence Division, WDGS, 23 March 1944, in ACSI #49, and also the Winkler-Bidwell material in ACSI #6, (especially 9–11), (classified).

14. McCloy to chief of staff, 20 June 1944, ACSI #49 (classified).

15. Memorandum from Nelson to Bissell, 22 June 1944, ACSI #49 (classified).

16. Memorandum from Bissell to DCS (drafted by Carter W. Clarke), subject: Intercept Facilities, 11 July 1944, ACSI #49 (classified).

17. In a subsequent memorandum (Bissell to DCS, Clarke drafter, 14 July 1944, ACSI #49), there is an accounting of the personnel to be affected by the transfer. As this is a statement of SSA/Second Signal Service strength as of July 1944, it is reproduced here to show how large this Washington-controlled portion of Army COMINT had become and that the transfer of personnel to MIS was no small matter:

STATION	OFFICERS	WARRANT OFFICERS	E.M.	CIVILIANS
AHS	729	4	1,459	5,853
VHFS (MS-1)	39	3	995	
Two Rock Ranch (MS-2)	20	3	578	
Miami (MS-3)	6		111	
Asmara (MS-4)	5	1	70	
Hawaii (MS-5)	7	2	164	
Amchitga (MS-6)	3		44	
Fairbanks (MS-7)	3		41	

Long Island (MS-9)	0	1	12	
Reseda, Cal. (MS-10)	0	1	12	
San Francisco (Signal Center COMINT Communications)	3	1	73	
Hq Alaskan Dept.	1	0	0	
TOTALS	818	17	3,600	5,853

18. Memorandum from Somerwell to chief of staff, 25 July 1944 (classified), and attached copy of memorandum from Ingles to ASF, same date, all in ACSI #49 (classified).

19. Various papers in ACSI #49.

20. Memorandum from McCloy to McNarney, 22 August 1944, ACSI #49 (classified).

21. Memorandum from Bissell to DCS, delivered to General Nelson by Colonel McCormack, 8 September 1944, subject: Intercept Facilities, ACSI #49 (classified). Attached to this is a paper entitled *Amplification of Reasons for the Transfer of Signal Security Agency from Signal Corps to the Military Intelligence Service* (classified).

22. Draft agreement prepared by CSO for signature of CSO and ACS, G-2, 30 November 1944, ACSI #49 (classified).

23. See Part 3(?) *History of Special Branch*.

24. See especially memorandum from Clarke to Bissell, 30 November 1944, for General Ingle's approach to Clarke and the latter's avoidance of the CSO.

25. Draft paper prepared by General Ingles, 4 December 1944, ACSI #49 (classified).

26. Memorandum from Bissell to DCS, 7 December 1944, subject: Signal Security Agency and Second Signal Service Battalion, ACSI #49 (classified). This memorandum acknowledges General Handy's verbal instructions.

27. Memorandum from Handy to ACS, G-2 and CSO thru CGASF, 10 December 1944, ACSI #49.

28. Memorandum from Bissell to CSO thru CGASF, 15 December 1944, ACSI #49.

29. Various memorandums and messages in ACSI #49.

30. Memorandum by General Stoner prepared for OCMH, quoted in *The Outcome*, 615, footnote 17.

31. *History of Special Branch*, 60–62, ACSI #2.

32. In a letter to the author, General Clarke has said that General Marshall delayed centralization in Europe because of British pressure. Clarke said that this is "one hell of a story" but that he would not disclose it. If this is the case, it is undoubtedly documented in some War Department records not seen by me.

33. Howe, Mss., chapter 7, no page numbers. Dr. Howe's study will be the authoritative account of U.S. Army tactical COMINT in Europe. I have drawn heavily on his work.

34. Howe, Mss., chapter 9, no page numbers.

35. This account of the 3252nd is based on interviews by the author and Henry F. Schorreck of Mr. Albert Jones, U.S. Army (Ret) and an NSA employee.

36. Jones was an SIS veteran who had been a charter member, as an enlisted man, of the Second Signal Service Company in 1939. His COMINT experience predated the activation of that unit. After commissioning in 1942, he went to the U.K. for assignment to Colonel Bicher's SIS ETOUSA.

37. Howe, Mss. chapter 9, no page.

38. See Howe, Mss, chapter 9 and elsewhere for the ongoing role of SIS ETOUSA, SID, and SID "D."

39. Howe, Mss, chapter 7. I have found no reports from permanent SSOs in Italy.

40. Memorandums from Bissell to Handy, Carter Clarke drafter, 11 March 1945, subject: ANCIB, ACSI #4, (classified).

41. Ibid.

42. See various memoranda in ACSI #4, March–April 1945.

43. Message #CRA8653, to Marshall from Sultan, 12 April 1945, ACSI #4 (classified).

44. Message #WAR67602 drafted by Carter Clarke, for Sultan from Marshall, 12 April 1945, ACSI #4.

45. Memorandum from Bissell to DCS, 14 April 1945, subject: Centralized Control of Signal Intelligence Activities in the Pacific and Far East, ACSI #4 (classified).

46. Memorandum from Ingles to Handy, 27 April 1945, ACSI #4 (classified).

47. Memorandum from Bissell to DCS (Clarke drafter), 5 May 1945, ACSI #4.

48. Message #WARX78834 for MacArthur, Sultan, and Wedemeyer from Marshall, drafted by Carter Clarke, 8 May 1945, ACSI #4 (classified).

49. These replies are in a memorandum from Bissell to chief of staff, 1 June 1945, ACSI #4 (classified).

50. Ibid.

51. Ibid., and in an attached paper, which is an elaboration to the basic memorandum.

52. Memorandum from Hull to Bissell, 7 June 1945, subject: Centralized Control of Signal Intelligence Units, ACSI #4 (classified).

53. Memorandum from Bissell to Hull, 14 June 1945, and drafts of messages, ACSI #4 (classified).

54. Memorandum for General Bissell from Colonel Hilles (MIS, London) quoting a message received from Carter Clarke, 19 June 1945, ACSI #40. Clarke recommended to Bissell that he force a command decision at the War Department rather than visit General Akin (classified).

55. Message from Bissell for Marshall and Handy quoted in memorandum from Carter Clarke to Handy, 5 July 1945, ACSI #4 (classified).

56. This message is quoted in an unsigned memorandum of 7 July 1945. The message had been released at 1810, 6 July, ACSI #40 (classified).

57. This message is quoted in an unsigned memorandum of 7 July 1945. The message was released at 1945, 6 July, ACSI #40 (classified).

58. D. Clayton James, *The Years of MacArthur,* vol. 2, (Boston, 1975), 770–776.

59. Message from Bissell to Clarke for Marshall and Handy, quoted in memorandum from Clarke to Handy, 10 July 1945, ACSI #4 (classified).

60. Memorandum from Bissell to chief of staff, 15 August 1945, subject: Centralized Control of Signal Intelligence Activities, ACSI #4.

61. Approval is in the form of signatures on Ibid. of General Hode (for Handy) and General Hull of OPD.

62. Memorandum from Bissell to Adjutant General, 4 September 1945, subject: Establishment of the Army Security Agency; AGO letter 6 September 1945 to commanding generals of the USAAF, AGF, ASF; commander in chief AFPAC; commanding generals of theaters; Defense Commands; Alaskan department; MDW; independent commands, ACSI #4.

63. AGO letter 19 September 1945 to the Chief of ASA and Chief of MIS, ACSI #4.

64. Memorandum for Captain Kinney and Captain Wenger from Captain J. V. Murphy, the deputy director of communications, 2 November 1944; also Communications Division Order No. 106-44, 13 Nov. 1944, signed by Captain Roy A. Gano, ADNC, OP-20-G Organization Folder.

65. The Murphy memorandum.

66. Order No. 106-44.

67. Supplement A (COMINT) to *History of Naval Intelligence*, A-11 (an interim study prepared by Captain Packard).

68. The functions of the organizations with the naval intelligence structure may be reviewed here. 3-GI, formerly OP-20-GI, was the intelligence correlating, reporting, and dissemination subdivision of the naval COMINT organization. The Far Eastern Section of ONI was officially known as OP-16-FE. As has been explained, OP-16-FE lost its role in COMINT evaluation in 1943. F-22 was the Pacific branch of F-20, the Combat Intelligence Division. Perhaps Pacific strategic intelligence was placed under 20-G because F-22 was properly fully involved in immediate, operational intelligence. In any case, the best information was COMINT, so strategic COMINT production and compilation were combined in the same place.

69. *GC History*, 46–47 (classified).

70. *GC History*, 48 (classified).

71. By CINCPAC/CINCPOA memorandum, serial 000793, 9 September 1944 (not seen) referenced in a CINCPAC/CINCPOA memorandum of 9 January 1945 addressed to the commander, Forward Area, Central Pacific; commanding general, U.S. Army Forces Pacific Ocean Areas; Island Commander, Guam; OIC, Joint Communications Activities, Guam, in *Catalogue*, 2.c.(14).

72. Ibid. See also memorandum OIC CICFOR to OIC Supplementary Radio Station ABLE, 20 August 1945, subject: CICFOR History, etc. Manuscript in vol. 4, Tab F, *SSO History*.

73. The 9 January 1945 CINCPAC/CINCPOA memorandum.

74. Ibid. The Army, of course, did not have a COMINT center in Hawaii, but SSOs were there.

75. The OIC CICFOR memorandum.

76. Ibid.

77. Manuscript report of Captain B. J. Merriam, Tab B, vol. 3, *SSO History*.

78. Ibid.

79. AG Letter 312.1, 24 June 1945, and attached paper headed "Conference on Low Level Signal Intelligence," same date, *Catalog* 5.i.

Glossary of Abbreviations

ACNO	Assistant Chief of Naval Operations
ACS	Assistant Chief of Staff
ADNC	Assistant Director of Naval Communications
AFPAC	Army Forces Pacific
AFSA	Armed Forces Security Agency
AHS	Arlington Hall Station
ANCIB	Army-Navy Communications Intelligence Board
ANCICC	Army-Navy COMINT Coordinating Committee
ASA	Army Security Agency
ASF	Army Services Forces
BP	Bletchley Park
BRUSA	British-U. S.
BSC	British Security Coordination
CA	Cryptanalysis
CBB	Central Brisbane Bureau
CBI	China-Burma-India (theater of operations)
CIC	Combat Information center
CICFOR	Combat Intelligence Center, Forward
CINCPAC	Commander in Chief, Pacific
CINCPOA	Commander in Chief Pacific ocean area
COI	Coordinator of Information
COMINCH	Commander in Chief U. S. Fleet
COMINT	Communications intelligence
COMSEC	Communications security
CONUS	Continental United States
CNO	Chief of Naval Operations
CSO	Chief Signal Officer
CSS	Chief of Secret Service
CZ	Canal Zone
DF	Direction finding

DMI	Director of Military Intelligence
DNC	Director of Naval Communications
DNI	Director of Naval Intelligence
ETOUSA	European Theater of Operations U.S. Army
FEAF	Far East Air Force
FBI	Federal Bureau of Investigation
FCC	Federal Communications Commission
FRUMEL	Fleet Radio Unit Melbourne (Australia)
FRUPAC	Fleet Radio Unit Pacific (Hawaii)
FUSA	First United States Army
GC&CS	Government Code and Cipher School
GHQ	General Headquarters
ICPOA	Intelligence Center Pacific Ocean Area
IIC	Interdepartmental Intelligence Conference
JCS	Joint Chiefs of Staff
JIC	Joint Intelligence Committee
JICPOA	Joint Intelligence Center Pacific Ocean Area
JMA	Japanese Military Attaché
JN	Japanese naval
JNA	Japanese Naval Attaché
MI	Military intelligence
MID	Military Intelligence Division
MIS	Military Intelligence Service
MS	Monitoring station
NDO	National Defense Organization
OCSigO	Office of Chief Signal Officer
ONI	Office of Naval Intelligence
OPD	Operations division
OSS	Office of Strategic Services
RAAF	Royal Australian Air Force
RAGFOR	Radio Analysis Group, Forward
RCN	Royal Canadian Navy

RES	Reserved
RFP	Radio fingerprinting
RI	Radio intelligence
RID	Radio Intelligence Division
RN	Royal Navy
RSM	Radio Squadrons Mobile
RSS	Radio Security Service
SHAEF	Supreme Headquarters Army Expeditionary Force
SI	Special intelligence
SID ETOUSA	Signal Intelligence Division European Theater of Operations, U. S. Army
SIGINT	Signals intelligence
SIS	Special Intelligence Service
SIS ETOUSA	Signal Intelligence Service European Theater of Operations, U. S. Army
SLU	Special Liaison Unit
SMI	Safeguarding Military Information
SRI	Signal Radio Intelligence
SSA	Signal Security Agency
SSR	Special Security Representatives
SSC	Signal Service Company
SSD	Signal Security Division
SSO	Special Security Officer
SSS	Signal Security Service
SWPA	Southwest Pacific Area
TA	Traffic analysis
USCG	United States Coast Guard
VCNO	Vice Chief of Naval Operations
VHFS	Vint Hill Farm Station
WDGS	War Department General Staff
WEC	Wireless Experimental Center

Sources

1. Unpublished Official Records

a. National Archives.

Record Group 173, "Federal Communications Commission: Radio Intelligence Division." (Portions of RG173 remain classified. The author had full access to all records.)

Record Group 165 "Military Intelligence Division."

b. NSA Historical Collection (NSAHC) maintained in the Center for Cryptologic History (CCH), S542.

(1) Army Records

A Chronology of Cooperation Between the SSA and the London Offices of GC&CS, prepared under the direction of the chief signal officer, 2 June 1945. A compilation of documents, mostly photocopies.

Cooperation with GC&CS 1940–45. A folder containing many ribbon copy memoranda.

British Liaison 1940–45, vol. 1. A folder containing many ribbon copy memoranda and agreements. It supplements the previous two collections.

History of the Central Bureau Brisbane: Technical Records. In two parts. Prepared at the Army Security Agency, 1949.

History of the Signal Security Agency in World War II. Prepared at the Army Security Agency, undated. See especially volumes 1 through 4. This is an extremely valuable work prepared by numerous contributors. It is, however, not greatly concerned with policy, liaison, or MIS, and any hint of controversy is absent.

Signal Security Division Annual Report for the Fiscal Year 1943.

SSA Folder 311.5 CXG-114 BII. This is a folder containing messages between SSA and Central Bureau Brisbane mainly during 1943.

Historical Reports of Monitoring Stations MS-2 to MS-10. These reports, which are not consistent in depth of content or general organization, are dated up to June 1944.

History of the Special Project Branch, SIS ETOUSA, also known as the *BEECHNUT Report*. This was prepared by Colonel Frank B. Rowlett in 1945.

History of Special Security Operations Overseas

Volume 1:	History of Supervisory Activities, MIS
Volume 2:	History of European Theater
Volume 3:	Armed Forces - Pacific Area
Volume 4:	Pacific Ocean Areas
Volume 5:	India-Burma and China Theaters

These five volumes are a collection of memoranda from the various SSOs to MIS in which these officers describe their experiences and make evaluations and occasional recommendations. Most were written in late 1945. This is an incredible collection of primary source material for Army COMINT history 1943–45. Volumes 1, 3, and 4 are ribbon copy and appear to be the only copies in existence. This compilation was directed by General Carter W. Clarke.

ACSI (Assistant Chief of Staff Intelligence) Books. These are numbered folders marked "ACSI #2," etc. The books were obtained in 1972 by the Cryptologic History Department from ACSI-USASSG (U.S. Army Special Security Group) files, the Pentagon, and were photocopied. The books contain MIS correspondence, studies, and interoffice notes from 1940 (pre-MIS) to 1945, relating to Army COMINT. This is an unparalleled course of information, and the author has heavily depended on the hundreds of documents therein.

Winkler-Bidwell Papers. This is actually a part of ACSI Book #6 and is in the form of a document headed "Answers to Questions Provided by Colonel Bruce W. Bidwell." It was prepared by Mr. Winkler (an ACSI and later DIA employee) in, perhaps, 1957. Colonel Bidwell was then writing an official history of MID (see below). Colonel Bidwell provided an excellent outline of MIS Special Branch operations 1942–45 and of the steps leading to the creation of ASA.

Report on E Operations of the GC&CS at Bletchley Park. Submitted to SSA by Mr. William F. Friedman, 12 August 1943.

Special Branch Histories. There are three separate items which I have numbered as follows:

Part 1 is *Origin and Functions of MIS Special Branch* prepared by Colonel Al McCormack, deputy chief of the branch, in the form of a memorandum to Carter W. Clarke, 15 April 1943. This is a fascinating, personalized, and interpretive account of great historic value. It is included in ACSI Book #2.

Part 2 is entitled *History of the Special Branch, MIS*. It is undated and more formal than Part I and covers the period from spring 1942 to June 1944, no date, no author (but quite possibly Colonel McCormack). It is found in ACSI Book #2.a.

Part 3 is entitled *History of Special Branch MIS, June 1944–September 1945*. Again there is no author or date. It too is found in ACSI Book #2.

U.S. Cryptologic Activities 1941–46, Part 2: Intercept and Processing. This was prepared by the Historian, NSA, 12 May 1953. There does not seem to be a Part 1. This study is by no means complete but does contain a great deal of data on traffic volume and the evolution of the various monitoring stations of SSA.

Reminiscences of Lieutenant Colonel Howard R. Brown. A manuscript prepared under the auspices of the chief signal officer, August 1945.

(2) Navy and Coast Guard Records

FBI-Coast Guard General File. This is a folder from Op-20-G files containing a major collection of COMINT-related correspondence regarding Op-20-G, ONI, Coast Guard, FBI, Army, FCC, and the British. Many of the items are ribbon copy. This was the most valuable source for the Navy view of COMINT policy and administration, especially 1941–43. It contains the oft-cited Kramer memorandum.

FCC and RI 1943–45. This is an Op-20-G correspondence file relating primarily to Navy-FCC COMINT relations from 1942–45.

Op-20-G Organization File

Op-20-G Organization post-1943 File

Op-20-G File

RI Dissemination File

GC Section History (tentative). This was written during 1945–46. It is an extremely detailed, if confusing, account of naval COMINT communications.

Wenger File – Canadian Y Organization

GY History File. This is a ribbon copy draft history of Op-20-G's attack on various Japanese codes and ciphers. It was probably prepared in 1945; it is unedited and somewhat disorganized, although very useful.

Nimitz Papers. These are COMINT-related extracts from the Nimitz Papers, Naval History Division, Personal Papers Series XIII, Item #40 (Personal Official Correspondence with Military Officers).

The Organization of U.S. Naval Communications Intelligence, Revised Edition, 15 November 1944.

Allied Communication Intelligence and the Battle of the Atlantic, 5 volumes, prepared by Op-20-G in 1945, no author. An exhaustive account of U.S. naval COMINT and the U-boat war. There are probably only two or three copies.

History of Coast Guard Unit #387, 1940–45. Copy #2 of 5. Prepared at Op-20-G in 1945 (?), no author. This is a detailed account of every German intelligence code and cipher (including ENIGMA) worked by the Coast Guard.

History of Naval Intelligence, Supplement A. (Prepared by Captain W. F. Packard, USN (Ret) as the COMINT supplement to an ongoing general history of naval intelligence.)

Catalog of Papers. This is a large collection of documents assembled at NSA in the early 1950s and covering Army and Navy COMINT policy matters from the 1930s through World War II.

    c. FBI Files

No general search of FBI records was made. See the footnotes and the correspondence and interviews portions of the sources section for additional information.

    d. Center for Military History (CMH), Department of the Army, Washington, D.C.

A History of the Military Intelligence Division, 7 December 1941–2 September 1945. Prepared by the Military Intelligence Division in 1946. No author.

History of the Military Intelligence Division, Department of the Army General Staff. This manuscript was prepared by Colonel (Ret) Bruce W. Bidwell during 1957–61, in five parts. Part Five covers World War II. This history seems to have been intended for eventual inclusion in the Army Official History series, but this did not take place. It was declassified by the adjutant general in 1973(?).

2. Correspondence with the Author

Brigadier General (Ret) Carter W. Clarke, former chief, Special Branch, MIS.

Colonel (Reserve) Abraham Sinkov, former head of the U.S. Army contingent, Central Bureau Brisbane.

Captain Wayman F. Packard, USN (Ret). Captain Packard provided the author with the results of his own ongoing research into naval intelligence. Of special interest were the transcripts of his interviews of Captain Rudolph Fabian, USN (Ret), former head of CAST and FRUMEL units.

3. Interviews and Oral History Programs

    a. NSA Historical Collection – Interview notes or transcripts.

Albert Jones, retired NSA employee who began his career in Army COMINT in 1937 (interviewed by the author and Mr. Henry F. Schorreck).

Edward W. Bromble, retired NSA employee who began his Army COMINT career in 1939 (interviewed by the author).

George E. Sterling, former head of the Radio Intelligence Division, FCC (interviewed by the author and Mr. Earl J. Coates).

Frank B. Rowlett, retired NSA employee who loomed large in U.S. COMINT from 1930–62 (interviewed by Messrs. Vincent Wilson, David Goodman, Earl J. Coates, and Henry F. Schorreck in various sessions during 1975 and 1976).

I. Woodrow Newpher and Paul Napier, retired heads of World War II-era FBI COMINT (interviewed by the author).

A. D. Kramer, Captain, USN (Ret). Transcript of a speech given at NSA in 1962.

Fred Welden, Captain, USN (Ret), who was in ONI September 1941 to the end of the war (interviewed by the author).

Elliott Glunt, NSA employee who was assigned to Op-19 (Radio Central, Navy Department) in 1941–44.

b. U.S. Naval Institute (USNI)

Bound transcripts of interviews conducted by Dr. John Mason, Oral History Director for USNI:

Rear Admiral Arthur J. McCollum, USN (Ret)

Rear Admiral John Redman, USN (Ret)

4. British Official Records

Government Code and Cipher School Histories, a multivolume work concerning GC&CS, 1939–45 (with significant earlier items too), prepared after the war. The specific volumes used are cited in the footnotes. This series is an unmatched record of intelligence organization, policy, and operations. Some of the volumes are superbly written and the authors, especially Frank Birch, show no hesitancy in describing controversy and personalities.

5. Congressional Reports And Hearings

U. S. Congress, House, *Hearings Before the Subcommittee of the Committee on Appropriations, House of Representatives, Seventy-eighth Congress, Second Session on the Independent Offices Appropriation Bill for 1945, 1149–1287.*

6. Published Official Histories

Conn, Stetson; Fairchild, Byron. *The Framework of Hemisphere Defense.* Washington, D.C.: Office of the Chief of Military History, 1960.

Davis, Vernon E. *The History of the Joint Chiefs of Staff in World War II.* 2 volumes. Historical Division, Joint Secretariat, Joint Chiefs of Staff, 1972.

Sterling, George E. "The U.S. Hunt for Axis Agent Radios." *Studies in Intelligence* (CIA), Spring 1960.

Terrett, Dulaney. *The Signal Corps: The Emergency.* Washington, D.C.: Office of the Chief of Military History, 1956.

Thompson, George R.; Harris, Dixie R.; Oakes, Pauline M.; Terrett, Dulaney. *The Signal Corps: The Test (December 1941 to July 1943).* Washington, D.C.: Office of the Chief of Military History, 1957.

Thompson, George R.; Harris, Dixie R. *The Signal Corps: The Outcome (Mid-1943 through 1945).* Washington, D.C.: Office of the Chief of Military History, 1966.

Troy, Thomas F. "The Coordinator of Information and British Intelligence," *Studies in Intelligence* (CIA), Spring 1974.

7. Secondary Sources

Berle, Beatrice B.; Jacobs, Travis B., ed. *Navigating the Rapids* (from the Papers of Adolf A. Berle). New York, 1973.

Koop, Theodore F. *Weapon of Silence.* Chicago, 1946.

Montgomery-Hyde, H. *Room 3603.* New York, 1965.

Nelson, Otto L. Jr. *National Security and the General Staff.* Washington, 1946.

Stimson, Henry L.; Bundy, McGeorge. *On Active Service in Peace and War.* New York, 1948.

Index

Abwehr traffic--109, 114

Agreement between GC&CS and War Department--108-109

"Agreement Regarding Special Material"--10

Akin, Colonel Spencer--3, 10-12, 17-18, 20, 31-32,33, 38, 40, 89, 90, 142, 153,154

Akin-Friedman proposals on U.S.-British COMINT cooperation--16-17

Alaskan Command--32, 124-125

Allen, Captain Archer--20

Allocation Committee--52

Anderson, Rear Admiral Walter S.--DNI, 10, 13, 17

Arlington Hall Station-- 37, 41, 42, 81, 84, 97, 100, 103, 108, 109, 110, 114, 120, 152

Army--1,2,6,8,9,10,11-18, 20, 23

Army Communications Service--33

Army-Navy agreement on collection--13

Army-Navy COMINT Coordinating Committee (ANCICC)--88, 133, 134, 135, 136, 137, 138

Army-Navy Communications Intelligence Board (ANCIB)--133, 137, 138, 139, 141, 151, 153

Army-Navy dissemination agreement (1939)--14, 153

Army Security Agency (ASA), establishment of--155

Army Services Forces (ASF)--34, 84

Ashly, Major James--141

Assistant Chief of Staff (ACS), G2--1,10, 13,16, 34-36, 40, 48, 49, 59, 81, 100, 103-104, 113, 126, 129, 134, 137, 138, 143, 145, 147-149, 151-153

Australia--31, 40, 46, 63, 67, 79, 81, 85, 88, 91, 105, 157

Australian Army--40, 88, 90

Bearce H.F.--as chief of Mexican diplomatic section, SIS, 3; as part of SIS Unit B, 33

BEECHNUT (Project)--110,111, 114, 149

Berle, Assistant Secretary of State Adolph A.--1, 31, 43, 48, 49

Bertolet, Commander Sam--45

Betts, Lieutenant Colonel (MID)--23

Bicher, Colonel George--41, 110, 150, 151

Birch, Frank--61, 119

Bissell, Colonel John T.--49

Bissell, Major General Clayton-- 137, 138, 143, 145, 147, 148, 149, 151, 152, 153, 154, 155

Blackburn, W.G.B.--(head of FBI cryptanalytic section), 9

Bletchley Park--14, 19, 20, 57, 58, 59, 101, 104, 105, 106, 108, 112, 113, 114, 121, 151

The Bombe--100, 101, 111
Booth, Wing Commander H. Roy--89
Bratton, Lieutenant Colonel Rufus (MID)--22, 23
British Joint Chiefs--105, 106, 107
British Secret Service (also see Secret Intelligence Service and MI-6)
British Security Coordination (BSC)--1, 14, 15, 51, 57, 60, 61, 62, 87, 97, 120, 126, 128, 129, 157
Brown, Captain Harold McD.--58, 87, 97
Brown, Lieutenant Harold R. (commanded MS-6)--31, 58, 87, 97, 11, 12
BRUSA Agreement, 1944--120, 121, 157
Bullock, Colonel Frank--36, 37, 50, 53, 80, 97, 100
Bundy, Major William--110
Burnett, Lieutenant Commander--20

"C" (see Stuart Menzies)
Calfee, Major--111
Campbell, Lieutenant K.E.--89
Carpender, Admiral--63
Cassidy, Captain W.G.B.--89
Cast--6, 7, 14, 20, 31, 32, 46, 63
Castner, Colonel L.V. (G-2, Alaskan Defense Command)--124
Central Bureau (see Central Bureau Brisbane)
Central Bureau Brisbane (CBB)--40, 81, 82, 83, 85, 86, 87, 88, 89, 90, 91, 135, 142, 143, 148, 151, 152, 153
Chappell, Walter (ONI)--2
Cheadle, Major John R. (U.K. liaison to SIS)--22
China-Burma-India (CBI) theater--80, 87, 141, 142, 143
Churchill, Winston--14, 105, 108
CICFOR (Combat Intelligence Center, Forward)--157, 158
Clandestine traffic/collection--8, 13, 46, 48, 49, 50, 51, 53, 55, 57, 61, 62, 78, 99, 102, 123-131
Clark, General Mark--151
Clark, Lieutenant Colonel H.L.--89
Clark, Major S.R.I.--89
Clarke, Carter W.--35, 36, 37, 39, 40, 49, 53, 81, 87, 88 89, 91, 93, 98, 99, 100, 101, 102, 103, 104, 106, 107, 108, 110, 113, 127, 128, 129, 133, 134, 135, 136, 137, 138, 141, 142, 144, 145, 146, 147, 149, 152, 153, 154, 155
Clarke, Squadron Leader W.J.--89
"COMB"--46, 120
Combat Information Center (CIC)--64, 105, 136, 157, 158
Combat Intelligence Division (F-2) -- 77, 78, 134, 135, 136

COMINCH--45, 46, 47, 51, 77, 78, 137, 156
Coordinator of Information (COI)--1, 3, 8, 21, 49, 50, 52
Cook, Lieutenant/Captain/Colonel Earle F.--12, 22, 114, 135
Corderman, Colonel W. Preston--80, 81, 100, 103, 106, 107, 108, 109, 114, 134, 136, 138, 147
Corregidor--6, 31
Cowgill, Lieutenant Colonel, MI-6--128
Crawford, D.M.--98
Currier, Prescott--19, 45

Daniels, Ensign--97
DeBayly, B.--62, 97
De LaFleur, Louis--49
Delimitations Agreement--1, 8
Dennis, Lieutenant Commander Jefferson--20
Denniston, Commander Alfred--21, 22, 57, 58, 108
Densford, Lieutenant Commander--43
DeWitt, General John--49
Dill, Field Marshall Sir John--59, 97, 98, 99, 100, 101, 102, 103, 104, 105, 106, 108, 109
Direction finding sites--6
    American Samoa
    Guantanamo, Cuba
    Point St. George, California
    Poyners Hill, North Carolina
Director of Naval Intelligence (DNI)--1, 10, 14, 17, 43, 47, 48, 52, 78, 91, 127, 128, 129, 137
Donovan, William J.--54
Doud, Major Harold--33, 92, 97
Drake, Major--61, 97
Driscoll, Mrs. Agnes--45
Dusenberry, Lieutenant Colonel--23

Eastman, Colonel Clyde--17
849th SIS--41, 42, 106, 151
Eighth Company, Presidio, San Francisco--3
Eighth RSM (Air Force)--157
Emmons, General Delos C.--16
Emory, Richard W. (CICFOR Communications Officer)--158
ENIGMA--19, 20, 22, 46, 58, 59, 60, 83, 97, 101, 103, 104, 105, 106, 107, 108, 109, 110, 111, 119, 126, 128, 130, 141
Erskine, Hugh--40, 89

European Theater of Operations, U.S. Army (ETOUSA)--40, 41, 42, 59, 81, 82, 100, 102, 110, 111, 112, 151
Evensson, Major Eric--33
Extension Agreement--119
EWT (OP-20-G material sent to GCCS)--21

Fabian, Lieutenant Rudolph--7, 63, 87, 88
Federal Bureau of Investigation (FBI)--1,2,7,8,9,10, 12, 13, 14, 15, 47, 48, 49, 50, 51, 53, 55, 56, 61, 62, 123, 124, 125, 126, 127, 128, 129, 130, 135, 136, 147
Federal Communications Commission (FCC)--9,12, 37, 48, 49, 50, 52, 54, 60, 61, 123, 124, 129, 135
Ferguson (Colonel) incident--127
Ferner, Robert O.--114
Filby, P. W.--114
First Radio Intelligence Company--3
Fleming, Commander Ian--21
FLORADORA--106
Fly, James L. (FCC chairman)--9, 10, 48, 49, 61, 124, 125
Ford, Lieutenant Commander--45
Fort Monmouth, New Jersey--3, 17, 18, 32, 37
Fried, Captain Walter J.--114
Friedman, Elizebeth--7, 9
Friedman, William F.--3,4,7,16,17, 19, 22,36,50, 53, 97, 103, 108
FRESCO (traffic forwarding code)--87
FRUMEL (Fleet Radio Unit Melbourne)--46, 61, 62, 63, 65, 80, 87, 88, 91, 120, 121, 135, 157
FRUPAC (Fleet Radio Unit Pacific)--46, 63,64,65, 66, 80, 87, 88, 91, 120, 121, 135, 157,

Gardner, Lieutenant Commander E.R.--12
GC&CS (Government Code and Cipher School) -- 14, 60, 98, 99, 100, 101, 103, 104, 107, 108, 109, 110, 111, 112, 113, 114
German diplomatic traffic--58, 110, 114
"German" station, Long Island--10
Ghormley, Rear Admiral Robert--16, 19
Glodell, Lieutenant Larry M.--34
Godfrey, Admiral John H.--21
Goggins, Commander--65
Gore-Brown, Lieutenant Colonel--112
"Green" ENIGMA--126
Greenwalt, Lieutenant jg--12
Guam--1,6,32, 67, 121, 142, 157

Halpin, Major Z.--89
Handy, General Thomas T.--138, 147, 151, 153, 154
Hastings, Captain Edward G. (U.K. COMINT Rep. in Washington)--21, 48, 51, 59, 60, 61, 87, 98, 99, 100, 101, 104, 107, 109, 114, 126
Hawaii--1, 3, 6, 10, 23, 24, 31, 46, 60, 63, 65, 67, 79, 80, 82, 85, 123, 124, 141, 142, 157, 158
Hayes, Captain Harold G.--22, 33, 41, 106
Henry, Major A.G.--89
Hillenkoetter, Commander--64
Hilles, Major F.W. --111
Hinsley, F.H.--120
Hodes, Brigadier General Henry--151, 152
Holbrook, Lieutenant Colonel Willard--50
Holden Agreement--61, 63, 88, 119, 121
Holden, Captain Carl--47
Hoover, J. Edgar--2, 9, 49, 125, 127, 128, 129
Horne, Vice Admiral Frederic J.--43, 44, 45, 47, 51, 52, 63, 65, 66, 77, 79, 91
Howeth, Linwood S.-- 157
Huddleston, Major Edwin W.--141
Hull, General John--153
Hyde, Captain H. Montgomery--15
Hypo--31, 32

Ingles, Colonel Harry C.--33, 91, 146, 147, 152
Intelligence Center Pacific Ocean Area (ICPOA)--63, 64
Intercept sites, OP-20-G--6
    Station A, Shanghai, China--6, 157
    Station B, Guam--6, 32
    Station C, Corregidor, Philippine Islands--6
    Station G, Amagansett, New York--6
    Station H, Heeia, Territory of Hawaii--6
    Station J, Jupiter, Florida--6
    Station M, Cheltenham, Maryland--6, 46
    Station O, San Juan, Puerto Rico--6
    Station S, Bainbridge, Washington--6, 79
    Station W, Winter Harbor, Maine--6
    Station U, Toro Point (previously Balboa), Canal Zone--6
Interdepartmental Intelligence Conference (IIC)--1, 49, 50, 51
Italian diplomatic traffic--3

Japanese Army traffic/codes--4, 31, 38, 39, 81, 82, 83, 84, 86, 87, 93, 133, 141, 152

Japanese diplomatic traffic--3, 4, 7, 9, 12, 13, 17, 23, 31, 133
Japanese naval systems--6, 7, 20, 23, 45, 46, 52, 61, 87, 88, 119, 135
Japanese navy fleet officers' code--7
Japanese Water Transport Code--82, 86
Jett, E.K.--10
JN-25--7, 20, 45, 46, 60, 79, 105, 121
JN-50--46
Johnson, Major Roy D.--59, 104, 110
Joint Chiefs of Staff--47, 53, 54, 123, 138
Joint Intelligence Center Pacific Ocean Area (JICPOA)--63, 64, 136, 142, 157
Joint Intelligence Committee (JIC)--2, 50, 52, 54, 55, 58, 77
Jones, Commander Leonard T.--53, 55, 62, 125, 129
Jones, Lieutenant Albert--149

Kimmel, Admiral Husband--6
Kinney, Captain Phillip R.--134, 136, 138, 155
King, Admiral Ernest J.--45, 47, 65, 77, 78, 91, 99
King-Marshall Agreement--133, 134, 135
Kirk, Captain Alan--15, 17
Knox, Secretary of the Navy--123, 124
Kramer, Lieutenant Commander A.D.--23, 45, 48, 49, 53
Kroner, Colonel Hayes--23, 34, 104, 105
Kullback, Solomon--3, 22, 33, 58, 59, 100, 126

Ladd, D.M. (FBI)--48, 49, 53
LA system--4
Layton, Commander/Captain Edwin T.--7, 64, 65
Leahy, Admiral--123, 124
Lee, Colonel/General Raymond E.--2, 16, 19, 34
Lehane, Captain B.--89
Littlefield, Major--111
Lothian, Lord (British ambassador to U.S./requests exchange of "technical information"--
    16
Loxley, Peter--113

Machine Section of the Special Cryptanalytic Unit (6812th SSO)--111
MacArthur, General Douglas--6, 31, 32, 40, 63, 86, 88, 90, 141, 142, 151, 152, 153, 154, 155
MacIntosh, Albert--62
MAGIC--13, 23, 36, 46, 83, 92, 93, 133, 144
Maidment, Captain Kenneth J.--61, 62, 97, 126

Marshall, General George C--36, 59, 98, 99, 100, 101, 102, 103, 104, 105, 106, 107, 108, 109, 112
Mason, Redfield--7
Mauborgne, General--11, 12, 13, 17, 18, 32, 33
McCabe, Colonel E.R.W.--10, 13
McCloy, John J. --35, 143, 144, 145, 146, 151
McCloy Board--143, 144, 145, 146
McCollum, Commander Arthur--21, 23, 43, 47, 63, 64
McCormack, Alfred--35, 36, 87, 100, 108, 113, 130, 133, 144, 147
McGrail, Major A.J. --33
McKee, Major Seth--111
McNarney, General--34, 91, 98, 102, 103, 146
Menzies, Stuart--56, 57, 99, 100, 104, 112
MERMAN (traffic forwarding code)--87
Mexican diplomatic traffic--3
MI-5--56
Miles, Sherman--13, 14, 17, 18, 20, 22, 23, 34
Military Intelligence Division (MID)--1, 2, 4, 10, 13, 14, 17, 18, 19, 22, 23, 32, 34, 35, 36, 46, 48, 50, 51, 92, 98, 99, 100, 108, 112, 143, 144, 145
Military Intelligence Service--34, 36, 37, 39, 40, 42, 52, 54, 56, 58, 62, 77, 81, 83, 84, 85, 86, 92, 93, 100, 107, 108, 110, 111, 112, 113, 126, 127, 129, 130, 133, 134, 135, 136, 137, 141, 142, 143, 144, 145, 146, 147, 148, 149, 150, 151, 152, 153, 155, 157
Minckler, Lieutenant Colonel Rex--22, 32, 36
Monitoring stations (MS)--3
   MS-1: Fort Monmouth, NJ--3, 32, 37, 38, 82, 85, 103
   MS-2: The Presidio of San Francisco--3, 32, 37, 39, 82, 83, 85, 143, 152
   MS-3: Fort Sam Houston--3, 82
   MS-4: Corozal, Canal Zone--3, 82, 85
   MS-5: Fort Shafter, Hawaii--3, 31, 39, 82, 85
   MS-6: Fort McKinley, Philippines--3, 4, 6, 7, 31, 82, 85
   MS-7: Fort Hunt, Virginia--3, 37, 82
   MS-8--85
   MS-11--157
   MS-15--39
   MS-91--39
Moore, Colonel John C. (signal officer for Army Eastern Defense Command)--49
Murmane, Lieutenant Colonel Charles R.--113
Murray, Colonel W.W.--97

Napier, Paul--8, 62
National Defense Organization (see also Radio Intelligence Division)

Nave, Captain T.E.--89
Navy--1, 2, 6, 7, 8, 9, 11, 12, 13, 14, 15, 16, 17, 18, 23
Navy Department--7, 23, 79, 80, 91
Negat--80, 156 (see also Supplementary Radio Activity, Washington)
Nelson, Colonel/General Otto L.--84, 109, 143, 145, 151
Newpher, Woodrow--129
Nimitz, Admiral--63, 64, 65, 66, 157, 158
Ninth Company, Fort Shafter--3
Norman, S.W.--61
Noyes, Admiral Leigh--11, 12, 13, 17, 43, 44

O'Connor, Colonel H.M.--114, 120
Office of Naval Intelligence (ONI)--1, 2, 7, 10, 13, 14, 21, 23, 36, 43, 45, 46, 47, 48, 49, 51, 52, 53, 54, 55, 63, 64, 65, 66, 77, 78, 119, 126, 127, 128, 129, 135
Office of Strategic Services (OSS)--1, 2, 54, 55, 77, 114, 125, 135, 143
Olmstead, Major General Dawson--32, 33, 36, 90, 91
OP-16FE (ONI)--77
OP-19--46
OP-20-G--6, 7, 10, 12, 14, 17, 19, 21, 22, 23, 24, 32, 43, 44, 45, 46, 47, 48, 51, 52, 53, 55, 56, 58, 60, 61, 62, 63, 65, 66, 77, 79, 80, 88, 90, 91, 92, 105, 119, 120, 121, 124, 125, 126, 130, 133, 134, 135, 136, 155, 156, 157
OP-20-GI--78
OP-20-GU (Coast Guard COMINT unit)--125, 127, 129, 130
OP-20-K--43
OP-20-Q--43
OP-20-3--156
Orr, Lieutenant Colonel Samuel M.--113

Pacific Fleet--6
PAIR traffic--114
Panama--1, 3, 18, 33, 39
Panama Signal Company, Canal Zone--3
Parke, Lieutenant Commander L.W.--45
Patterson, Assistant Secretary of War Robert P.--16
Pearl (low-level cryptographic systems)--143
Pearl Harbor--2, 3, 4, 6, 7, 9, 14, 20, 22, 23, 32, 33, 34, 35, 43, 56, 58, 60, 64, 65, 79, 81, 120, 135, 136, 157
Perdue, Major--133
Petrie, David--56
Philippines--1, 3, 4, 6, 14, 20, 31, 32, 40, 46, 88, 124, 142, 153, 158
Picking, Captain Sherwood--21

Portugal, diplomatic codes, traffic--4, 55
Pound, Admiral Sir Dudley--21
PQR (GCCS material sent to OP-20-G--21
Prather, Louise--34
Puerto Rico--1, 6, 10
PURPLE system/machine--4, 5, 7, 12, 13, 14, 18, 19, 20, 45, 103, 105, 107

Radio Intelligence Division (RID)--10, 32, 39, 48, 53, 54, 56, 61, 62, 123, 124, 125, 129, 130
Radio Security Service (RSS)--57, 62, 102
RAGFOR (Radio Analysis Group, Forward)--121, 157, 158
Raven, Lieutenant Frank--45
Redman, Brigadier--107, 108, 109, 110
Redman, John--43, 44, 47, 48, 49, 51, 52, 53, 63, 65, 66
Redman, Joseph--43, 44, 47, 63, 65, 90, 91, 92, 93, 119, 120, 121, 125, 138
RED system--4, 5, 12
Regnier, Colonel W.M.--18
Richardson, Admiral James O.--6
Rochefort, Lieutenant Joseph--7, 63, 64, 65
Roosevelt, President--1, 8, 13, 14, 16, 20, 50, 54, 59, 108, 124
Rosen, Lieutenant Leo--19, 22
Rowlett, Frank B.--3, 22, 97, 110
Royal Australian Air Force (RAAF)--40, 85, 86, 88, 89, 90
Royal Australian Navy--63
Royal Canadian Navy--61
Royal Marines--21
Royal Navy--14, 61, 119
Runnals, Captain John F.B.--141

Sadtler, Colonel Otis K.--33
Safeguarding Military Information (SMI) section--35
Safford, Commander Laurance--7, 10, 11, 12, 17, 43, 63, 155
Samoa--1, 6
Sandford, Lieutenant Colonel A.W.--87, 88, 89
Sandwith, Captain H.R.--58, 60
Scherr, Major Joseph--31, 40
Schuermann, Admiral Roscoe E.--47, 78, 127, 128
Schukraft, Lieutenant/Captain Robert E.--12, 33, 34, 62
Seaman, Captain John W.--114
Second Signal Service Battalion--37, 82 (detachments), 85 (realignment)
Second Signal Service Company--3, 33

Second Signal Service Detachment--157
SERENA (traffic forwarding code)--87
Services of Supply (see Army Services Forces)
Seventh Company, Fort Sam Houston--3
SID "D"--151
Signal Intelligence Detachment 9251-A--41
Signal Intelligence Service Division (see Signal Security Agency)
Signal radio intelligence (SRI) companies--38, 39, 40, 41, 42, 81, 82, 86, 91, 103, 137, 143, 146, 148, 149, 150, 151, 152, 153, 155

    102d SRI: 39, 125
    111th ": 86, 157
    112th ": 86
    114th " : 151
    117th ": 42
    118th " : 151
    121st " : 86
    122d " : 41
    123d " : 42
    124th ": 149
    125th " : 39, 86
    126th " : 40, 86
    128th " : 41
    130th " : 157

Signal Security Agency--40, 84, 143
Signal Security Division (see also Signal Security Agency)
Signal Security Service (see also Signal Security Agency)
Signal Service companies (SSC)--38, 149
Sinkov, Abraham--3, 19, 22 33, 40 86, 89, 102
Sinkov-Rosen mission to UK--19, 20 22
Sixteenth Naval District--6
SLU detachments--107, 112, 113, 150, 151
Small, Albert W.--114
Small, Major B.E.--89
Smedberg, Captain W.R. III--136, 137, 138
Smith, General John--143
Smith-Hutton, Captain--134
Snow, Major (Special Branch liaison officer to the Navy)--134
Somervell, Lieutenant General Brehon B.--34, 145, 146
Southwest Pacific theater (SWPA)--38, 40
Spain, diplomatic codes/traffic--4, 55

Portugal, diplomatic codes, traffic--4, 55
Pound, Admiral Sir Dudley--21
PQR (GCCS material sent to OP-20-G--21
Prather, Louise--34
Puerto Rico--1, 6, 10
PURPLE system/machine--4, 5, 7, 12, 13, 14, 18, 19, 20, 45, 103, 105, 107

Radio Intelligence Division (RID)--10, 32, 39, 48, 53, 54, 56, 61, 62, 123, 124, 125, 129, 130
Radio Security Service (RSS)--57, 62, 102
RAGFOR (Radio Analysis Group, Forward)--121, 157, 158
Raven, Lieutenant Frank--45
Redman, Brigadier--107, 108, 109, 110
Redman, John--43, 44, 47, 48, 49, 51, 52, 53, 63, 65, 66
Redman, Joseph--43, 44, 47, 63, 65, 90, 91, 92, 93, 119, 120, 121, 125, 138
RED system--4, 5, 12
Regnier, Colonel W.M.--18
Richardson, Admiral James O.--6
Rochefort, Lieutenant Joseph--7, 63, 64, 65
Roosevelt, President--1, 8, 13, 14, 16, 20, 50, 54, 59, 108, 124
Rosen, Lieutenant Leo--19, 22
Rowlett, Frank B.--3, 22, 97, 110
Royal Australian Air Force (RAAF)--40, 85, 86, 88, 89, 90
Royal Australian Navy--63
Royal Canadian Navy--61
Royal Marines--21
Royal Navy--14, 61, 119
Runnals, Captain John F.B.--141

Sadtler, Colonel Otis K.--33
Safeguarding Military Information (SMI) section--35
Safford, Commander Laurance--7, 10, 11, 12, 17, 43, 63, 155
Samoa--1, 6
Sandford, Lieutenant Colonel A.W.--87, 88, 89
Sandwith, Captain H.R.--58, 60
Scherr, Major Joseph--31, 40
Schuermann, Admiral Roscoe E.--47, 78, 127, 128
Schukraft, Lieutenant/Captain Robert E.--12, 33, 34, 62
Seaman, Captain John W.--114
Second Signal Service Battalion--37, 82 (detachments), 85 (realignment)
Second Signal Service Company--3, 33

Second Signal Service Detachment--157
SERENA (traffic forwarding code)--87
Services of Supply (see Army Services Forces)
Seventh Company, Fort Sam Houston--3
SID "D"--151
Signal Intelligence Detachment 9251-A--41
Signal Intelligence Service Division (see Signal Security Agency)
Signal radio intelligence (SRI) companies--38, 39, 40, 41, 42, 81, 82, 86, 91, 103, 137, 143, 146, 148, 149, 150, 151, 152, 153, 155

    102d SRI: 39, 125
    111th ": 86, 157
    112th ": 86
    114th ": 151
    117th ": 42
    118th ": 151
    121st ": 86
    122d ": 41
    123d ": 42
    124th ": 149
    125th ": 39, 86
    126th ": 40, 86
    128th ": 41
    130th ": 157

Signal Security Agency--40, 84, 143
Signal Security Division (see also Signal Security Agency)
Signal Security Service (see also Signal Security Agency)
Signal Service companies (SSC)--38, 149
Sinkov, Abraham--3, 19, 22 33, 40 86, 89, 102
Sinkov-Rosen mission to UK--19, 20 22
Sixteenth Naval District--6
SLU detachments--107, 112, 113, 150, 151
Small, Albert W.--114
Small, Major B.E.--89
Smedberg, Captain W.R. III--136, 137, 138
Smith, General John--143
Smith-Hutton, Captain--134
Snow, Major (Special Branch liaison officer to the Navy)--134
Somervell, Lieutenant General Brehon B.--34, 145, 146
Southwest Pacific theater (SWPA)--38, 40
Spain, diplomatic codes/traffic--4, 55

Special Branch--35, 36, 56, 81, 83, 84, 92, 93, 100, 107, 111, 112, 126, 133, 134, 136, 144, 145, 147
Special Cryptanalytic Unit (6813th SSO)--111
Special Intelligence Service (SIS)--1, 3, 4, 6, 7, 9, 10, 12, 13, 14, 16, 19, 21, 22, 31, 32, 33, 34, 35, 36, 37, 38, 39, 40, 41, 42, 45, 46, 50, 52, 53, 56, 58, 59, 60, 62, 80, 81, 82, 84, 100, 102, 106, 109, 110, 111, 137, 143, 148, 151, 152, 153
Special Intercept Unit (6811th Special Security Detachment)--111
Special Service Branch (see Special Branch)
SSO (Special Security Officer system)--88, 90, 107, 110, 111, 112, 136, 141, 142, 143, 144, 145, 149, 150, 151, 157, 158
SSRs (Special Security Representatives)--112
Station Glenn--8
Stephenson, William--2, 14
Sterling, George--10, 54, 62, 124
Stevens, Major Geoffrey--22, 59
Stevens, Petty Officer H.L.--89
Stimson, Henry L.--13, 22, 35, 81, 144, 146
Stone, Captain Earl E.--47, 66, 90, 91, 92, 127
Stoner, Brigadier General Frank--33, 36, 91, 148
Strong, General George V.--16, 17, 18, 19, 35, 36, 48, 54, 59, 81, 84, 85, 89, 91, 92, 98, 99, 100, 101, 102, 103, 104, 105, 107, 108, 110, 126, 133, 143
Sultan, Lieutenant General Dan--151, 152
Supplementary Radio Activity, Washington (see also Negat)-155, 156
Sutherland, General Richard K.--142

Talbert, Major Ansel E.M.--112, 113
Tanner, Major G.A.--89
Taylor, Telford--62, 97, 107, 108, 110, 111, 114, 130, 141
Tenth Company, Fort Mills, Philippines--3
Thompson, Major John R.--142
Thornett, E.B.C.--114
Thornton, R.E.--62
3-N Agreement--128, 129
3250th Signal Service Company--149
3251st Signal Service Company--149
3252d Signal Service Company--149
3-U.S.--111, 112, 113, 130, 149, 150, 151
Thumb (TA and DF)--143
Tiltman, Colonel John--58, 97, 99, 100
TINA--65
Tizard, Sir Henry--16

Train, Rear Admiral Harold--47, 91, 92
Travis, Sir Edward--57, 61, 99, 100, 101, 102, 108, 109
Travis-Strong Agreement--109, 110, 111, 114, 120
TUNA (collective address)--46, 120
TUNNEY--107
Turing, Dr. Alan--98, 99, 100, 101, 102, 103, 126
Turner, Admiral R.K.--23
Twitty, Brigadier General Joseph--64
Two Rock Ranch--37, 38, 39, 82, 83, 85

ULTRA--141
ULTRA Dexter--141
ULTRA officers--112, 113
United States Coast Guard (USCG)--7, 8, 10, 12, 13, 14, 37, 48, 49, 50, 51, 53, 55, 60, 62, 125, 126, 130
U.S. Army Forces British Isles (see European Theater of Operations U.S. Army (ETOUSA)
U.S.- British COMINT conference in Singapore--20
USCG-FBI relations--10

Vichy France traffic--4, 6, 9, 37, 45, 78
Vint Hill Farm Station (VHFS)--37, 41, 42, 82, 85, 103
VVV TEST-AOR case--8

Walsh, Flight Lieutenant J.--89
Ward, Flight Lieutenant P.F.--89
War Department--16, 17, 18, 34, 36, 37, 39, 40, 49, 50, 51, 53, 59, 81, 82, 86, 88, 90, 91, 97, 98, 99, 101, 103, 106, 108, 109, 110, 111, 113, 124, 141, 142, 143, 145, 149, 151, 152, 153, 154, 155
WEC--87, 143
Weeks, Robert--19
Welb, Tom (FBI)--127
Welker, Lieutenant Commander--43, 45
Wenger, Joseph--44, 46, 48, 49, 52, 53, 55, 60, 87, 88, 92, 119, 126, 129, 133, 134, 135, 136, 137, 138, 155, 156
Western Defense Command--32, 39, 49
Wilkinson, Admiral T.S.--43, 47, 48
Wireless Experimental Center (WEC)--83, 87, 143
Wrangham, Archie--21

XX Committee--56

Yardley, Herbert O.--22
Y Board--57, 60, 102
Y Committee--57, 60
Y Northwest Africa Committee--41